MW01252920

Varieties of Capitalism, Types of Democracy and Globalization

This book combines two strands of international political economy; examining how capitalism and democracy shape and are shaped by each other. Although until now considered separately, this path-breaking book proposes an innovative view of a political-economic system that inextricably links the model of capitalism to the type of democracy, where continuation is mutually reinforced.

Advanced countries have achieved postwar affluence by adopting one of two contrasting models of capitalism; liberal market economies or coordinated market economies, and two opposing types of democracies: consensus or majoritarian democracies. Expert contributors in the field consider the question of whether and how globalization is transforming the postwar political-economic systems of advanced countries such as Britain, France, Germany, Italy and Japan, as well as the question of how it is shaping democracy and capitalism combinations in former socialist countries in Eastern Europe and the new "capitalist" China. The book examines various topics, including party system change, a political dilemma of the established party, and corporate governance reforms, to posit an original and innovative theory of international political economy.

Variety of Capitalism, Types of Democracy and Globalization will be of interest to students and scholars of comparative politics, political economy and globalization.

Masanobu Ido is Professor of Political Science at Waseda University, Tokyo, Japan.

Routledge advances in international political economy

Varieties of Capitalism, Types of Democracy and Globalization

Edited by Masanobu Ido

Routledge
Taylor & Francis Group

LONDON AND NEW YORK

First published 2012
by Routledge
2 Park Square, Milton Park, Abingdon, Oxon OX14 4RN

Simultaneously published in the USA and Canada
by Routledge
711 Third Avenue, New York, NY 10017

Routledge is an imprint of the Taylor & Francis Group, an informa business

British Library Cataloguing in Publication Data
A catalogue record for this book is available from the British Library

Library of Congress Cataloging in Publication Data
Varieties of capitalism, types of democracy and globalization/edited by
Masanobu Ido.
   p. cm. – (Routledge advances in international political economy)
   Includes bibliographical references and index.
   1. Capitalism. 2. Democracy. 3. Globalization. I. Ido, Masanobu, 1957–
HB501.V3555 2012
   330.12'2–dc23   2011038920

ISBN: 978-0-415-67150-7 (hbk)
ISBN: 978-0-203-12398-0 (ebk)

Typeset in Times New Roman
by Wearset Ltd, Boldon, Tyne and Wear

Printed and bound in the United States of America by Publishers Graphics,
LLC on sustainably sourced paper.

Contents

viii *Contents*

Figures

Tables

Contributors

Laszlo Bruszt is Professor of Sociology at the European University Institute (Florence). In his earlier research he has dealt with issues of economic and political transformation in the post-communist countries. His more recent studies focus on the interplay between transnationalization, institutional development and economic change in evolving market economies. He co-edited with Ronald Holzhacker *Transnationalization of Economies, States, and Civil Societies* (Springer, 2009) and co-authored with David Stark *Post-socialist Pathways: Transforming Politics and Property* (Cambridge University Press, 1998).

Luigi Burroni is Associate Professor of Economic Sociology at the University of Teramo, Italy. His recent publications include: "Local Governance in Hard Times," in *Socio-Economic Review* (with C. Crouch, M. Kaminska and A. Valzania, 2008), "The Governance of the Shadow Economy," in *E&P C. Government and Policy* (with Colin Crouch, 2008), "Italy. Rise, Decline and Restructuring of a Regionalized Capitalism," in *Economy and Society* (with Carlo Trigilia, 2010) and "Flexicurity: A Conceptual Critique," in *European Journal of Industrial Relations* (with Maarten Keune, 2011).

Helen Callaghan is a senior research fellow at the Max Planck Institute in Cologne. Her current research focuses on the politics of corporate governance in EU member states.

Masanobu Ido is Professor of Political Science at Waseda University in Tokyo. He has published books and articles widely in the field of comparative political economy, with special emphasis on contemporary Japan.

Hideko Magara is Professor of Political Science at Waseda University in Tokyo and member of the Council of the House of Representatives Electoral Districts. She has published books and articles on political parties and political reforms in Italy and Japan. Magara was formerly President of the Japan Association for Comparative Politics (2008–2010) and is an associate member of the Science Council of Japan (since 2007).

Christopher A. McNally is Associate Professor of Political Economy at Chaminade University and Fellow at the East-West Center in Honolulu, USA. His research focuses on comparative capitalisms, especially China's capitalist transition. He has edited four volumes, including *China's Emergent Political Economy – Capitalism in the Dragon's Lair* (Routledge, 2008).

T. J. Pempel is Professor of Political Science at the University of California, Berkeley. He is the author of numerous books and articles on Japanese politics and political economy as well as on East Asian regional activities.

Philippe C. Schmitter has been on the faculty of the European University Institute (EUI) from 1996 to 2004, after ten years at Stanford University. Currently, he has been a recurrent visiting professor at the Central European University in Budapest, at the Istituto delle Scienze Humanistiche in Florence and the University of Siena. Schmitter has conducted research on comparative politics and regional integration in both Latin America and Western Europe, with special emphasis on the politics of organized interests. He has been the recipient of numerous professional awards and fellowships, including the award for lifetime achievement in European politics by the ECPR in 2008, the award for lifetime achievement in the study of European integration by EUSA, the Mattei Dogan Prize of the IPSA and the Johan Skytte Prize by Uppsala University – all in 2009.

Arpad Todor is a Ph.D. student at European University Institute and expert within the Ecopolis and Asociatia Pro Democratia Romanian NGOs. He has authored two books and several public policy studies. His areas of interest cover: varieties of capitalism, fiscal policy, evolutionary institutionalism, environmental policy and political party financing.

Carlo Trigilia is Professor of Economic Sociology at the University of Florence, where he is also Director of the European Center for Local and Regional Development. Among his publications: "Social Capital and Local Development," in *European Journal of Social Theory* (2001), *Economic Sociology: State, Market and Society in Modern Capitalism* (Blackwell, 2002), "Italy. Rise, Decline and Restructuring of a Regionalized Capitalism," in *Economy and Society* (with Luigi Burroni, 2010) and "Social Class" in the *International Encyclopedia of Political Science* (Sage, 2011).

Acknowledgments

This book is the result of the research project "Party System Change and the Transformation of Production Regime," financed by the Japan Society for the Promotion of Science, Grant-in-Aid for Scientific Research (B) (18330028) (Project Leader: Masanobu Ido), for the Japanese academic years 2006–2009. All contributors to the volume presented the earlier versions of their chapters in the meetings held in Hakone, Kyoto, and at Waseda University in Tokyo, in 2006, 2007 and 2008, respectively. I am particularly grateful to Prof. Schmitter for his invaluable advice on the necessity to broaden the scope of research to relationships between Varieties of Capitalism (VoC) and Types of Democracy (ToD), rather than restricting it to the impacts of party system on VoC change. I believe this refocusing and the adoption of the general framework of ToD–VoC interactions in the entire project has enabled the collection of chapters contained in this volume by scholars specialized in such diverse areas in the world to become a theoretically coherent volume with a global appeal. I would also like to express my gratitude to Prof. T. J. Pempel, who has suggested that Dr. Helen Callaghan and I coauthor the introduction to the edited volume. Finally, I would also like to thank the three anonymous reviewers for Routledge for their constructive comments that have helped me improve the final product.

M. I.

Part I
Theory and measurement

1 Introduction

Varieties of capitalism, types of democracy, and globalization

Helen Callaghan and Masanobu Ido

How do types of democracy relate to varieties of capitalism? And how does their relationship mediate the political and economic pressures that arise from globalization? By addressing these questions, the present volume bridges a gap between comparative politics and political economy that had grown wider over time.

The relationship between democracy and capitalism has drawn scholarly attention ever since both systems first emerged, with few possible connections left unexplored. On the pessimistic side, some, following Marx, claim that capitalism subverts democracy, by producing an unequal distribution of wealth that distorts political competition. Others, following Friedman and Schumpeter, retort that democracy subverts capitalism, by empowering political majorities to take market-distorting actions. On the optimistic side, some argue that democracy supports capitalism, by necessitating the welfare adaptations that allow the market economy to survive without a larger and more costly repressive apparatus. Others claim that capitalism supports democracy by raising the standard of living to a level that allows citizens to engage in politics.

As democracy and capitalism evolved over time and spread around the globe, scholars began to discern *varieties* of capitalism and *types* of democracy. The ensuing research led to increasing sub-disciplinary specialization. Studies of capitalist diversity, including Hall and Soskice (2001), Amable (2003), Hollingsworth *et al.* (1994), Crouch and Streeck (1996) and Whitley (1999) mainly explore how institutional arrangements and governance mechanisms in the economic realm (e.g., worker participation rules, skill formation systems, employment protection, corporate finance, etc.; market-based versus network-based or hierarchical coordination) affect economic performance, measured in terms of economic growth, competitiveness, employment rates, etc. Studies of democratic diversity, including Lijphart (1999), Sartori (1994) and Held (2006), mainly explore how institutional arrangements in the political realm (e.g., voting rules, concentration of executive power, executive-legislative relations, division of power, etc.) affect various aspects of democratic policy-making, including political equality, voter participation, party competition, state capacity, accountability, corruption, etc.

For the past two decades, the impact of "globalization" has been a major theme in political economy as well as in comparative politics, without, however, there being much dialogue across sub-disciplinary boundaries. The Varieties of Capitalism (VoC) debate on whether globalization would cause models of capitalism to converge long focused on the *economic* pressures associated with intensified competition on capital and product markets. Believers in a unique most competitive set of institutional arrangements argued that diversity would end once market pressures were strong enough to ensure that only the fittest companies survive (e.g., Hansmann and Kraakman 2001). Believers in multiple roads to competitiveness questioned the inevitability of market-driven convergence. Assuming that different models equip firms to perform better at some activities and worse at others, they argued that growing international trade might even increase diversity by encouraging a global division of labor (e.g., Porter 1990; Hall and Soskice 2001). VoC scholars have only recently come to recognize that the battle of the systems is fought in the political as well as in the economic realm, over distributional as well as efficiency matters (e.g., Hancké *et al.* 2007; Callaghan 2010).

Conversely, Types of Democracy (ToD) research on whether globalization would cause party systems to transform has emphasized *political* reasons for persistent divergence without exploring the mediating role of economic structures. Azmanova (2004) and Kriesi *et al.* (2008) argue that globalization transforms the political space in West European countries by generating new conflicts between winners and losers that cross-cut traditional structural and political cleavages. To explain why the impact of globalization on party systems varies across countries, Kriesi *et al.* (2008: 10) point to cross-national differences in the political and institutional context in which parties are embedded. They view globalization as creating political potential which is then translated into political programs, strategies and votes according to the local political context. Relevant variables include the size of the niche for new parties (determined, among other factors, by strength of traditional political divisions and the polarization of the party system), institutional entry barriers for new parties (including those posed by the electoral system), strategic choices made by incumbent parties (to ignore, accommodate or fight new demands) and the country's cultural heritage regarding issues such as the conceptualization of nationhood and citizenship. The *economic* context is discussed mainly to highlight similarities across the six West European countries included in their sample: as highly advanced industrial economies, all are assumed to develop similar cleavages dividing the winners and losers from globalization. Kriesi *et al.* do not discuss the possibility that the identity and number of winners and losers from globalization may differ across varieties of capitalism.

The present volume connects these two literatures by exploring the following questions: first, how do varieties of capitalism relate to types of democracy? Second, how, if at all, do the consequences of globalization for democracy differ across varieties of capitalism? Third, how, if at all, do the consequences of globalization for capitalism differ across types of democracy?

How do varieties of capitalism relate to types of democracy?

To examine the relationship between VoC and ToD, the volume proceeds in two steps. First, we propose new ways of systematically measuring and documenting the elective affinities between varieties of capitalism and types of democracy. Second, we present case studies of countries hitherto neglected by the main-stream literature on VoC and ToD that draw on a range of quantitative and quali-tative techniques to highlight various aspects of the complex causal relationship between VoC and ToD.

Step 1: measurement

Most previous efforts to uncover elective affinities fail to provide a comprehen-sive picture because they narrowly focus on specific components of VoC and ToD. Index measures of shareholder orientation and of electoral proportionality or left-party dominance are especially widely used. Pagano and Volpin (2005) examine the relationship between the electoral system (majoritarian or propor-tional representation (PR)) and shareholder protection as well as employment protection, finding that PR is negatively correlated with the former and posi-tively correlated with the latter. Roe (2003: 50–60) examines the relationship between "strength of social democracy" and diffusion of share ownership, finding that countries with stronger social democratic values tend to have more concentrated share ownership. Gourevitch and Shinn (2005: 72–75) examine the relationship between ToD (consensus or majoritarian, classified by measuring "political cohesion") and diffusion of share ownership as well as minority share-holder protections, finding that consensus democracies are associated with more concentrated ownership and weaker shareholder protections. Callaghan and Höpner (2005) study a roll call vote in the European Parliament to examine the relationship between left/right party affiliation and political support for liberal takeover legislation. They find that MEPs from non-liberal market economies were more likely to reject liberal EU takeover legislation, regardless of their party affiliation.

Amable (2003: 181–197) goes further by correlating a wide range of indic-ators distinguishing ToD and VoC. Among other things, he finds that the polit-ical systems associated with market-based and social democratic varieties of capitalism differ with regard to the degree of concentration of political parties, constitutional rigidity, number of veto players, degree of interest group plural-ism, proportionality of the electoral system, and the number of seats in the lower chamber obtained by parties on the left.[1]

Schmitter and Todor's contribution to this volume (Chapter 2) complements Amable's inductive approach by deductively deriving generic dimensions (namely stateness, decision-making, territory and function) that potentially fit both VoC and ToD, and by visualizing the degree of overlap between the corre-sponding institutional arrangements in the political and economic realm by means of an innovative spiderweb technique.

Step 2: explanations

Previous attempts to explain observed elective affinities between specific elements of VoC and ToD fail to provide a comprehensive picture because they typically consider only specific elements in the complex web of causal relationships, because empirical evidence is mostly drawn from a narrow set of Western advanced industrialized democracies, and because they neglect the impact of globalization

The effect of ToD (more specifically: electoral systems) on VoC is the focus of studies by Gourevitch and Shinn (2005), Pagano and Volpin (2005), Iversen (2005), Iversen and Soskice (2006) and others. Three causal mechanisms are identified. First, voting rules affect policy output – and hence the legal and regulatory framework of VoC – by determining the weight attached to the preferences of different subgroups among the electorate. Majoritarian systems force politicians to woo the median voter, while proportional representation gives voice to a wider range of constituents. Second, voting rules influence preferences, by determining the credibility of long-term political commitments. Majoritarian systems, like that of Britain, are more prone to radical policy swings than PR systems, and rational voters anticipating such swings should be less willing to support policy measures or enter political bargains with pay-offs premised on long-term continuity. Third, voting rules directly influence elements integral to the VoC, such as interest group association. Martin (2006) claims that gaps in party representation caused by the majoritarian electoral system were filled by highly politicized business organizations that were unable to cooperate with other class factions, reducing the capacity of US employers to create coordinating institutions and to express collective interests in economic developmental and social policies.

A smaller subset of studies on the effect of ToD on VoC focuses on party competition (specifically: strength of the left) instead of electoral rules. In Mark Roe's (2003) influential argument, "social democracy" – through its presumed negative effect on shareholder rights – is the main determinant of cross-national differences in ownership dispersion. Roe assumes that minority shareholders in countries where social democratic values prevail have more reason to fear that their interests will be trampled on, inducing owners to hold larger blocks of shares. The power resource literature on welfare state development identifies the historical strength of the left as a key explanatory variable for the size and structure of welfare states (e.g., Esping-Andersen 1990). Iversen and Stephens (2008) build on this work in their study of partisan influences on skills regimes.

The reverse effect – of VoC on ToD – is explored by Cusack *et al.* (2007), Callaghan (2009) and Perotti and von Thadden (2006), among other. Causally, VoC are said to affect actors' preferences via their material interests, and these preferences in turn are thought to shape aspects of ToD. Cusack *et al.* (2007) argue that preferences shaped by VoC affect the choice of electoral system. They build on previous work by Hall and Soskice, Svenson, Mares, Thelen and others whereby employer preferences depend on the production strategies in which companies engage.[2] Based on this, Cusack *et al.* maintain that low economic coordination at the end of the nineteenth century bred class conflict that led parties on the right to favor majoritarian institutions as the best protection against the rising left. Where economic coordination was high, employers and skilled workers shared an interest in institutions that would protect investment in co-specific assets, leading parties on the right to support proportional representation. Callaghan (2009) and Perotti and von Thadden (2006) argue that VoC affects patterns of party competition. Callaghan's study on the politics of takeover regulation assumes that parties cater to their core clienteles and argues that, where both upscale socioeconomic groups and working-class clienteles are shaped by the structure of corporate ownership. Perotti and von Thadden's study on the allocation of corporate control to banks rather than equity holders assumes that parties cater to the median voter and argues that, where wealth is concentrated among richer voters, a political majority has more at stake in the form of firm-specific human capital, and therefore supports dominance by banks. If instead the median voter has a sufficient financial stake, she supports equity dominance, which results in riskier investment strategies and possibly higher innovation, at the cost of greater individual risk-bearing.

The present volume conceptualizes these various causal links as elements of a positive feedback loop (solid lines in Figure 1.1) that is responsible for the

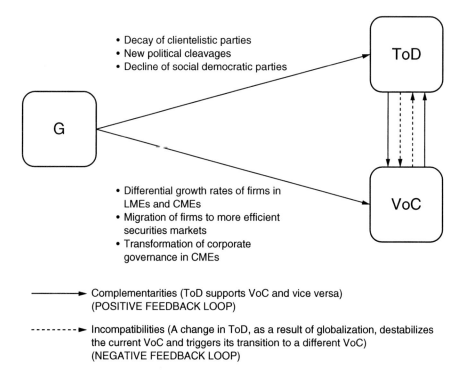

Figure 1.1 Globalization, ToD and VoC change.

formation and reproduction of two clusters of advanced countries, respectively characterized by Majoritarian-LMEs (Liberal Market Economies) and Consensus-CME (Coordinated Market Economies) combinations. Chapter 2 draws on terminology from the literature on institutional change to systematize some of the generic processes at work (namely functional adjustment, path dependency, critical juncture, diffusion). Beyond that, we also draw attention to the negative feedback loop (broken lines in Figure 1.1) that is set in motion by globalization. Alongside technological development and population aging, increasing cross-border mobility of goods, services, capital and workers contributes to putting the established ToD-VoC combinations under strain. Chapter 2 labels the generic processes at work by employing the terms bricolage, radical reform and – again – diffusion. The assembled case studies start from the assumption that the impact of globalization on the relationship between ToD and VoC is shaped by both positive and negative feedback loops. To obtain a comprehensive picture, each chapter focuses on a different aspect of this complex causal web.

Economic pressures of globalization and their political impact

Previous work on the economic pressures of globalization has focused on their impact on economic behavior. As noted above, the debate on whether globalization would cause varieties of capitalism to converge long centered on whether companies in CMEs derived competitive advantages or disadvantages from labor market protections, stakeholder-oriented corporate governance and other regulatory constraints. According to some, the purely economic mechanisms of differential growth rates (Hansmann and Kraakman 2001), migration of companies to more efficient securities markets (Coffee 1999), changes in the composition of corporate ownership (Goyer 2007)[3] and increased shareholder-value pressure (Ahmadjian and Robbins 2005; Dore 2000; Jackson 2005) would, given increased capital mobility, threaten CMEs. According to others, the economic mechanism of comparative advantage would ensure continued institutional differentiation as part of a global division of labor (Hall and Soskice 2001). Hall and Thelen assert that firms' "defection," or economic exit, generates changes in VoC (Hall and Thelen 2009).

The present volume focuses on how globalization affects the political behavior of economic actors. While we concur that globalization, by transforming corporate governance systems, changes the preferences of firms in CMEs, we explore more closely how this change of preferences is reflected in political processes. Firms in CMEs that turn into "global players" with an increasingly short-term perspective are lobbying their governments to adopt neo-liberal policies such as privatization of state enterprises, deregulation of labor markets, abolition of various regulations in domestic markets, and conclusion of Free Trade Agreements (FTAs) with foreign countries. Consequently, economic regulations have diminished considerably in CMEs. For example, according to Ido's chapter in this volume (Chapter 3), from the late 1980s to 2003 the strictness of employment protection regulations has decreased significantly in CMEs and Mixed Market Economies (MMEs), while increasing slightly in LMEs. Whether the changed preferences of firms in CMEs result in a transformation of their production regimes into LMEs depends on the political dynamics of production regime reorganization. To this end, Pempel's chapter in this volume (Chapter 6) describes the changing political strategies of large Japanese manufacturers.

Prior research on the economically induced political consequences of globalization has also neglected the possibility that these consequences differ across varieties of capitalism. The hypothesis springs to mind when the comparative politics literature is confronted with related research in the field of political economy. As reviewed above, Azmanova (2004) and Kriesi *et al.* (2008) argue that globalization transforms the political space in West European countries by generating new conflicts between winners and losers that cross-cut traditional cleavages. Meanwhile, Hall and Soskice (2001) and others suggest that the distribution of the winners and losers from globalization differs across VoC, because international trade encourages companies to specialize in those market segments where their national production regime offers comparative institutional advantages. While unskilled workers suffer through globalization in all advanced industrialized economies, the size of this group varies across market segments and, by extension, across countries. Beyond the scope of the present volume, systematic examination of this hypothesis merits further research.[4]

Political pressures of globalization

Previous work on the political pressures of globalization has largely treated the state as a "black box." Political consequences such as the reduced scope for government action, including autonomous macroeconomic and industrial policies as well as the maintenance of a substantial welfare state (Berger 2000) were explained as the direct effects of globalization, which the powerless state was unable to oppose.

We open this "black box" and question the assumption of powerlessness by examining how political institutions mediate the pressures associated with globalization (cf. Keohane and Milner 1996). Prior research on veto points and veto players (Tsebelis 2002) suggests that political institutions shape processes and outcomes. For example, neo-liberal reforms are harder to carry out in corporatist countries because such reforms are opposed by powerful organized workers, and policy adjustments tend to be slower in consensus democracies, where the "losers" of globalization are represented in inclusive electoral institutions (Swank 2002). Recent modifications of electoral systems, party systems and party organizations in several advanced countries provide a good opportunity to further advance this research. While ToD as a whole have remained stable, a wave of electoral system reforms during the 1990s has increased the number of countries with "mixed-member" systems, i.e., hybrid of proportional and majoritarian electoral systems (Gallagher and Mitchell 2005). In the cases of Italy and

Japan, newly introduced more majoritarian electoral systems have produced more bipolar party systems. Chapters 5, 6 and 7 examine whether such changes in the constituent elements of ToD have engendered changes in the VoC of these countries.

Regarding the impact of globalization on the dynamics of party competition, the existing literature offers two strands of research. The first focuses on the difficulties of left-leaning parties to protect their traditional working-class clienteles from the consequences of increased labor market competition (Berger 2000). Traditionally the interests of low-skilled workers in CMEs were firmly protected by corporatist institutions and duly represented in national politics by strong social democratic parties. Globalization is said to hit unskilled workers hardest by putting them in direct competition with those in poorer countries like China and India, hence leading to a decline in their bargaining power and in the political fortunes of social democratic parties. The second strand concentrates on the difficulties of clientelistic parties of the center and the right to protect their supporters from the consequences of increased product market competition. According to this account, the Christian democrat and conservative parties in several MME and CME struggled because globalization reduced the rents of their large firms and the agricultural sector (Kayser 2007; Kitschelt 2007). Golden (2004) cites globally-oriented small firms in the "Third Italy" as an example of actors who opted for "political exit" in response to the new economic opportunities of the Single European Market. In her view, their withdrawal of support was one of the critical factors that contributed to the collapse of the DC (Christian Democrats: Democrazia Cristiana). The breakup of the center occupied by the DC led to the reshuffling of the postwar Italian party system as a whole with the emergence of Forza Italia and the Lega Nord on the right in the ideological spectrum. Chapter 6 in this volume describes comparable developments in Japan. While it has brought the dominant parties to a head, globalization is opening the possibility for new groups to gain political representation and thereby reshape their VoC. For example, center-left parties in France, Germany, Italy and the United States turned to shareholders during the 1990s to form a new social class alliance with a segment of finance and the middle class (Cioffi and Höpner 2006). In general, dominant parties need to adapt their support bases in response to changing economic conditions if they want to remain dominant. As Pempel (1990: 349) puts it, they require "the Machiavellian capacity to betray some portions of the party's original support group in order to attract newer more vital support." Prime Minister Koizumi proved his "Machiavellian capacity" when he promoted neo-liberal "structural reforms," by replacing a section of the Liberal Democratic Party's (LDP) original supporting social class alliance (i.e., agricultural population, storekeepers and rural areas) with globalized firms and urban population. If such a project succeeds, the LDP will be transformed from a conservative party that places some emphasis on social compensation into a liberal party with an unabashed pro-market orientation.

The "new politics" of production regimes

The pressures described above have prompted a shift in ToD-VoC combinations by altering the nature of production regime politics in two ways. First, they have affected party organization. In the "old politics" of production regimes, mass parties that relied on organized interests such as unskilled workers and farmers played the leading role in the creation of postwar VoC. Today, outsiders of the postwar ToD-VoC combinations and even individual populist leaders are promoting neo-liberal policies against the opposition of the vested interests. The party politics literature has also identified these new phenomena, including the emergence of populism, presidentialization of politics (Poguntke 2005), decline of mass parties and their replacement by cartel parties (Mair 1997). Schmitter's "radical reforms" scenario is pertinent here. Second, they have affected the ideological positioning of parties. Parties that traditionally supported highly regulated and protected markets have become more neo-liberal. Adams *et al.* (2009) found that parties of the center and the right have adjusted their ideologies in response to globalization because of their being office-seeking cadre parties rather than policy-seeking mass parties of the left. Such a transformation of the party of the right is vividly exposed by Pempel's analysis of the LDP under Koizumi in this volume (Chapter 6). In sum, VoC can be expected to change in response to one of several political developments associated with globalization. Previously marginalized groups may promote alternative social class alliances (from "outside"); members of the previously dominant social group may choose political "exit," or exercise political "voice"; or the ruling party, for its own political survival, opts to reorganize its supporting social class alliances (from "above"). Throughout these processes, projects of reorganizing the social class alliances are taking place inside several dominant parties or across the lines of political parties. These projects might lead to the transformation of conservative parties into pro-market liberal parties with new neo-liberal policy packages (e.g., Japan), or the emergence of a new more bipolar party system with new "right parties" (Forza Italia and Lega Nord) replacing the traditional center party (DC) (the case of Italy).

Outline of the volume

In Chapter 2, Schmitter and Todor not only provide an explanation of the causal mechanisms that sustain the ToD-VoC combinations as well as those that will transform them, but also offer a "spider web" analysis of ToD-VoC combinations of advanced countries. In the innovative "spider web" analysis, Schmitter and Todor decompose each of VoC and ToD into multidimensional entities with "radials" and "spokes" and test for associations between them. Following Aristotle, Schmitter and Todor also suggest the likely superiority of "mixed" regimes in terms of political and economic performance.

Chapter 3 takes the party system – one of the few time-varying institutions of the ToD – as an independent variable and examines how its cross-national difference and its change over time impacted on the changes in the two key domains of VoC., i.e., corporate governance and labor market, for the OECD countries. Ido finds that majoritarian democracies have increased the sizes of their stock markets while maintaining their liberal labor markets, whereas consensus democracies have expanded the number of atypical workers while maintaining their bank-based corporate governance. In explaining the causal mechanism that led to these contrasting outcomes, Ido emphasizes the importance of contrasting preferences of business parties in these two types of democracies.

Chapter 4 illustrates how "political feedback effects from the structure of the political economy sustain distinctive VoC (Hall 2007: 81)." Callaghan argues that differences in the dispersion of corporate ownership, which characterize different VoC, help explain why party positions on corporate governance vary across countries and over time. She shows that British, French and German political debates over takeover regulation since the 1950s differ significantly along several dimensions, including the pattern of left/right competition and the timing of debate, and that these differences correspond to differences in the structure of corporate ownership. To explain the observed correlation, Callaghan assumes that parties cater to their core constituents, and provides reasons for why ownership structure shapes the preferences of both upscale socioeconomic groups and working-class clienteles.

Chapters 5 through 7 focus on Italy and Japan, which have experienced major changes in their party systems. With the collapse of the DC, the Italian party system has changed from polarized pluralism to a bipolar system with high fragmentation. In Japan, since the electoral reform in the 1990s, transformation of its party system from an LDP-led predominant party system to a two-party system is now under way. Moreover, both Berlusconi and Koizumi, arguably the two most "populist" leaders in advanced countries, have exploited the use of media in their appeal to the general public in order to put their neo-liberal economic programs into practice.

In Chapter 5, Burroni and Trigilia see the basic character of the Italian VoC in the territorial disparity of its productive organization (i.e., coexistence of different "models of capitalism"). In Italy in the 1990s, technocratic governments promoted extensive neo-liberal reforms of the economy, which included inflation and wage control, industrial relations reform, pension reform, and privatization of its gigantic state-holding companies. These wide-ranging reforms can be considered as a case of what Schmitter calls "radical reforms" promoted by outsiders. However, under the new fragmented bipolar party system where both right and left camps were internally divided, this experiment of "radical reforms" soon lost momentum. Nevertheless, they note that despite such stagnation of national economic reforms (what they call "incomplete reformism"), small-scale firms in industrial districts have realized substantial development, and hence reinforced the hybrid character of the Italian VoC. Their evidence counters Hall and Soskice's thesis that "pure systems perform better than hybrid ones" and supports Schmitter's Aristotelian view of the superiority of "mixed" regimes.

In Chapter 6, Pempel argues that with protected domestic markets in the postwar period, the LDP has assured economic development and its political domination, by promoting the development of large firms (or the "productivity" sector, according to Pempel's catchy expression) with various protection measures and subsidies and redistributing part of the fruits of economic development to the dependent social groups (or "pork" sector) in return for their votes. However, having increased production in the overseas facilities, globalized large manufacturers that no longer need government protection are now asking the government to deregulate and liberalize the economy (i.e., their preferences were "transformed"). The LDP in turn, which cannot afford to continue the redistribution to the "pork" sector, has been facing a crisis of political domination. Pempel interprets the political achievement of Koizumi who, with his "presidential" – even close to "populist" – style of policy-making, realized sweeping neo-liberal "structural reforms," including privatization of the Japan Post and his project of "reorganizing" the LDP into a neo-liberal party, in the context of the LDP's political dilemma.

Chapter 7 takes party system changes as a dependent variable. Magara asks why electoral reforms during the 1990s in Italy and Japan produced opposite political outcomes. Japan's LDP returned to power after a short period in opposition, while the largest opposition party, the Social Democratic Party of Japan, has virtually disappeared from the political scene. On the other hand, in Italy, DC disappeared, while the PCI (Italian Communist Party: Partito Comunista Italiano) was transformed into a center-left party (PDS [Democratic Party of the Left: Partito Democratico di Sinistra], then DS [Democrats of the Left: Democratici di Sinistra], and now PD [Democratic Party: Partito Democratico]) and came into power. Magara explains these contrasting outcomes as a result of interactions among factions within the establishment (reformers and status quo seekers) and factions within the opposition (realists and ideologists).

In Chapter 8, McNally argues that the case of contemporary China presents a rare opportunity to trace the evolution of a variety of capitalism under intense globalization. He calls China's emerging capitalism a "competitive state coordinated economy," again a new variety of capitalism, which we cannot find in Hall and Soskice's volume. China's competitive state coordinated economy is a hybrid variety of capitalism that comprises two sectors, i.e., a state-led sector and that of small-scale private producers. He finds the basic reason why China's "new capitalism" takes such a form in its decision to embrace globalization and its historically-inherited social institutions such as Guanxi practice. On the other hand, McNally deems contemporary China an "authoritarian regime" that has only a small chance for a democratic transition, at least in the near future, because of the dependence of its capitalists, professionals and workers on the CCP-led state.

In Russia and Eastern Europe, large-scale political and economic changes have occurred since the late 1980s. The magnitude of these changes is far greater than those in advanced countries. On the political plane, what these countries have experienced were not transitions from a type of democracy to another type, but transitions from dictatorships to democracies. On the economic plane, what they underwent were not transitions from a variety of capitalism to another variety, but transitions from controlled economies of communism to capitalist economies. Reflecting such a gigantic magnitude of their political and economic changes, in Chapter 9 Bruszt focuses on political regimes (democracies, hybrid regimes and dictatorships), instead of party systems, in his explanation of the emerging variety of capitalism in post-communist Russia and Eastern Europe.

Notes

1 Specifically, Amable (2003) finds that the number of seats in the lower chamber obtained by parties on the left is positively correlated with the degree of coordination of wage bargaining, the intensity of employment policies, centralization of financial systems and the extent of the welfare state.
2 Employers engaged in strategies that rely on firm-specific skills are said to be more supportive of policy measures that enhance job security (thereby encouraging investment in firm-specific skills) than employers engaged in strategies that rely on the flexibility to restructure at short notice.
3 Goyer (2007) distinguishes foreign shareholders into types in terms of their differential impact upon the adoption of long-term horizons by manufacturing firms – one is pensions that take a long-term view and the other is mutual/hedge funds that take a short-term view.
4 Obvious methodological difficulties preclude rigorous quantitative testing. Most prominent is the general problem of over-determination associated with the small number of cases: the universe of advanced industrial democracies is too small to allow controlling for the many variables other than VoC that also influence party system change. The problem is compounded by strong elective affinities between VoC and ToD. There are few if any cases that vary along the VoC dimension and other relevant variables but fall into the same ToD category. As a result, it is impossible to determine whether variation in the effect of globalization on party systems are due to differences in VoC, due to differences in ToD, or neither, or both. A third problem is the lack of socioeconomic data on the distributional consequences of globalization for different VoC. Such data would not solve the over-determination problem. However, if it turned out that the number and identity of losers does not differ significantly across VoC, the hypothesis could be rejected nonetheless.

References

Adams, J., Haupt, A. B. and Stoll, H. (2009). What moves parties? *Comparative Political Studies*, 42(5), 611–639.
Ahmadjian, C. L. and Robbins, G. E. (2005). A clash of capitalisms: foreign shareholders and corporate restructuring in 1990s Japan. *American Sociological Review*, 70(3), 451–471.
Amable, B. (2003). *The Diversity of Modern Capitalism*. Oxford: Oxford University Press.
Azmanova, A. (2004). The mobilisation of the European Left in the early 21st century. *European Journal of Sociology*, 45, 273–306.
Berger, S. (2000). Globalization and politics. *Annual Review of Political Science*, 3(1), 43.
Callaghan, H. (2009). Insiders, outsiders and the politics of corporate governance: how

ownership structure affects party positions in Britain, Germany and France. *Comparative Political Studies*, 42, 733–762.

Callaghan, H. (2010). Beyond methodological nationalism: how multilevel governance affects the clash of capitalisms. *Journal of European Public Policy*, 17, 564–580.

Callaghan, H. and Höpner, M. (2005). European integration and the clash of capitalisms: political cleavages over takeover liberalization. *Comparative European Politics*, 3, 307–332.

Cioffi, J. W. and Höpner, M. (2006). The political paradox of finance capitalism: interests, preferences, and center-left party politics in corporate governance reform. *Politics & Society*, 34(4), 463–502.

Coffee, J. C., Jr. (1999). Future as history: the prospects for global convergence in corporate governance and its implications. *Northwestern University Law Review*, 93(3), 641–708.

Crouch, C. and Streeck, W. (eds.) (1996). *The Political Economy of Modern Capitalism: Mapping Convergence and Diversity*. London: Francis Pinter.

Cusack, T. R., Iversen, T. and Soskice, D. (2007). Economic interests and the origins of electoral systems. *American Political Science Review*, 101, 373–391.

Dore, R. P. (2000). *Stock Market Capitalism: Welfare Capitalism: Japan and Germany versus the Anglo-Saxons*. New York: Oxford University Press.

Esping-Andersen, G. (1990). *Three Worlds of Welfare Capitalism*. Princeton: Princeton University Press.

Gallagher, M. and Mitchell, P. (eds.) (2005). *The Politics of Electoral Systems*. New York: Oxford University Press.

Golden, M. A. (2004). International economic sources of regime change: how European integration undermined Italy's postwar party system. *Comparative Political Studies*, 37(10), 1238–1274.

Gourevitch, P. and Shinn, J. (2005). *Political Power and Corporate Control: The New Global Politics of Corporate Governance*. Princeton: Princeton University Press.

Goyer, M. (2007). Capital mobility, varieties of institutional investors, and the transforming stability of corporate governance in France and Germany. In B. Hancke, M. Rhodes and M. Thatcher (eds.), *Beyond Varieties of Capitalism: Conflict, Contradiction, and Complementarities in the European Economy*. New York: Oxford University Press, 80–104.

Hall, P. and Soskice, D. (eds.) (2001). *Varieties of Capitalism: The Institutional Foundations of Comparative Advantage*. Oxford: Oxford University Press.

Hall, P. A. (2007). The evolution of varieties of capitalism in Europe. In B. Hancke, M. Rhodes and M. Thatcher (eds.), *Beyond Varieties of Capitalism: Conflict, Contradiction, and Complementarities in the European Economy*. New York: Oxford University Press.

Hall, P. A. and Thelen, K. (2009). Institutional change in varieties of capitalism. *Socio-Economic Review*, 7(1), 7–34.

Hancke, B., Rhodes, M. and Thatcher, M. (eds.) (2007). *Beyond Varieties of Capitalism: Conflict, Contradictions, and Complementarities in the European Economy*. Oxford: Oxford University Press.

Hansmann, H. and Kraakman, R. (2001). The end of history for corporate law. *Georgetown Law Journal*, 89, 439–468.

Held, D. (2006). *Models of Democracy*. Third Edition. Palo Alto: Stanford University Press.

Hollingsworth, J. R., Schmitter, P. C. and Streeck, W. (eds.) (1994). *Governing Capitalist Economies*. New York: Oxford University Press.

Iversen, T. (2005). *Capitalism, Democracy, and Welfare*. Cambridge: Cambridge University Press.

Iversen, T. and Soskice, D. (2006). Electoral institutions and the politics of coalitions: why some democracies redistribute more than others. *American Political Science Review*, 100, 165–181.

Iversen, T. and Stephens, J. (2008). Partisan politics, the welfare state, and three worlds of human capital formation. *Comparative Political Studies*, 41, 600–637.

Jackson, G. (2005). Stakeholders under pressure: corporate governance and labour management in Germany and Japan. *Corporate Governance: An International Review*, 13(3), 419–428.

Kayser, M. A. (2007). How domestic is domestic politics? Globalization and elections. *Annual Review of Political Science*, 10(1), 341–362.

Keohane, R. O. and Milner, H. V. (eds.) (1996). *Internationalization and Domestic Politics*. Cambridge: Cambridge University Press.

Kitschelt, H. (2007). Citizen-politician linkages: an introduction. In H. Kitschelt and S. Wilkinson (eds.), *Patrons, Clients, and Policies: Patterns of Democratic Accountability and Political Competition*. New York: Cambridge University Press.

Kriesi, H., Grande, E., Lachat, R., Dolezal, M., Bornschier, S. and Frey, T. (eds.) (2008). *West European Politics in the Age of Globalization*. Cambridge: Cambridge University Press.

Lijphart, A. (1999). *Patterns of Democracy: Government Forms and Performance in Thirty-Six Countries*. New Haven: Yale University Press.

Mair, P. (1997). *Party System Change: Approaches and Interpretations*. New York: Oxford University Press.

Martin, C. J. (2006). Sectional parties, divided business. *Studies in American Political Development*, 20, 160–184.

Pagano, M. and Volpin, P. (2005). The political economy of corporate governance. *American Economic Review*, 94(4), 1005–1030.

Pempel, T. J. (ed.) (1990). *Uncommon Democracies: The One-Party Dominant Regimes*. Ithaca: Cornell University Press.

Perotti, E. and von Thadden, E. (2006). Corporate governance and the distribution of wealth: a political-economy perspective. *Journal of Institutional and Theoretical Economics*, 162, 204–217.

Poguntke, T. (ed.) (2005). *The Presidentialization of Politics: A Comparative Study of Modern Democracies*. New York: Oxford University Press.

Porter, M. E. (1990). *The Competitive Advantage of Nations*. New York: Free Press, Macmillan, Inc.

Roe, M. J. (2003). *Political Determinants of Corporate Governance – Political Context, Corporate Impact*. Oxford and New York: Oxford University Press.

Sartori, G. (1994). *Comparative Constitutional Engineering*. New York: New York University Press.

Swank, D. (2002). *Global Capital, Political Institutions, and Policy Change in Developed Welfare States*. New York: Cambridge University Press.

Tsebelis, G. (2002). *Veto Players: How Political Institutions Work*. Princeton: Princeton University Press.

Whitley, R. (1999). *Divergent Capitalisms: The Social Structuring and Change of Business Systems*. Oxford: Oxford University Press.

2 Varieties of capitalism and types of democracy*

Philippe C. Schmitter with Arpad Todor

The relationship between capitalism and democracy has been an extensively studied and "essentially contested" one. We now know that all "real-existing" democratic polities (REDs) also have "real-existing" capitalist economies (RECs),[1] but that not all capitalist economies have democratic polities.[2] From this we can infer that some variety of capitalism (VoC) may be necessary for some type of democracy (ToD), but not sufficient. Inversely, we can infer that having a democratic political regime is neither a necessary nor a sufficient condition for the survival or success of a capitalist economy.[3]

Capitalism would seem, therefore, to be logically (and probably also temporally) prior to democracy.[4] Its initial historical agent, the bourgeoisie, played a central role in the transition from autocracy (at least, in Europe) and its subsequent side-product, the industrial proletariat, was a key protagonist in expanding further its inclusiveness and scope. On the other hand, the third wave of democratization, especially in the post-communist countries, exhibited an alternative causal path. Democratic institutions are chosen by design prior, or simultaneously, with the transition from a socialist planned to a capitalist market economy. In other words, the usual assumption is that the VoC determines the ToD – except in Central Eastern Europe and (some parts of) the former Soviet Union where this pattern was inverted.

But this tells us little about the relation that may develop historically (and, especially, exist contemporarily) between different VoCs and different ToDs. We have a general warrant for assuming that they are likely to be related – if only on the grounds that if capitalism is related to democracy, then subtypes of both are also likely to be related to each other, and that the VoC is probably going to be the causal agent – at least, initially. For example, Boix (2003) subsumes capitalism and democracy under the broader notion of asset distribution. "Real-existing" democratization – that is formal equalization of power resources across individuals and social groups – depends on a relatively equal distribution of economic assets, a high degree of capital mobility and an effective distribution of power that limits the ability to repress or outmaneuver opponents. Lasting democratic regimes can thrive in countries where either economic equality or capital mobility are high or where circumstances limit the concentration of the coercive capacity of elites. However convincing this argument may seem, it is too generic to predict the outcome of the continuous interaction between various VoCs and ToDs.

If this rational-logical assertion were not enough, we also have the "practical" essays in The Federalist Papers written by Alexander Hamilton at a particularly crucial early stage in the choice of regime-level institutions for the United States that clearly argue in favor of such a connection. Unless the United States adopted a set of "reasonably centralized" and "calculatedly limited" institutions of a "republican" form of government democracy, he argued, it will not be capable of sustaining and, much less, furthering its capitalist development. We do not know the counter-factual answer to what would have happened had the United States retained its "confederal" set of more dispersed and directly democratic institutions, but we certainly can testify to the subsequent emergence of a vigorous liberal market VoC.[5]

Four casual mechanisms

So much for the abstract theoretical and concrete practical arguments about the relation between REC and RED. What about the specific causal mechanisms that might be connecting them over more or less lengthy periods of time? What are the generic interactions that might be linking the two and can therefore be relied upon to explain why changes in one VoC or ToD will produce corresponding changes in each other? In this section we explore the four most important mechanisms and their inherent limitations in mapping out these causal connections.

1   The most obvious mechanism is "functional adjustment," namely, that the reproductive and growth needs of REC cause a predictable and corresponding change in RED. The ToD, therefore, consists of an apposite political solution to the needs determined by different VoCs – perhaps with an intervening lag in time due to resistance by those actors who benefit from the previous ToD. Conversely, political change can determine automatic strategic adaptation from capital owners. Moreover, it is often assumed that once this functional adjustment has taken place, both REC and RED enter into a state of equilibrium until some exogenous event or process disturbs their relationship.

On the other hand, as Greif and Laitin (2004) argue, subsequent shocks may be generated by endogenous evolutions of quasi-parameters associated with the co-functioning of a specific constellation of VoC and ToD. According to Martin and Swank (2008: 181), the relationship between VoC and ToD is mediated by the tendency of proportional, multiparty systems to foster social corporatist business organizations, and the tendency of two-party systems and federalism to promote pluralistic organizations. Thus, the developmentalist intention to develop peak business associations adjusted to the existing political institutions, producing pluralist associations, in the United States, instead of centralized, organized and hierarchical *social corporatist* groups in Europe.

Only a moment's historical reflection should suffice to discard the omnipresence and efficacy of this mechanism. Needs have to be perceived by actors; theories have to be invented to explain why particular changes in institutions or practices will produce the supposedly necessary effects; individuals and organizations have to be mobilized to act collectively in conformity to these perceived needs and theories. Needless to say, at every stage, conflicts are likely to emerge among actors with varying capacities to defend and advance their interests – and different ToDs enhance these capacities and channel them through pre-established representative institutions and decision-making agencies. The stickiness of specific choices, especially through their institutionalization, is bound to limit the overall feedback capacity of even the best intentioned functionalist mechanisms. The end result will most probably be a compromise among political forces that will almost surely be less than optimally functional from the perspective of the needs of a specific variety of REC.

2   The next most obvious mechanism is *"path dependency,"*[6] namely, that whatever the initial relationship between REC and RED, the actors involved will increasingly benefit from reproducing that past relationship – even when it is suboptimal from the perspective of capitalism and/or democracy as a whole. Some combination of sunken material costs, entrenched habits of behavior, established normative justifications, legal-constitutional obstacles, power resources of existing beneficiaries and the sheer uncertainty of the costs and benefits involved in shifting to a different relationship in the future contributes to keeping both the VoC and the ToD on the same evolutionary path. All one should expect are minor incremental adjustments on both sides of the equation.

Again, historical reflection suggests that, in terms of frequency of occurrence, path dependency has been more likely than functional adjustment, but it does not always prevail. One important limitation in using path dependency as an analytical tool is that usually it can only be identified in long-term processes, and can accommodate almost any kind of relationship. It is almost impossible to falsify statements about path dependencies. Incremental changes in either REC or RED can accumulate and gradually affect the market competitiveness or the balance of political forces to the extent that a new relationship emerges – usually as the unintended product of reform measures designed for other purposes. In a recent book, John Campbell (2004: 69–74) has re-introduced the French expression, *bricolage*, in order to capture the process of institutional change within the limits of path dependency – while noting that, given the accumulation of such experiences plus the unintended consequences that can generate, these seemingly incremental and tentative efforts at repairing the practices embedded in a particular path can eventually result in the shift to another path.

3   More infrequently, *critical junctures* can occur – either as the result of exogenous events or endogenous contradictions – that may compel actors to shift their expectations to a dramatically different path.[7] Usually those advocating

such a shift can be found among the persons marginalized and victimized by the previous connection between VoC and ToD or, more likely, some type of autocracy (ToA). But not infrequently, firms, parties, movements and persons who were previous beneficiaries and even supporters of the *ancien régime* under special circumstances – international war and severe economic depression have been the most common – may defect from the status quo and mobilize disaffected and impotent groups. On the basis of either the desperation of past losers or the anticipated reaction of past winners, a critical mass of actors emerges that is willing to bear the uncertain "transition costs" of moving toward different institutions of either REC or RED. The normal term for such a change, when it involves widespread violence and encompasses a wide range of institutions, is *revolution*. Perhaps because the countries we are interested in seem incapable of accomplishing changes in institutions of such a magnitude, we tend to exclude this generic mechanism from consideration.[8] Let us think in terms of the mechanism of *radical reform*. However, the "real-existing socialisms" of Eastern Europe and the former Soviet Union remind us that something like revolution does exist – although sometimes as a mechanism for the shift from a variety of non-capitalism and a type of non-democracy.[9]

4   In the present context of rapidly expanding communications across political boundaries, another causal mechanism has become increasingly significant: *diffusion*. One can no longer assume that political and economic units are coincident with each other at the national level and, hence, that national actors choose their institutions only on the basis of their own historical legacies or contemporary endowments. Every unit is in contact with each other and, thanks to globalization, is in competition with each other to some extent. Messages circulate freely and consequentially, especially those that contain some information about "best practices" that are alleged to convey comparative economic or political advantage. On the one hand, the conviction that the VoC or ToD of one's competitor is somehow superior can provide a powerful incentive for imitation – and the fact that it is so demonstrably superior serves to reduce both the search costs and uncertainty of benefits that previously inhibited switching to a different path.[10] On the other hand, the recent literature on transnational networks[11] stresses that diffusion happened through non-competitive methods as a side effect of networking effects.

As strong as the urge to mimic winners has become, it has also become equally apparent that this is not an easy task. Somewhere in the specification of the "proper/optimal" relationship between VoC and ToD, imitators have often ignored the contextual features that made the original model work well. Strict transfers of such practices or institutions rarely produce similar effects and by the time the imitators have understood and incorporated these seemingly extraneous features, the reforms become so transformed and compromised in the process that they make only a marginal positive contribution, if one at all. John

Campbell (2004: 79–86) has labeled such mechanisms of cross-border adaptation to diffusion as *"translations."*[12] Also, some models depend on some *institutional complementarity* with one or several non-transferable features like location comparative advantages.

One (complex) operationalization

What would be the best way to test for the relationship between VoC and ToD? Obviously, a compelling answer to the nature of this VoC–ToD relationship hinges critically on how one specifies the varieties and types and how one subsequently derives valid measures for their multiple components. The purpose of this section is precisely to define and to operationalize these variables and, then, to test for their co-variation

The simplest way to do this would be to dichotomize both of them. VoC becomes either (1) a *Liberal Market Economy (*LME);[13] or (2) a *Coordinated Market Economy* (CME).[14] ToD becomes either (1) a *Majoritarian (or Westminsterian) Democracy* (MD); or (2) a *Consensual (earlier called Consociational) Democracy* (CD).[15] And, sure enough, when these are cross-tabulated, a rough correspondence emerges.[16] It is stronger between LMEs and MDs, as exemplified by the tight Anglo-American–Canadian–Australian cluster, than between CMEs and CDs, formed more loosely by the Scandinavian countries, Austria, Germany and Switzerland. However, a substantial number of rich capitalist economies and stable political democracies prove difficult to classify. We suspect that if one were to apply this mode of analysis to cross-sections of a longer historical period, the association would prove even weaker and the number of "unclassifiable cases" would be much greater.

Recently, there has also been a flood of econometrically inspired analyses that have "proven" that specific political traits of well-established democracies – electoral laws, party systems, partisan complexion of governments, executive formats, territorial arrangements, etc. – are significantly associated with one or another of the components of VoC and with differences in aggregate performance: growth, employment, public expenditure, income inequality, etc.[17]

Nevertheless, from the perspective of this chapter, these findings are simply not convincing. The LME/CME and MD/CD dichotomies are too primitive in their attempt to capture variation and, as we shall see, too inconsistent in their allegedly covariant sub-components[18] The bi-variate cross-tabulations or regression analyses of these isolated variables also violate the central principle behind the effort to conceptualize both VoC and ToD – namely, that what counts are precisely not single traits but distinctive clusters or profiles. There is no theoretically grounded reason to expect that, say, the electoral system or the banking system alone will produce reliable and significant variation in macro-level outcomes across all units. What counts is the "variety" or "type," i.e., the *ensemble or Gestalt* of traits, with their related institutional complementarities It is only when the single trait is embedded in a more encompassing whole that the anticipated effects are likely to emerge and to persist. For this reason, only an empirical

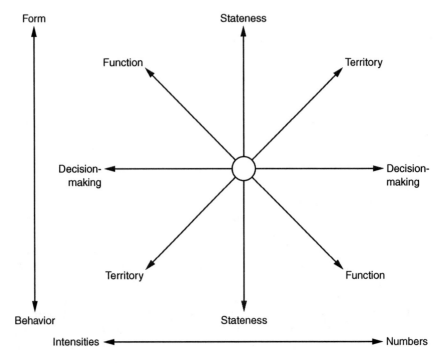

Figure 2.1 Generic properties of VoC and ToD.

technique that is capable of capturing, displaying and analyzing the multiple variables that are conceptualized as forming a distinctive variety or a type will suffice. Moreover, provided the scale of measurement is more discrete than a dichotomy, this technique should provide a reliable basis for generating intermediate varieties/types and not just the proximity of single cases to one or another of extreme varieties/types.

In the analysis that follows, VoC and ToD are explicitly treated as multidimensional economic and political constructs, not as a bundle of presumed independent variables as in the econometric literature. Each of the two will be initially disaggregated into four + two generic dimensions ("radials") that are shared and then each of these radials will be further defined in terms of two subcomponents ("spokes"), one based on formal organizational properties and the other on observed behavioral outcomes. Each of the 12 spokes will then be operationalized by apposite quantitative measures and only when they have been tested for patterns of association will it become apparent whether the dichotomous LME/CME and MD/CD clusters really exist and are capable of bearing the inferences that have been associated with them.

Four + two radials

The literatures on capitalism and on democracy are not only prolific, but they are rich in suggestions concerning what dimensions of variation are relevant for proceeding *per genus et differentiam*, i.e., for distinguishing subtypes of each of them. Political science has been especially attentive to this conceptual challenge and to uncovering significant differences in the stability of regimes, the distribution of benefits and the quality of performance according to subtypes of democracy. Instead, economic science once it fell under the hegemony of neo-liberalism abolished such a concern with institutional and behavioral differences[19] and postulated a single trans-national, trans-cultural and trans-historical model of capitalism that served as an almost universally accepted basis for further deductive assumptions. Only a group of political economists/political scientists thought that there might be different varieties of "it" with different rules and relationships and that these other configurations might even be capable of persisting as long and performing as well as the neo-liberal one. Those scholars who have jumped on the VoC bandwagon in recent years, however, have been almost as prolific in suggesting dimensions of variation as their ToD forerunners.

Our task has been to shift through these suggestions and to try to find a limited number of meta-dimensions that potentially apply to both VoC and ToD. The four + two that have been selected seem to fit that bill, but they are but a first approximation.

1 *Stateness.* This is the most obvious variable that both capitalism and democracy have in common. Without it, neither would exist nor persist. Only the most hardcore libertarian or anarchist could argue that the state should be abolished or allowed to wither away – unless he or she would also prefer to destroy both capitalism and democracy. Their common embeddedness in a system of public authority that is capable of exercising (even of monopolizing) legitimate coercion over a distinctive territory is a sine qua non for ensuring that market contracts will be observed and that elected officials will be able to respond effectively to citizen demands. Economic and political actors will differ over how much and what kind of stateness is desirable: liberal individualists will argue that "He who governs least, governs best" and social collectivists will say that "We who govern most, govern most fairly," but neither would deny the need for some stateness.[20]

2 *Rules for decision-making.* Both REC and RED have to make decisions about the allocation of resources – private and public. In the former case, most of these are disguised as virtually invisible and routine choices by producers and consumers interacting in markets of differing degrees and types of competition. In the latter, they usually involve highly formalized and controversial choices made by citizens when voting in elections and by politicians when governing in public offices – and these are converted into explicit laws and regulations that are binding on everyone and not just on

those that made them. In both cases, however, what counts in determining the outcome are the rules under which competition takes place, i.e., who can participate, what resources they can bring to bear and what mechanisms determine the resulting distribution of costs and benefits.

3   *Territorial representation.* Both economies and polities occupy particular physical spaces such that the location within which their transactions occurs makes a difference – *pace* the recent literature on globalization that pretends that territorial constraints have been eliminated (or, at least, made much less relevant). Consumers and citizens, producers and rulers recognize this and they channel expectations and make demands accordingly, usually through intermediaries that represent their interests. Again, this may seem much less relevant in the case of economic actors.[21] Political actors, as long as they are compelled to operate with the system of national states, are much more acutely aware of the extent of coincidence between the boundaries of private markets and public authorities.

4   *Functional representation.* At the core of capitalism and democracy lie two intrinsic interest conflicts: (1) between workers and the owners of productive enterprises; and (2) between citizens and the rulers of authoritative institutions. Not uncommonly, the personnel in these two categories coincide or, at least, they occupy mutually distinctive positions of power. To deal with these conflicts, both have developed systems of bargaining or regulating the interaction between organizations representing the functional interests of conflicting classes, sectors and professions. Needless to say, these are not the only conflicts that capitalists and politicians have to resolve in order to perpetuate their dominant status, but they have proven to be the most enduring.

5   *Asset specificity.* Actors in the economy and polity have different initial endowments and subsequent resources that they can bring to bear in order to influence outcomes. The orthodox "liberal" theories of both realms strongly emphasize the provision of the least specific of assets. These are presumably something that all actors have and can distribute freely in response to any preference: namely, "citizenship" and "consumer sovereignty." In the real worlds of capitalism and democracy, however, assets are not only less equally distributed, but they involve qualitative distinctions that limit their utility. Depending on type of education, initial career choices, willingness to move, procedures for nominating candidates and barriers to entry and inclusion, some actors can find themselves with personal and collective assets that can only be used for specific purposes.

6   *Gender discrimination.* Among the actors with different material endowments and cultural resources that can be expected to receive discriminatory treatment in both the economy and polity are women. They were initially excluded from access to ownership and managerial roles in production and citizen roles in collective decision-making. Belatedly and often as the result of collective action, they have improved their status in both domains, although the timing and circumstances of this process have varied considerably across the rich

democracies of the OECD. This has left a good deal of variation in the extent to which something approaching gender equality has been realized among them.

Eight + four spokes

Having identified above the four + two "radial" properties that REC and RED seem to have in common according to their respective literatures, we can now proceed to measuring their occurrence across 19 of the OECD member countries.[22] The radials of stateness, decision-making, territorial and functional representation, asset specificity and gender discrimination are highly abstract in nature and, therefore, cannot be subject to measurement directly. There has been some discussion of potential indicators by analysts of both VoC and ToD, but there is no accepted standard for measuring them; therefore, we have had to select from a number of measures and our choices may not always be the most apposite. Only further experimentation with alternative ones will correct for this possible source of distortion.

Each of the radials for VoC and ToD has been divided into two "spokes." The first attempts to capture the formal or institutional aspects of the corresponding radial and the second the empirical consequences that might have been produced by those institutions. For example, stateness in ToD is measured first by total central government revenues as a percentage of GNP and then by the number of government employees as a proportion of the total economically active population. In VoC, it is first measured as the percentage of the total banking system that is owned by all levels of the state and then by an index of economic liberalization. Our expectation is that the two spokes of the same radial will be positively correlated, but not perfectly so. If there is no correlation and, even worse, if it is negative, the indicators are probably wrong – unless the discrepancy is due to measurement error.

The raw data have been transformed into rank-orders. Since our "sample" consists of 19 OECD member states, each of the ten spokes for VoC and the ten for ToD can only vary from one to 19. In the interest of clarity of exposition, we have assigned the top ranking (1) to those countries that, theoretically speaking, score closest to the "*liberal*" ideal and the bottom rank (19) to those that should be closest to the "*social*" end of the continuum. Henceforth, our extremes – for both VoC and ToD – will be labeled as **liberal and social capitalism and liberal and social democracy**. And the closer a given country comes to obtaining a similar rank-ordering across all of the ten spokes, the more it presumably resembles the ideal-types anchoring the extreme ends of these continua. Those in the middle will be labeled as "hybrids."

What will first concern us, therefore, is the rank consistency within in each country and then across them. This transformation has several important consequences. It evens out the scores between countries and reduces potential distortion due to outliers. It may even correct for some measurement error due to minor differences in data collection. It also has the effect of making the data much easier to display visually and to analyze comparatively. However, it also enhances the importance of intermediate cases that might have only minor variations in "real" data and this improves the likelihood of our discovering hybrid or mixed profiles of VoC and ToD – exactly the opposite of the bias built into the usual dichotomous treatment that both have received.

All indicators are scored for values as close as possible to 1995, although none of them are believed to vary greatly from year-to-year. A more thorough investigation of the VoC–ToD relationship would, of course, examine changes in these indicators over a much longer period and presumably contribute to answering the particularly vexing question of causality.

The VoC spokes

The following are the operational indicators that have been chosen for the varieties of capitalism:

1 *Stateness*: for this radial, there exists a multiplicity of potential indicators all having to do with the intervention (or lack thereof) by public officials, elected or appointed, in the conduct of economic firms. Without a doubt, stateness has declined over recent decades, either as the result of explicit public policy of liberalization and privatization or as the side-product of globalization and regionalization that have undermined the capacity of state institutions to act efficiently and effectively.

   VoC 1A. The importance of all banks that are state-owned in proportion to the total holdings of all banks (inverted so that the lower the public holding the lower the rank).[23, 24]

   VoC 1B. A composite measure of "economic freedom" from public constraints in the form of business taxation, labor relations and other regulations.[25]

2 *Decision-making*: along this dimension the major discussion in the recent literature has focused on the nature of "corporate governance," i.e., whether managers of private enterprises are subject to greater influence and control by shareholders or whether they are protected by legal or cross-holding arrangements. A more standard concern has been with the degree of market competition and the role of potentially oligopolistic large firms.

   VoC 2C. Composite indicator of corporate governance.[26]

   VoC 2D. Indicator of concentration of ownership in largest firms.[27]

3 *Territory*: economists have generally not been concerned with spatial referents in their work.[28] By-and-large, where enterprises are located across an entire economy and how this has affected their external political and social relations has not been considered important – even though there does exist a lively discussion in economic sociology about the impact of precisely these features. In the absence of any potential indicator or any available data, we have chosen to substitute measures for the nature of the financial system which everyone seems to agree is a very important radial for different VoCs.

VoC 3E. Market capitalization as a percentage of GNP.[29]

VoC 3F. Composite indicator of shareholder rights.[30]

4   *Function*: all economies are composed of multiple sectors that produce different goods and services and these tend to have different forms of organization at the firm level and different degrees of competition and coordination at the aggregate or "meso" level. Contrary to the literature that tends to assign a single "generic" label to the entire VoC, e.g., "liberal" or "coordinated," these chains of producer-to-producer relations may vary considerably within the same national economy and, if so, their relative importance becomes a crucial determinant of the VoC. Moreover, "natural" forms of protection from internal competition as well as governmental forms of protectionism from external competition tend to distinguish between "sheltered" and "exposed" sectors.

VoC 4G. Index of labor coordination.[31]

VoC 4H. Indicator of employment protection.[32]

5   *Asset specificity*: there has long been a political economy literature arguing that concentrated dependence on a particular commodity has a broad and determinant impact on the VoC. In its most extreme contemporary version, petroleum, and so-called "lootable assets" such as diamonds and rare minerals, have produced even more dramatic and perverse outcomes. None of the countries in the OECD sample exhibit such concentrations in their productive or trading systems (with the partial exceptions of Norway and earlier the Netherlands), but they do have significant variation in the domestic importance of different productive sectors and the composition of their exports. Strangely, the VoC literature has focused exclusively on the nature of vocational training and its impact on intra-class income distribution – more perhaps a result of previous research by its authors than of theoretical reflection.

VoC 5I. Percentage of post-secondary students in vocational training.[33]

VoC 5J. Earning inequality among full-time employees.[34]

6   *Gender discrimination*: the two dimensions upon which "real-existing" capitalism has been accused of systematically discriminating against women involve their access to positions of management and their remuneration for performing equal tasks.

VoC 6K. Women as a percentage of total CEOs in large enterprises.[35]

VoC 6L. Wage disparity between men and women.[36]

Our test for internal validity rests on the rank-order correlations between the two spokes of each of the six VoC radials. They should all be positive since they are supposed to be measuring different aspects of the same variable, and it would be even better if they were "statistically significant," i.e., not likely to have emerged randomly. Table 2.1 demonstrates that the first assumption was correct. As expected, all of the Spearman's Rho correlations between spokes of the first four radials are positive with the weakest coming between the two indicators of finance capitalism: market shares and shareholder rights, and the strongest

Table 2.1 Rank-order correlation between VoC spokes: Spearman's Rho

Dimension	Interaction	Significance
Stateness	VoC 1A × VoC 1B = +0.439	Sig. (2-tailed) = 0.068
Decision-making	VoC 2C × VoC 2D = +0.551	Sig. (2-tailed) = 0.014
Territoriality	VoC 3E × VoC 3F = +0.578	Sig. (2-tailed) = 0.010
Functionality	VoC 4G × VoC 4H = +0.694	Sig. (2-tailed) = 0.001
Asset specificity	VoC 5I × VoC 5J = +0.779	Sig. (2-tailed) = 0.001
Gender discrimination	VoC 6K × VoC 6L = +0.577	Sig. (2-tailed) = 0.015

emerging between the two indicators of functional or class relations: labor coordination and employment protection.

The first indicator of stateness, public ownership of banks, is especially positively and highly correlated almost across the board, first with its corresponding spoke, government employment (0.439) and then with VoC 2C (0.729), VoC 2D (0.533), VoC 3E (0.767), VoC 3F (0.742), VoC 4G (0.681) and VoC 4H (0.486). This is a truly amazing performance for a single variable. The second stateness spoke also does well in predicting the other dimensions of VoC, but not quite as well. The two measures of asset specificity, namely, those related to extent of vocational training and equality of inter-class income, are highly correlated with each other (0.779), but weakly correlated with all of the other VoC spokes which is a hint that it is not a generic component of VoC or that we have not operationalized it properly.

Hidden within these encouragingly positive correlations are some interesting divergences within individual countries.[37] For example, Spain ranked highly liberal (fifth) in its low state ownership of banks, but highly social (fifteenth) in its restrictions on economic freedom. Austria and Germany have high proportions of state banks (nineteenth and seventeenth respectively), but did relatively well in terms of the composite index of economic freedom (seventh and eighth). In addition to these deviant cases, there were two "puzzling" ones on this stateness spoke: Sweden and Switzerland, but in opposite directions. The decision-making radial had fewer deviant cases. France was social in terms of more restrictive corporate governance provisions (fifteenth), but very liberal (fourth) in terms of low level of banking concentration. Australia was deviant in the opposite direction (sixth and sixteenth). The shareholder radial is more difficult to interpret since one of its spokes (VoC 3E: shareholder rights) is a classification system with many tied-ranks. As mentioned, the functional or class conflict radial is so tight that there are neither deviant nor puzzling cases.

The first "plausibility probe" that goes beyond the usual suspects in the literature involved asset specificity, strangely conceptualized in terms of the importance for vocational training of workers. In Table 2.1, the two indicators we have chosen – the one measuring directly the proportion of age-eligible persons in vocational training course and the other measuring earnings equality among regular employees – are very highly correlated at the national level (+0.779).

As a second "plausibility probe," we also entered a sixth radial in an effort to capture differences in the gendered nature of VoC, the spokes being measured by rank-orderings of the proportion of women as officers in major corporations and general wage equality between men and women – both from the *World Economic Forum's Report on The Global Gender Gap, 2007.*[38] These two indicators are, not surprisingly, related to each other (+0.577)

The ToD spokes

The following are the operational indicators that have been chosen for the types of democracy:

1   *Stateness*: for this radial, the political science literature is massive, but ambiguous with regard to measurement. The most obvious measure for its first spoke is the capacity of the state (at the central level) to extract resources via taxation, fees, etc. from the citizenry on the assumption that this capacity is not only an indicator of the exercise of legitimate coercion over a given territory, but also of the state's potential role in policy intervention affecting the livelihood of its citizenry. The more social the democracy the higher the rank-ordering. The indicator for the second spoke is much less obvious. As a first approximation, we have used employment at all levels of government as a proportion of the total economically active population, but this may be subject to distortion in those cases where state activities are performed by private subcontractors or by semi-public institutions. The "liberal" end of the spoke should indicate a smaller proportional level of government receipts and less public employment.

  ToD 1A. Central government receipts as a percentage of GNP.[39]

  ToD 1B. Government employment at all levels as a proportion of total economically active population.[40]

2   *Decision-making*: again the political science literature on this radial in REDs offers a surfeit of possible indicators, based on two generic dimensions: the relation between citizens and their representatives and the relation between different governing institutions. The first should measure the extent to which ruling institutions "check and balance" each other and are constitutionally autonomous. The second indicator tries to capture the extent to which the party system is dominated (presumably as the result of free, fair and competitive elections) by a single party – regardless of the ideological orientation of that party or of the electoral system involved. Liberal REDs are expected to have more elaborate systems of horizontal accountability and more competitive party systems. Social REDs should have less constrained structures of authority and to have more dominant party systems.[41]

  ToD 2C. A combination of the number of veto points and institutional limits on central state executive and legislative authority.[42]

  ToD 2D. Average extent of hegemony by the leading party in executive authority from 1950 to 1998.[43]

3   *Territory*: in REDs, the representation of territorial constituencies is largely a function of the operation of the party system and multiparty electoral competition. In this regard two dimensions or spokes have usually been stressed: (1) the number of political parties that are effectively present, i.e., occupy a seat or seats in the lower house of national parliaments; and (2) the extent of disproportionality in the distribution of these seats. The usual assumption is that "liberal" democracies tend to have fewer effective parties than "social" ones and, hence, tend to form governments based on a single or small number of parties. One way this partisan concentration is accomplished is through electoral systems that "punish" voters who do not choose a winning candidate. "Social" democracies typically have proportional systems that ensure that such votes are not thrown away and that territorially based minorities, whatever their social basis, are ensured a presence in the legislative process Needless to say, many other sources of variation have been extensively discussed in the literature on ToD, for example, the ideological distance between competing parties, the extent of mal-apportionment across constituencies, the margin of victory for winning parties or coalitions, not to mention the eternal favorite, the nature of the electoral system itself. Again, the indicators we have chosen should be supplemented or revised in further research.

ToD 3E. Number of effective political parties.[44]

ToD 3F. The index of disproportionality in territorial representation.[45]

4   *Function*: all varieties of capitalism generate systematic differences in reward and security for groups of persons that exercise different functions in their systems of production and distribution. Dealing with conflicts between these classes is a common element in all types of democracy that varies in accord with the extent of self-organization and consciousness of these groups, as well as the rules that emerge historically in response to such conflicts. At the liberal end of the continuum, the formation of trade unions was initially resisted by authorities as an "obstacle" to economic freedom and subsequently left to the voluntary choice of workers, while at the social end these same public authorities (often controlled by governments with strong social democratic parties) facilitated membership and even granted privileged access to their organizations. Employers responded (often reluctantly) by organizing themselves and entering into more or less stable bargaining arrangements at varying levels of aggregation ranging from the plant to the sector to the entire economy. As a result of these differing patterns of negotiation (captured in part by the conceptual distinction between pluralist and corporatist systems of interest intermediation), REDs adopted quite different policies with regard to tolerating or facilitating trade union membership. In liberal REDs, they tended to result in lower membership densities; in social REDs, they approached almost universal levels of membership for workers and professionals.

ToD 4G. Mean score on corporatism indicator.[46]

ToD 4H. Trade Uuion membership as a percentage of total economically active population.[47]

5   *Asset specificity*: discussions about ToD have completely ignored this variable. Indeed, it is not easy to imagine why it should be relevant or how it should be measured. In any democracy, the most specific asset is citizenship – equal status of individuals with regard to a specified set of rights and obligations. Needless to say, not all citizens take equal advantage of these rights or obligations, but they should be entitled in principle to do so. The more the holders of these citizenship properties are protected against others (foreigners, resident aliens) making competing claims, the higher should be the asset specificity of acting within a given ToD. At the extreme, in totalitarian autocracies, citizens benefit (or suffer) from extreme asset specificity since they cannot leave nor can foreigners enter without the explicit consent of public authorities. Contemporary REDs are much more tolerant, but they do vary considerably in the extent to which they permit foreigners to reside in their territory and to which they permit these "denizens" to acquire citizenship.

   ToD 5I. Non-nationals legally resident (denizens) as a percentage of total population.[48]

   ToD 5J. Difficulty for denizens to acquire national citizenship.[49]

6   *Gender discrimination*: democratic theory, once it had "digested" and then taken for granted the enfranchisement of women, shifted its attention to their success in gaining access to specific elite positions, namely, (1) in parliaments (usually the lower one if there are two); and (2) in cabinets formed by winning parties or coalitions. At the liberal end of the continuum, this process of transformation was left to the "normal" channels of choice and representation by political parties and, hence, gender equality has taken longer and been less comprehensive. At the social end, REDs have usually adopted specific government or party policies designed to accelerate this process, e.g., by quotas, and to extend it to a wider set of political positions.

   ToD 6K. Women in cabinet positions.[50]

   ToD 6L. Women in parliament.[51]

The correlation between the two indicators of stateness: total central government receipts and total government employment is strong (0.621), as expected. The puzzling cases (those with more than five and less than ten differences in rank) are the United States and Portugal with low proportional receipts, but

Table 2.2 Rank-order correlation between ToD spokes for each radial: Spearman's Rho

Dimension	Interaction	Significance
Stateness	ToD 1A × ToD 1B = +0.621	Sig. (2-tailed) = 0.005
Decision-making	ToD 2C × ToD 2D = +0.519	Sig. (2-tailed) = 0.023
Territoriality	ToD 3E × ToD 3F = +0.605	Sig. (2-tailed) = 0.006
Functionality	ToD 4G × ToD 4H = +0.839	Sig. (2-tailed) = 0.000
Asset specificity	ToD 5I × ToD 5J = +0.493	Sig. (2-tailed) = 0.068
Gender discrimination	ToD 6K × ToD 6L = +0.786	Sig. (2-tailed) = 0.000

relatively more government employees. The United Kingdom and Netherlands got it the other way round. No case is deviant according to our standard.

The correlation between formal institutional concentration and domination by a single competitive party on the decision-making radial is positive and strong (0.519). For example, Japan is the only deviant case with a rank of 19 in party domination and only 11 in dispersion of formal institutions. The United States, Australia and Italy are puzzling in that their less concentrated systems of executive decision-making are combined with more competitive electoral systems.

The territorial radial as measured by the number of effective parties in the electorate and the extent of disproportionality in the distribution of votes won and seats allocated in the lower house of the legislature is quite strongly correlated (0.605). Theoretically speaking, this conforms to expectations since underlying both are similarities in electoral systems, especially the difference between majoritarian, first-past-the-post, single-member (liberal) ones and various types of proportional, multi-member (social) ones – not to mention the German mixed system. Switzerland is a deviant case with relatively few parties in the electorate (third) and a highly proportionate allocation of legislative seats. Belgium is also deviant in the same fashion. Portugal is even more deviant in the opposite direction, eighteenth with its large number of parties and yet fourth in terms of proportionality! Austria is "puzzling" in the same regard.

The two spokes of the functional radial that measure the pattern of interaction between organized capital and labor and that of membership in trade unions are very strongly correlated (0.839). Only Ireland is deviant according to our criteria. It has a much more liberal (or pluralist) industrial relations system (third) and relatively high levels of trade union density (fifteenth).[52] Belgium, Denmark, Italy, Australia, Canada and the United Kingdom are "puzzling" in the same way. Inversely, Germany and Japan have smaller densities of membership than one might expect from their higher scores on corporatism.

The ToD spokes intended to represent asset specificity through conditions for nationalization of citizenship (ToD 5J) and proportion of foreign residents (ToD 5I) are positively correlated (0.493), but weakly related to most of the other ToD variables, except (strangely) for the one measuring the number of political parties (0.537) and (less strangely) the ones measuring the corporatist nature of industrial relations (0.463) and proportionate membership in trade unions (0.551).

The spokes measuring women in parliament and in cabinet positions are very strongly related (0.812), as one might suspect. Moreover, both of them have a number of strong associations with other ToD variables. In other words, the more women occupy leading political roles, the more social is the type of democracy in general. And the strongest single predictor of greater gender equality in politics is the mean score for corporatism (+0.607). My conclusion is that the political, as opposed to the economic, treatment of women is an integral component of different types of democracy – but this is not the case for varieties of capitalism.

The internal validity between the two spokes of ToD radials is generally less impressive than that between the VoC ones. This could either imply that the operational indicators of the former are less valid or that, of the two underlying conceptual models, the types of democracy may be based on a less coherent set of assumptions about the interrelationship between institutions and behaviors than the varieties of capitalism. It might also be that the weaker empirical clustering of ToD variables is indicative of a very important empirical difference, namely, that the choice of political regime characteristics is less functionally determined and more path dependent than that of VoC. In the latter case, competition between private firms and across national economies is more compelling and the units involved are better equipped to adjust to changes in consumer preference and technology; whereas, in the former, the dynamics of interaction between political parties, employer associations, trade unions, state agencies and their respective publics are constrained by relatively fixed barriers such as constitutions and legal norms and by deeply entrenched identities and interests that ensure an increasing marginal return to the persistence of institutions, i.e., to path dependency. Also capitalist firms may be more open to imitating the success of their competitors at home or abroad. Political actors may be reluctant to do so for fear of being accused of lacking patriotism by their more nationalist competitors.

Another sign of this apparently generic difference between varieties and types can be gleaned from the differing importance of stateness. In the former, as we observed, VoC 1A (government ownership of banks) correlated positively and strongly with virtually all of the other VoC spokes; whereas, in the latter, ToD 1A (central government receipts as a percentage of GNP) was also positively associated with the other ToD spokes, but more weakly so. Nevertheless, in both cases, stateness is the most powerful predictor of variation in the other dimensions of VoC and ToD. It deserves the theoretical status of "Master Variable" in both of the macro-configurations of national political economy.

With regard to both VoC and ToD, the measures of correlation are usually higher for the raw scores (Pearson Product Moment) than for the rank orderings (Spearman's Rho). This could be a simple artifact of the way in which the two statistical instruments are calculated, or it could have interpretive significance. We mentioned above that the transformation from the former to the latter diminishes the importance of outlying cases – whether high or low – and stretches out the scores of those cases that cluster toward the mean. If the distribution of values in each of the spokes is roughly normal, this suggests that the prevailing "dichotomous" treatment of VoC and ToD in the literature may have some merit. Two "extreme and tight" clusters of cases at the high (liberal/majoritarian) and low (coordinated/consensus) ends of the continuum and a larger number of more-or-less indistinguishable and mixed cases in the middle would explain why the raw scores are more strongly associated than the rank orderings.[53]

Two × 19 circles?

If the recent literatures on VoC and ToD were completely accurate (and if our indicators are valid), the plotting of the radials for each of the 19 countries

Table 2.3 Aggregate rank order and standard deviations of the four VoC radials and their eight spokes

	Rank	(Score)	Standard deviation
Liberal capitalism			
United Kingdom	1.	(1.5)	0.5
United States	2.	(1.6)	1.1
Canada	3.	(4.0)	2.8
Ireland	4.	(5.9)	2.4
Switzerland	5.	(6.4)	3.8
Australia	6.	(7.0)	3.9
			Average SD = 2.1
Hybrid capitalism			
Japan	7.	(7.5)	7.0
Netherlands	8.	(8.0)	2.6
Denmark	9.	(9.9)	2.0
Sweden	10.	(10.4)	4.1
Spain	11.	(10.9)	3.6
France	12.	(11.3)	3.3
Finland	13.	(12.0)	2.9
Belgium	14.	(12.5)	4.3
			Average SD = 3.8
Social capitalism			
Germany	15.	(13.9)	4.8
Portugal	16.	(13.9)	4.5
Norway	17.	(14.1)	2.7
Austria	18.	(16.4)	4.5
Italy	19.	(16.9)	1.5
			Average SD = 2.8

should produce 40 (almost) perfect circles. If economic and political institutions and practices were really as functionally "complementary" as these theories suggest, the rank-orderings of their measures should result in the most liberal cases, i.e., with the scores closest to 1 on both VoC and ToD variables, clustering in a tight circle at the center of the diagram and those with social capitalism and democracy should form a large outer circle. Although both literatures have little to say about the cases in between these extremes, we might also expect a similar functionalist logic to apply such that these hybrids could also have their own set of complementary institutions and, therefore, be circular and consistent with their intermediate scores.[54]

The 19 VoC cases group rather well into three categories, as expected: (1) liberal, (2) hybrid and (3) social. The distribution of data seems to support one of the key assumptions of the VoC literature – namely, that there are two more institutionally consistent varieties at the far ends of a continuum. The hybrids in the middle rank less consistently. This is illustrated by the tendency for lower standard deviations in a country's rank-orderings, the closer it approximates one or the other of the extreme ideal types. There are a few exceptions, however. Denmark and the Netherlands are unusually consistent cases of hybridity;

Table 2.4 Rank ordering of VoC cases by their standard deviations

1. United Kingdom	0.5
2. United States	1.2
3. Italy	1.5
4. Denmark	2.0
5. Ireland	2.4
6. Netherlands	2.6
7. Norway	2.7
8. Canada	2.8
9. Finland	2.9
10. France	3.3
11. Spain	3.6
12. Switzerland	3.8
13. Australia	3.9
14. Sweden	4.1
15. Belgium	4.3
16. Portugal	4.5
17. Austria	4.5
18. Germany	4.8
19. Japan	7.0

Australia has rather mixed rankings for an otherwise liberal economy. Japan is by far the most erratic performer with a SD of 7.0; the United Kingdom is the least erratic (at the liberal end of the continuum) with a SD of 0.5. Not surprisingly, the United States also emerges as consistently liberal.

What is much less supportive of that literature is its assumption that "pure" types (LMEs and CMEs in their jargon) perform better. This topic has *not* been an explicit concern in this chapter, but a quick glance would reveal a lot of variation in growth, inflation and unemployment rates within each of the clusters – certainly now, but also in the recent past. Hall and Gingerich test the hypothesis that growth is higher in purer types of VoC with robust positive results for the 1971–1997 period.[55] If, however, they are ranked by their institutional consistency (as indicated by their respective standard deviations), the order that emerges would seem to conform better to expectations about performance. Even so, two of the most celebrated (and presumably best performing CMEs) – Austria and Germany – would not seem to have the hypothesized "institutional complementary." Rather, they (and Japan even more so) look decidedly heterodoxical.

The types of democracy are a bit more difficult to classify than the varieties of capitalism. They too cluster numerically and can be labelled safely as liberal, hybrid and social, but this produces some strange pairings. Spain emerges in Table 2.5 as more liberal than Australia, Switzerland or the United Kingdom. The clue to these counter-intuitive aggregate scores is to be found in the standard deviations. They are much higher than for VoC and the two "extreme" types, liberal and social, have higher SD scores than the hybrid ones. The social democratic cluster is easily recognizable (Austria, Finland, Denmark, Norway and

Table 2.5 Aggregate rank order and standard deviations of the four ToD radials and their eight spokes

	Rank	(Score)	Standard deviation
Liberal democracies			
United States	1.	(3.8)	3.2
Spain	2.	(2.8)	2.8
Australia	3.	(3.3)	3.3
Canada	4.	(7.3)	5.7
United Kingdom	5.	(7.5)	6.5
			Average SD = 4.3
Hybrid democracies			
Portugal	6.	(7.8)	4.5
Switzerland	7.	(7.9)	6.9
France	8.	(8.3)	5.0
Germany	9.	(9.5)	5.5
Japan	10.	(9.5	5.3
Italy	11.	(10.3)	4.2
Belgium	12.	(10.4)	5.0
Ireland	13.	(10.4)	2.2
Netherlands	14.	(10.5)	6.0
			Average SD = 4.9
Social democracies			
Austria	15.	(12.4)	5.7
Finland	16.	(13.4)	4.5
Denmark	17.	(14.1)	4.1
Norway	18.	(15.5)	3.0
Sweden	19.	(17.0)	2.4

Sweden – in that order), although one might have expected the Netherlands to have been placed in it.

Again, it is the standard deviations that are as revealing as the rank-order correlations. This time the "extremes" of liberal and social democracy do not have much more consistent institutional rankings. The United Kingdom and Switzerland are both near the "liberal" end, but have two of the highest SDs. Austria, close to the "social" end, also has a high SD, but Sweden, the most "social" of all, has a very low one. We conclude that ToDs have less "complementary" rules and practices than VoCs. Whether this has important implications for the quality of their respective democracies is something we cannot assess in this chapter.

The "fit" between VoC and ToD

Finally, we are able to address the question we began with: how do the two patterns "fit" with each other. Our initial orienting hypothesis was that they should be positively and significantly correlated – although since we only have been exploiting synchronic data (*c.*1990 or longer term averages around this date), we can not assert anything about their diachronic relationship. The literature,

Table 2.6 Aggregate rank order of standard deviations from the eight ToD spokes

Standard deviation	Country
2.3	Sweden
3.2	United States
3.3	Spain
3.5	Ireland
3.9	Australia
4.1	Germany
4.2	Denmark
4.3	Italy
4.6	Portugal
4.8	Finland
5.1	Belgium
5.4	Austria
5.6	Netherlands
5.8	Norway
5.8	Canada
6.1	Japan
6.2	France
6.6	UK
6.7	Switzerland

however, confidently assumes that historically it has been the VoC that has determined the ToD.[56]

Taking into consideration 19 of the richest OECD countries, the relationship is a very significant +0.475. On the basis of our conceptualization of the key dimensions (the "Radials") and our admittedly more tentative operationalization

Table 2.7 The rank order relation between the compound rank-orders for VoC and ToD

	VoC ranking	ToD ranking	(Disparity)
United Kingdom	1.	4.	(−3)
United States	2.	1.	(+1)
Canada	3.	7.	(−4)
Ireland	4.	14.	(−10)
Switzerland	5.	5.	(0)
Australia	6.	3.	(+3)
Japan	7.	9.	(−2)
Netherlands	8.	12.	(−4)
Denmark	9.	17.	(−8)
Sweden	10.	19.	(−9)
Spain	11.	2.	(+9)
France	12.	10.	(+2)
Finland	13.	16.	(−3)
Belgium	14.	11.	(+3)
Germany	15.	8.	(+7)
Portugal	16.	6.	(+10)
Norway	17.	18.	(−1)
Austria	18.	15.	(+3)
Italy	19.	13.	(+6)

of their variables (the "Spokes"), we confidently conclude that *the varieties of capitalism and the types of democracy are predictably and positively related to each other.* The more liberal, hybrid or social is the one; the more liberal, hybrid or social is the other. Moreover, this relationship holds not just at the extremes, but throughout the full range of variation.

If we begin with the assumption that capitalism is usually prior to democracy and provides much of the impetus for and the constraints within which democracy operates, this leads us to the conclusion that ToD should be embedded within VoC, rather than the contrary. We have symbolized this by the pluses and minuses in the rank disparities in Table 2.6. A minus indicates that the country has a less liberal type of democracy than one would expect given its more liberal variety of capitalism, a plus that its VoC is more social than its ToD. Several countries seem to have the VoC and ToD they deserve: the United States (+1), Norway (–1), Switzerland (0), Belgium (+3), Australia (+3), Japan (–2), Austria (+3) and Finland (–3) are almost exactly where one would expect them to be. Others come close to a putative "equilibrium" with a disparity of six ranks or less: France (+4), United Kingdom (–4), Canada (–4), Netherlands (–4), Italy (+6) and Germany (+6). The puzzling cases are Denmark (–8), Sweden (–9), Ireland (–9) and Spain (+9), but the only really deviant one is Portugal (+10). Its democracy is much more liberal (sixth) than its economy (sixteenth). So, while the general VoC–ToD relationship holds up remarkably well, there are sufficient exceptions to keep comparative analysts busy for some time.

In Figure 2.2, the composite rank-orderings for VoC and ToD are superimposed upon each other which permits a visualization of puzzles and deviations noted above. Portugal's large "blue" social capitalism extends far beyond its liberal democracy; Sweden, Denmark and Ireland have the opposite misfit. Their social democracies reach beyond their expected levels of social capitalism. Spain looks like a mild version of the Portuguese misfit.

Our second basic assumption has been that both the varieties of capitalism and the types of democracy share the same defining dimensions that we have called "radials," i.e., (1) stateness, (2) decision-making, (3) territory and (4) function. This is a much more demanding one to prove empirically. The correlation of aggregate rank orderings of VoC and ToD that we have just discovered could obtain – even if the presumably corresponding spokes did not correlate with each other. All it proves is that there are general configurations that are related to each other, not that each of the four radials is related to its allegedly corresponding one.[57]

Table 2.8 Stateness radial: correlation between VoC and ToD spokes: Spearman's Rho

	ToD 1A	*ToD1B*
VoC 1A	0.342	0.407
Sig. (2-tailed)	0.152	0.084
VoC 1B	0.443	0.620
Sig. (2-tailed)	0.066	0.006**

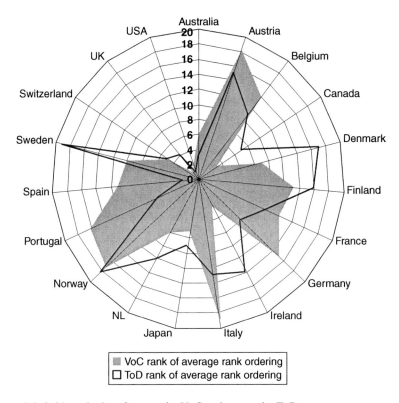

Figure 2.2 Spiderweb plot of composite VoC and composite ToD.

At the top or institutional end, the relationship between central government receipts and state role in the banking system is weak (0.342), but that between a higher degree of freedom from economic regulation and the proportion of government employees is high (0.620). Moreover, the other two cells show positive relationships. Which suggests that there is some merit in the assumption of a common stateness dimension to both VoC and ToD.

Table 2.9 Decision-making radial: correlation between VoC and ToD spokes: Spearman's Rho

	ToD 2C	*ToD 2D*
VoC 2C	−0.262	−0.262
Sig. (2-tailed)	0.279	0.279
VoC 2D	−0.024	−0.061
Sig. (2-tailed)	0.923	0.805

A similar notion that this communality also applies between decision-making in firms and in political institutions is firmly rejected by the matrix in Table 2.9.

Table 2.10 Territorial radial: correlation between VoC and ToD spokes: Spearman's Rho

	ToD 3E	*ToD 3F*
VoC 3E	0.181	0.436
Sig. (2-tailed)	0.459	0.062
VoC 3F	0.714	0.573
Sig. (2-tailed)	0.001	0.010

The pattern revealed in Table 2.10 shows a strong relationship between our territorial radials, which is surprising since we admitted having difficulty coming up with equivalent measures for this VoC spoke. Three of the cells are strongly correlated, with an astonishing high correlation between VoC 3F (shareholder rights) and ToD 3E (the number of effective parties in the electorate).

Table 2.11 Functional radial: correlation between VoC and ToD spokes: Spearman's Rho

	ToD 4G	*ToD 4H*
VoC 4G	0.530	0.438
Sig. (2-tailed)	0.020	0.061
VoC 4H	0.590	0.292
Sig. (2-tailed)	0.008	0.224

When it comes to dealing with the relations between capital and labor at the plant or sectoral level and through the political role of their class associations, we discover a set of very high correlations across the two realms, except for that between VoC 4H (the level of employment protection) and ToD 4H (the density of trade union membership). It would seem that lots of members is not a necessary condition for high state regulation of the labor market, especially when the latter is the product of policies inherited from a previous autocratic regime, e.g., Spain and Portugal. Nevertheless this radial is almost as strong a candidate for communality as stateness.

Table 2.12 Asset specificity radial: correlation between VoC and ToD spokes: Spearman's Rho

	ToD 5I	*ToD 5J*
VoC 5I	0.540	0.332
Sig. (2-tailed)	0.038	0.226
VoC 5J	0.571	0.325
Sig. (2-tailed)	0.026	0.237

Asset specificity has not performed well in terms of its connections with other dimensions of either VoC or ToD – leading us to suggest its removal from the analysis – but it is interesting to note how much the nature of a given country's vocational training system tends to be correlated with the proportion of foreigners resident in it (the more foreigners, the less important is vocational training). Could it just be that this indicator of asset specificity is less a characteristic of VoC than of ToD?

Table 2.13 Gender discrimination radial: correlation between VoC and ToD spokes: Spearman's Rho

	ToD 6K	*ToD 6L*
VoC 6K	–0.509*	–0.439
Sig. (2-tailed)	0.037	0.078
VoC 6L	–0.275	–0.135
Sig. (2-tailed)	0.254	0.582

The correlation between our gender discrimination variables in different VoC and ToD is nil – confirming our suspicion that this variable is much more affected by political policies and party competition than by economic calculations and the decisions of firms and plants.

To summarize with regard to the six radials thought to be in common and, hence, to characterize both the varieties and the types, stateness, territory and function conform to this assumption. The radials for decision-making and gender discrimination do not. And the asset specificity radial has a partial set of associations for which we have no explanation.

Eventually, a conclusion

There is no way that we can conclude this study by exploring the causal relation between VoCs and ToDs. We have shown that a general correlation exists between the two, as well as more specific correlations between the radials and spokes that we have used to characterize each of them. But our data preclude even speculating about the causality embedded in the historical processes that have brought them together. We have good reason to believe that the two have had a difficult and, at times, tumultuous relationship. And that, over time, the causal one may have become the affected one – and vice versa. But eventually they managed to converge into what seem to be a self-reinforcing set of rules and practices, even if the performance is not optimal. For the foreseeable future, varieties of capitalism and types of democracy seem to be condemned to coexistence – whether they enjoy it or not.

The second way to conclude this synchronic and descriptive study of the relation between VoC and ToD would have been to test for the impact of our findings upon economic and/or political performance. The major hypothesis "out there" is that the purer varieties of national capitalism closer to the liberal or social poles of the continuum should grow faster, produce less unemployment and have more stable currencies. Presumably, a similar hypothesis could be entertained for the more liberal or social types of national democracy. They should have more stable governments, more satisfied citizens and a higher quality of democracy.

Here, the problem is not the existence or cost of obtaining relevant data. There is an excess of them, especially for OECD countries. What currently makes such an assessment impossible is the existence of extraordinarily great, recent fluctuations in these performance data – without any corresponding changes in the basics of VoC or ToD. Countries that were triumphantly declared "miraculous" just a few years ago have become the most "miserable" ones today. And those that were decried for the "rigidity" of their economic policies or the "unresponsiveness" of their political systems are now doing relatively better than their competitors. In other words, whatever results one might obtain by correlating performance data with VoC or ToD would vary radically according to the time period used to aggregate them.

The safest assumption would seem to be that no variety or type, however pure, can guarantee optimal performance all of the time. This depends on the business or product cycle, trends in consumer preference, the random generation of innovations, shifts in citizen interests and the salience of social cleavages, fads and fashions in public policy, the constraints and opportunities generated by international exchanges, etc. And Aristotle may have had the best answer some time ago. It is those much deprecated "mixed" regimes that may have the "requisite diversity" that enables them to perform well (if not optimally) in different circumstances.

Appendix 1

Table 2.14 Rank scores for VoC spokes

Country	VOC 1A	VOC 1B	VOC 2C	VOC 2D	VOC 3E	VOC 3F	VOC 4G	VOC 4H
Australia	9	5	6	16	6	4	5	5
Austria	19	7	19	15	19	13	19	17
Belgium	14	13	13	17	10	19	7	8
Canada	1	9	3	7	5	1	3	4
Denmark	7	11	7	10	11	13	10	5
Finland	15	—	8	9	14	10	14	10
France	11	14	15	4	12	10	12	10
Germany	17	8	17	5	13	17	17	16
Ireland	6	10	4	6	9	4	4	7
Italy	16	19	18	19	17	17	15	9
Japan	1	4	10	3	2	4	18	14
Netherlands	8	6	11	12	7	4	8	19
Norway	18	12	11	11	16	13	16	10
Portugal	13	16	16	19	18	4	13	19
Spain	5	15	13	14	14	10	8	15
Sweden	12	18	8	13	8	4	10	17
Switzerland	10	1	5	7	3	13	6	3
UK	1	2	2	1	1	1	2	2
United States	1	3	1	1	4	1	1	1

Table 2.15 Rank scores for ToD spokes

Country	TOD 1A	TOD 1B	TOD 2C	TOD 2D	TOD 3E	TOD 3F	TOD 4G	TOD 4H
Australia	4	5	7	14	5	1	8	9
Austria	12	14	3	8	8	13	19	18
Belgium	14	11	4	4	19	7	10	12
Canada	9	13	12	15	4	14	1	1
Denmark	18	17	12	5	15	10	15	15
Finland	17	15	15	3	16	9	12	16
France	15	16	9	1	7	19	7	5
Germany	8	6	1	7	9	12	14	12
Ireland	7	12	12	13	10	18	9	8
Italy	11	9	6	12	17	15	4	9
Japan	5	1	11	19	11	1	11	11
Netherlands	16	2	7	6	13	16	16	6
Norway	13	18	19	16	14	1	18	16
Portugal	3	10	16	11	3	11	5	6
Spain	6	7	9	10	6	1	3	2
Sweden	19	19	19	17	12	17	17	18
Switzerland	1	3	1	2	18	8	13	14
UK	10	4	16	18	2	1	6	2
United States	2	8	4	9	1	1	1	4

Appendix 2

Spiderweb plots of VoC and ToD for all Japan and Germany.

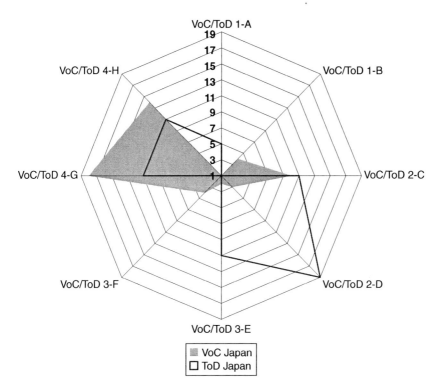

Figure 2.3 Japan.

Note
To illustrate the potential of using this visual methodology for analyzing specific cases and making cross national comparisons, we have included the spiderwebs of Germany and Japan – two countries whose recovery from World War Two has frequently been contrasted. In each case, we have super-imposed its Type of Democracy upon its Variety of Capitalism. In the German case, the two are roughly coordinate with a relatively low standard deviation in rank-orderings – but contrary to the literature that stresses Germany as the archetype of a "Coordinated Market Economy," it is a clear hybrid according to our operationalization. The Japanese case is quite exceptional in that the two profiles are radically in-congruent and the variation among the characteristics of both its VoC and its ToD is the greatest of all the 19 OECD countries.

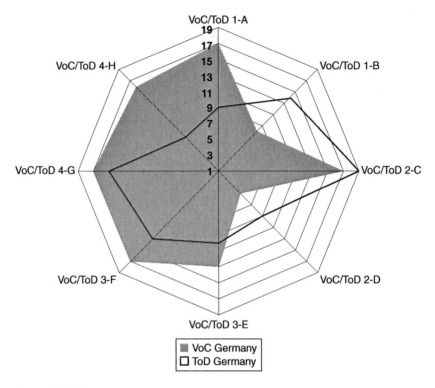

Figure 2.4 Germany.

Notes

* This chapter is the result of a comparative research endeavor supported by the Japan Society for the Promotion of Science Grant-in-Aid for Scientific Research (B) (18330028), Masanobu Ido (Project head) "Party System Change and the Transformation of Production Regime" headed by Masanobu Ido from Waseda University. We are indebted to both of them and to the other participants in this project: Laszlo Bruszt, Helen Callaghan, Hideko Magara, Christopher McNally, Takashi Oshimura, T. J. Pempel and Carlo Trigilia for a simulating set of papers and discussions. Without the spiderwebbing wizardry of Alexander Trechsel, we would not have been able to make it.

1 A "real-existing" democracy (or RED in our terminology) has three characteristics: (1) it calls itself democratic; (2) it is recognized by other self-proclaimed democracies as being "one of them"; and (3) most political scientists applying standard procedural criteria would code it as democratic. The same criteria apply to "real-existing" capitalism (REC). Their resemblance to the ideal types of democracy or capitalism as advocated in theory or described in many civics and economics textbooks is coincidental. In practice, both are the products of a complex set of historical compromises that have resulted in "mixed" regimes.

2 Of course, a country could create democratic institutions faster than it could create a functioning capitalist economy. We refer here to long-term relationships.

3　Indeed, there is a burgeoning literature on the emergence and even success of so-called "Authoritarian Capitalism" with China, Singapore and Vietnam as leading exemplars, and Russia as a more ambiguous one. The idea of "Authoritarian Capitalism" finds its earlier expression in the late development patterns observed by Gerschenkron (1962) and then in the vast literature on the "developmental state" in East Asia, such as Johnson (1982); Deyo (1987); Amsden (2001); Gold (1986). Somewhat more conceptual is Evans (1989). On China, Vietnam and Russia the most prominent comparative work is probably McCormick and Unger (1996).

4　There is one possible exception in early modern Europe, namely, Switzerland. This country managed to practice a peculiar type of small-scale (communal and cantonal) democracy before it became capitalist, although it should be noted that the cantons in the plains (as opposed to the original mountain ones) were oligarchic patrician regimes and they were the first to become capitalist. Of course, in the classical case of Athens, democracy also preceded capitalism, although there has been a recent debate in *The Economist* about the nature of this sequence and the prior importance of silver mining.

5　Although it is worth mentioning that the United States' VoC only really "took off" after an intervening political event of great importance, namely, the civil war and its suppression of the slave economy of the south.

6　Pierson (2000).

7　For an innovative effort to conceptualize and analyze such a moment, see Bodenstein and Schneider (2006).

8　Although we would like to remind the reader that the very first case in the most recent wave of democratizations was Portugal where it was (at least, initially) accompanied by violently induced, large-scale changes in both economic and political institutions.

9　There has been some discussion about whether the transformations in CEE and the FSU deserve the qualification "revolutionary." Timothy Garton Ash (1989) has tried to resolve the issue by calling them "refolutions," fusing the concepts of revolution and reform. Perhaps this is what we mean by radical reform.

10　Although one should add that allegedly superior models of the relationship between capitalism and democracy have shown a remarkable tendency to be short-lived. Contemporary history is littered with the wreckage of such national successes, all of which were subsequently proven to be either vulnerable or inimitable or both.

11　Bruszt and Holzhacker (2009).

12　We have excluded from my list of mechanisms the one that is most widely diffused among contemporary North American political scientists (and, for some time, among their economist brethren), namely, rational choice, for the simple reason that it is not a causal mechanism – at least not until its proponents shift from merely stipulating that individuals with perfect information for surveying alternative courses of action, assess the constraints they face and select that one which optimizes their self-interest. Only when they succeed in actually demonstrating empirically that actors do act in this matter and have the "preferences" routinely attributed to them, do we have reason to consider it a potential causal mechanism.

13　We would prefer "Competitive Market Economy" – but that would produce two CME acronyms.

14　Hall and Soskice (2001).

15　Lipjhart (1999).

16　Amable (2004).

17　Good examples of this approach are a classical article by Persson *et al.* (2000) where presidentialism and legislative cohesion are used to predict different levels of state spending, analogous to the difference between LMEs and CMEs. Gourevitch and Hawes (2001). Peter Hall (2007) provides an important "qualitative" example of approaching this issue from a more comprehensive perspective in which variables such as "partisan complexion of government" differ in their effect depending on their association with other regime characteristics. He is also one of the few to recognize "reverse causality" in which the VoC can influence the ToD, although he concludes: "Over the long term, however, political feedback effects from the structure of the political economy sustain distinctive VoC" (2007: 81).

18 For example, Boagards (2000).
19 And, accordingly, it abolished the subject of "Comparative Economic Systems" from its curriculum.
20 Which makes it all the more surprising that the VoC literature makes virtually no reference to this obviously crucial "radial" property. Presumably, this was the result of a momentary distortion due to the hegemony of neo-liberal ideology, but even if one restricts one's thinking to the last 30 years in rich capitalist democracies, there is abundant evidence that state intervention had not disappeared from the national practices of capitalism. Admittedly, the trend in most cases was toward privatization and deregulation and the policies decided (but not always implemented) by the EU did place greater restrictions on the overt use of public favoritism and funding by its member governments – nevertheless, there has been plenty of evidence of activity by state officials during this period. Some of these interventions, protections and subsidies were quite overt, even if they disregarded EU, WTO and other strictures. Just imagine trying to classify the agricultural sector anywhere in the OECD as "stateless."
21 Which helps to explain why the academic discipline of economics can appear to be so utterly indifferent to such factors. Only recently has it "discovered" geography and location.
22 New Zealand, South Korea and Greece were excluded due to data problems and this should be resolved in future versions of this analysis. Iceland and Luxembourg have been deliberately excluded due to their much smaller size. Other present OECD members such as Hungary, Mexico, Slovakia and Turkey have been excluded due to their markedly different levels of capitalism and democracy.
23 La Porta *et al.* (2001).
24 Previously, this might have been measured by the turnover of all publicly owned productive enterprises as a percentage of total turnover, but there has been so much privatization of this type of business that it seems no longer valid.
25 All data are from the 1995 Heritage Economic Freedom Index but for Belgium, Denmark, Finland, Netherlands, Norway and Switzerland are for the year 1997 (cf. www.heritage.org/Index/Explore.aspx).
26 From Hall and Gingerich (2009: 458).
27 From de Jong and Semenov (2006: 148, Table 1), Table 1: Levels of ownership concentration across countries.
28 Although geographical economics became more influential and has resulted in a recent Nobel prize for Paul Krugman.
29 From Beck *et al.* (2002: 27–29, Table 1. Bank Concentration and Competition and Banking Crises).
30 From Stulz (2005: Table 1: The Data, Column "Antidir" or anti-director's rights (i.e., the LLSV index of minority protection)).
31 From Hall and Gingerich (2009: 458).
32 From Kelly and Hamann (2007: Table 4, "Employment protection legislation in 19 OECD countries late 1980s–2003," Column Late 1990s – itself from (and completed by us with) OECD, *Employment Outlook*, 2004, chapter two "Employment Protection Regulation and Labour Market Performance," p. 112, Table 2.A2.1. "Indicators of the strictness of employment protection for regular employment", Column Overall strictness of protection against dismissals, Late 1990s (cf. www.oecd.org/dataoecd/8/4/34846856.pdf)).
33 From OECD (2000: 170, Table 2.2. "Estimated distribution of upper secondary students by the main education and training pathways after compulsory education (1996 or closest year)", Column General Education (100-x)).

34 From Kelly and Hamann (2007: Table 5, "Gross earnings inequality (90:10 ratios) for full time employees in 19 OECD countries 1980–84 to 1995–99," Column 1990–1994 – and 1995–1999 when data non available in 1990–1994 – itself from (and completed by us with) OECD (2004), Chapter three "Wage-Setting Institutions and Outcome", Table 3.2: "Trends in earnings dispersion, 1980–2001," p. 141).

35 World Economic Forum Report on the Global Gender Gap, 2007. Available at: www. weforum.org/pdf/gendergap/report2007.pdf (survey data, responses on a 1–7 scale (1 = worst score, 7 = best score)).

36 World Economic Forum Report on the Global Gender Gap, 2007 Available at: www. weforum.org/pdf/gendergap/report2007.pdf (survey data).

37 As a rough measure of rank-order discrepancies, we have used the following: rule of thumb: if a country had a disparity of more than five rank orders between spokes of the same radial, it was considered a "puzzling" case. When the disparity reached ten or more, we labeled it as a "deviant" case.

38 Available at: www.weforum.org/pdf/gendergap/report2007.pdf.

39 OECD (1998: 46).

40 OECD (1998: 39).

41 These operationalizations should be revisited in future versions, especially to take into account the extent to which higher courts are empowered to review and potential reverse decisions made by popularly elected representatives.

42 Schmidt (2000: 352).

43 Schmidt (2000: 381).

44 In "Comparative Welfare States Data Set" assembled by Evelyne Huber, Charles Ragin and John D. Stephens, December 1997, and updated by David Brady, Jason Beckfield and John Stephens, April 2004. Available at: www.lisproject.org/publications/welfaredata/welfareaccess.htm.

45 Herfindahl Index from Beck *et al.* (2001).

46 Siaroff (1999).

47 Trade Union Density from OECD (1998: 44).

48 In "Comparative Welfare States Data Set."

49 This is an indicator obtained by multiplying the coded date for the requirements for obtaining legal residence by the requirements for obtaining citizenship.

50 In "Comparative Welfare States Data Set."

51 In "Comparative Welfare States Data Set."

52 Actually, Ireland shortly after this variable was measured (*c*.1990) engaged in a protracted process of policy concertation in which business associations and trade unions were major participants, thereby reducing its deviant status.

53 We have placed the raw data, i.e., the rank orderings for all 19 countries, on VoC and ToD in Appendix 1.

54 Actually, in the case of VoC, these mixed cases are more often regarded as less well performing precisely because their degree of institutional complementarity is lower. Hence, at least for the VoC webs, we should anticipate that they will form more erratic and inconsistent patterns. The ToD literature has virtually nothing to say about those democratic regimes that cannot be classified as either "majoritarian" or "consensual."

55 Hall and Gingerich (2009: 471).

56 For a recent analysis of the proposition that "differences in the structure of economies" produced significant change in electoral systems in early Western democracies, see Cussack *et al.* (2007). For a contracting recent explanation that such choices emerged from the preferences of competing parties, see Penadès (2006). In both case, the analysis focuses on only one aspect of ToD – not even one that we regard as "radial."

57 We also experimented with the role of two other radials: asset specificity and gender discrimination. Neither of the two was significantly associated with VoC, but

women's role in politics corresponded closely with ToD. The more social the democracy, the more women held important positions in its executive or legislative institutions. Liberal democracies clearly suffered from greater gender discrimination.

References

Amable, B. (2004). *The Diversity of Modern Capitalism*, Oxford: Oxford University Press.

Amsden, A. H. (2001). *The Rise of "the Rest": Challenges to the West from Late-Industrializing Economies*, New York: Oxford University Press.

Ash, T. G. (1989). "Reflution: the Springtime of Two Nations," *New York Review of Books*, July 5.

Beck, T., A. Demirguc-Kunt and R. Levine (2002). "Bank Concentration and Crises," *NBER Working Papers*, 9921. Available at: siteresources.worldbank.org/DEC/Resources/crisis.pdf.

Beck, T., G. Clarke, A. Groff, P. Keefer and P. Walsh (2001). "New Tools in Comparative Political Economy: The Database of Political Institutions." *World Bank Economic Review*, 15(1), 165–176.

Boagards, M. (2000). "The Uneasy Relationship between Empirical and Normative Types in Consociational Theory." *Journal of Theoretical Politics*, 12(4), 395–423.

Bodenstein, T. and G. Schneider (2006). "Capitalist Junctures: Explaining Economic Openness in the Transition Countries," *European Journal of Political Research*, 45(3), 467–498.

Boix, C. (2003). *Democracy and Redistribution*, Cambridge: Cambridge University Press.

Bruszt, L. and R. Holzhacker (eds.) (2009). *The Transnationalization of Economies, States, and Civil Societies*, New York: Springer.

Campbell, J. (2004). *Institutional Change and Globalization*, Princeton: Princeton University Press, 69–74.

Cussack, T., T. Iversen and D. Soskice (2007). "Economic Interests and the Origins of Electoral Systems," *American Political Science Review*, 101(3), 373–392.

de Jong, E. and R. Semenov (2006). "Cultural Determinants of Ownership Concentration Across Countries," *International Journal of Business and Ethics*, 2(1–2), 145–165.

Deyo, F. (ed.) (1987). *The Political Economy of East Asian Industrialism*, Ithaca: Cornell University Press.

Evans, P. (1989). "Predatory, Developmental and Other Apparatuses: A Comparative Political Economy Perspective on the Third World State," *Sociological Forum*, 4(4), 561–587.

Gerschenkron, A. (1962). *Economic Backwardness in Historical Perspective*, Cambridge, MA: Harvard University Press.

Gold, T. B. (1986). *State and Society in the Taiwan Miracle*, Armonk: M. E. Sharpe.

Gourevitch, P. and M. Hawes (2001). "Political Institutions and National Production Systems in the Globalized Economy," paper presented at the conference on "Business Interests and the Varieties of Capitalism: Historical Origins and Future Possibilities," University of North Carolina, Chapel Hill, November 2–3, 2001.

Greif, A. and D. Laitin (2004). "A Theory of Endogenous Institutional Change," *American Political Science Review*, 98(4), 633–652.

Hall, P. A. (2007). "The Evolution of Varieties of Capitalism in Europe," in B. Hancke, M. Rhodes and M. Thatcher (eds.) *Beyond Varieties of Capitalism*, Oxford: Oxford University Press.

Hall, P. A. and D. W. Gingerich (2009). "Varieties of Capitalism and Institutional Complementarities in the Political Economy: An Empirical Analysis," *British Journal of Political Science*, 39(3), 449–482.

Hall, P. A. and D. Soskice (eds.) (2001). *Varieties of Capitalism: The Institutional Foundations of Comparative Advantage*, Oxford: Oxford University Press.

Johnson, C. (1982). *MITI and the Japanese Miracle*, Palo Alto: Stanford University Press.

Kelly, J. and K. Hamann (2007). "Does Varieties of Capitalism Explain National Patterns of Labor Relations?" paper prepared for delivery at the Midwest Political Association Meeting, Pal House, Chicago, April 12–15.

La Porta, R., F. Lopez-de-Silanes and A. Shleifer (2001). "Government Ownership of Banks," Harvard University, John F. Kennedy School of Government, Working Paper Series, number SWP 01–016.

Lipjhart, A. (1999). *Patterns of Democracy. Government Forms and Performance in Thirty-Six Countries*, New Haven: Yale University Press.

McCormick, B. L. and J. Unger (eds.) (1996). *China after Socialism: In the Footsteps of Eastern Europe or East Asia?* Armonk: M. E. Sharpe.

Martin, C. J. and D. Swank (2008). "The Political Origins of Coordinated Capitalism: Business Organizations, Party Systems, and State Structure in the Age of Innocence," *American Political Science Review*, 102, 181.

OECD (1998). *The public employment service*, Paris: OECD.

OECD (2000). *From Initial Education to Working Life: Making Transitions Work*, Paris: OECD.

OECD (2004). *Employment Outlook*, Paris: OECD.

Penadès, A. (2006). "The Institutional Preferences of Early Socialist Parties: Choosing Rules for Government," Estudios: Working Papers, Instituto Juan March, 226 (May).

Persson, T., G. Roland and G. Tabellini (2000). "Comparative Politics and Public Finance," *The Journal of Political Economy*, 108(6), 1121–1161.

Pierson, P. (2000). "Increasing Returns, Path Dependence and the Study of Politics," *American Political Science Review*, 94, 251–267.

Schmidt, M. (2000). *Demokratie-theorien*, Opladen: Reske + Budrich.

Siaroff, A. (1999). "Corporatism in 24 Industrial Democracies: Meaning and Measurement," *European Journal of Political Research*, 36, 175 205. Available at· www.sociol.unimi.it/corsi/polcomp/materials/siaroff.pdf.

Stulz, R. M. (2005). "The Limits of Financial Globalization," *ECGI – Finance Working Paper* No. 75.

Part II

Changing ToD–VoC combinations in advanced democracies

3 Party system change and the transformation of the varieties of capitalism*

Masanobu Ido

Introduction

Recent globalization of the world economy has raised the question of which type of economic system will be able to survive in this new environment of unprecedented competitiveness. Some argue for the superiority of the market-based economic systems of Anglo-Saxon countries, whereas others maintain that the German, Japanese, and Scandinavian economies, in which strategic coordination among social partners (e.g., employers, trade unions, and banks) plays a key role, are at least equally as competitive. In this debate on the "varieties of capitalism (VoC)," Hall and Soskice (2001) called the market-coordinated economic system of Anglo-Saxon countries "liberal market economy (LME)" and contrasted them with the strategically coordinated German and Japanese economies, which they called "coordinated market economies (CMEs)." One of the most interesting recent developments in this field of comparative capitalisms is empirical testing of the claim that the types of democracy (majoritarian vs. consensus) are associated with these two opposing VoC, LME and CME (e.g., Gourevitch and Shinn 2005). In these studies, both the type of democracy and VoC are conceptualized as fixed systems rather than the ones that undergo a process of transformation. However, recently, researchers have questioned the adequacy of such a conceptualization. Many studies on the "hybridization" of CME have cast doubts on the contemporary validity of the clear LME–CME distinction of advanced economies proposed by Hall and Soskice (2001) (Campbell and Pedersen 2007; Deeg and Jackson 2007; Jackson 2005). On the other hand, the electoral reforms in countries such as Italy, Japan, and New Zealand in the 1990s (D'Alimonte 2005; Katz 2005; Reed 2005; Vowles 2005) and the growing political importance of new right-wing parties have transformed the party systems – one of the key components of the type of democracy – of several European countries (Kriesi *et al.* 2008).[1]

Building on these new insights, I suggest in this chapter that the type of democracy intermediates the impact of globalization on the VoC. In particular, I will focus on the structure of the party system – one of the time-varying aspects of the type of democracy – and relate it to recent changes in the VoC. For this purpose, panel analyses of the OECD countries for the period 1983–2004 were conducted for two of the key social institutions of VoC, the labor market and corporate governance. (Corporate governance is here defined as the mechanisms by which suppliers of finance assure return on their investments.) The clear finding is that majoritarian democracies have advanced the liberalization (the growth of the stock market) of their corporate governance while maintaining their liberal labor markets, whereas consensus democracies have "liberalized" their traditionally rigid labor markets through the expansion of atypical workers while maintaining their bank-based corporate governance. This chapter is divided into four sections. The second section examines the present state of VoC in advanced countries. I will argue that the adjustment to globalization has ended the clear distinction between LME and CME among advanced economies in the postwar era and has produced ambiguity regarding the VoC. The third section presents a hypothesis of dual transformation of both the type of democracy and the VoC and describes the pattern of changes in party systems of advanced countries. In the final section, by conducting panel analyses of the data on advanced countries in the past two decades, this study investigates the impact of party systems and their changes on the transformation of VoC.

"Hybridization" of CME and blurred boundaries between LME and CME

The VoC theory distinguishes among advanced economies and groups them into two types, LME and CME. Both these economies achieve efficiency but in different ways. According to Hall and Soskice (2001), the authors of the theory, both LMEs and CMEs are characterized by different combinations of their key institutions, for instance, employment systems, financial markets, and training systems. These combinations are consistent (or mutually complementary) in both LMEs and CMEs in different forms, which assures their efficiency. For instance, in LMEs, fluid labor markets that provide a mobile workforce to firms and stock market-based financial systems complement each other, and in CMEs, rigid labor markets that protect the employment of loyal core workers and bank-based financial systems complement each other but in different ways. Figure 1.1 provided in the study by Hall and Soskice (2001) demonstrated a distinct clustering of advanced economies into LME and CME on the two axes of labor market and corporate finance.

A number of scholars have recently argued that there has been a "hybridization" of VoC (i.e., through changes within the respective VoC) but not a complete transition from CME to LME or vice versa (Campbell and Pedersen 2007; Deeg and Jackson 2007; Jackson 2005). In this literature, Germany – an archetypical CME – is cited as a case of such "hybridization." According to Deeg and Jackson (2007), Germany has recently introduced some elements of LME into its corporate governance while maintaining its basic CME character in other areas. This process of combining elements of the opposite VoC with its original VoC has reshaped the German economy as a newer hybrid form of VoC. A similar hybridization process is said to have occurred in Denmark with the introduction of substantial LME elements into the labor market (Campbell and Pedersen 2007). Although less drastic in degree than Germany and Denmark, other CMEs have also moved in the direction of LME as a result of recent reforms in the labor market and corporate governance. Such changes in the economies of advanced countries have reduced the distinction between LMEs and CMEs. In the following passages, I will examine changes in the two key institutions of VoC, the labor market and corporate governance, to show that globalization has actually diminished the LME–CME distinction considerably in the last two decades.

Liberalization of labor markets in CMEs

In the post-World War II period, workers' employment and labor conditions were protected by rigid labor laws in CMEs, whereas employers faced less constraints in the hiring and dismissal of workers with fewer and less rigid labor laws in LMEs. However, since the 1990s many advanced countries that have adopted CME have resorted to large-scale labor market reforms. These reforms have increased the flexibility of labor markets by instituting fixed-term contracts and expanding temporary and part-time workers while maintaining the protection of regular workers (OECD 2006). The most renowned "success story" of such labor market reforms in CME is undoubtedly Denmark's "flexicurity" system. The combination of the country's traditionally less rigid labor market, stricter conditions for unemployment insurance, and tying of its provision of benefits to records of workers seeking employment as well as its active labor market policy, has assured Danish employers wider discretion in the hiring and dismissal of workers while softening the economic and social impact of unemployment on workers. Campbell and Pedersen (2007) claim that together with Danish institutions' decentralization of the active labor market policy, the country's welfare state, and its collective bargaining system, the adoption of this "flexicurity" system indicated a move of the Danish political economy in the direction of LME. With the legalization of temporary workers and relaxation of national labor protection laws in the 1990s, other CMEs have also "liberalized" their labor markets by instituting changes that allow them to be more responsive to fluctuations in the market. These CMEs are also undergoing a process of "hybridization," for instance, in the form of a transition from pure CMEs to a more hybrid VoC that combines the elements of both CME and LME to form more liberal labor markets. Figure 3.1 indicates that most CMEs (notably Sweden, Germany, and Belgium) have actually reduced their employment protection levels, at least in terms of the strictness of their employment protection legislation (EPL),[2] in the past two decades.

Growing importance of stock markets in corporate finance

Since the 1990s, most advanced countries have liberalized their financial markets. In order to gauge liberalization in financial markets, I will examine

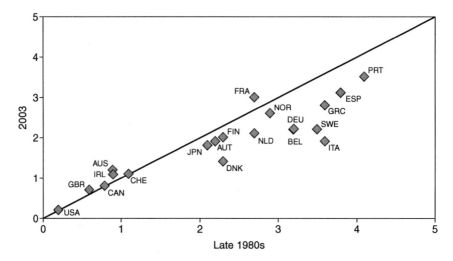

Figure 3.1 Changes in rigidities of EPL in OECD countries, late 1980s vs. 2003 (sources: OECD, 1999, 2004).

Notes
There are two versions of EPL: overall EPL versions 1 and 2. The former does not consider collective dismissals, but is available from the late 1980s. The latter does consider collective dismissals, but has data only for the late 1990s and 2003. In this figure, values of the overall EPL version 1 in the late 1980s and in 2003 are compared.

Sample (20 countries): Australia (AUS), Austria (AUT), Belgium (BEL), Canada (CAN), Denmark (DNK), Finland (FIN), France (FRA), Germany (DEU), Greece (GRC), Ireland (IRL), Italy (ITA), Japan (JPN), New Zealand (NZL), Norway (NOR), Portugal (PRT), Spain (ESP), Sweden (SWE), Switzerland (CHE), the UK (GBR), and the United States (USA).

changes in stock market capitalization. Stock market capitalization measures the size of a country's stock market (that is, the value of its listed shares) in relation to its GDP. Thus, a country with a high value of stock market capitalization has a large stock market in relation to the size of its economy. LMEs usually have developed stock markets and hence have a high score in terms of stock market capitalization value. In contrast, CMEs usually have less developed stock markets and score low in terms of stock market capitalization value. I use data regarding the ratio of stock market capitalization to GDP reported in Beck *et al.* (2000) for the period 1989–2004. Figure 3.2 illustrates the general trend toward the liberalization of financial markets in advanced countries from the 1989–1992 period to the early 2000s.[3] All of the 19 advanced countries have increased their ratios of stock market capitalization to GDP in this period. Notably, Switzerland had the highest increase in the value of its stock market capitalization, from 0.75 to 2.30.

As Figure 3.3 shows, the clustering of the two types of capitalist economies, CMEs and LMEs, along the two axes of the labor market and corporate governance was less distinct and the boundary between them blurred considerably in the early twenty-first century. In particular, significant increases in stock market

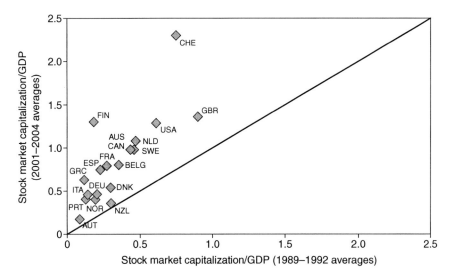

Figure 3.2 Changes in stock market capitalization/GDP in advanced countries (source: Beck *et al.* 2000).

Sample (19 countries)
Australia (AUS), Austria (AUT), Belgium (BEL), Canada (CAN), Denmark (DNK), Finland (FIN), France (FRA), Germany (DEU), Greece (GRC), Italy (ITA), Netherlands (NLD), New Zealand (NZL), Norway (NOR), Portugal (PRT), Spain (ESP), Sweden (SWE), Switzerland (CHE), the UK (GBR), and the United States (USA)

capitalization of CME countries, such as Switzerland and Finland, as well as significant decreases in the strictness of labor market protection (of EPL) in Sweden, Belgium, Germany, and Denmark contributed to this change. In the post-World War II "Golden Age" of capitalism, CMEs, located in the upper left hand corner, combined strong protection of workers with less developed stock markets, whereas LMEs, located in the lower right-hand corner, combined weak protection of workers with develped stock markets. Today, LMEs (Australia, Canada, the United States, the UK, Ireland, and New Zealand) constitute a loose cluster that spans a wide range horizontally and lies under a loose wide cluster of CMEs. In actuality, the countries that occupy the upper left-hand corner are mixed market economies, such as Portugal, Greece, and Italy, and CMEs such as Norway, Germany, and Austria.

Types of democracy and VoC change

Dual transformation of VoC and the types of democracy

In the literature on the VoC, several scholars have recently proposed a correlation between the types of democracy (majoritarian vs. consensus) and the

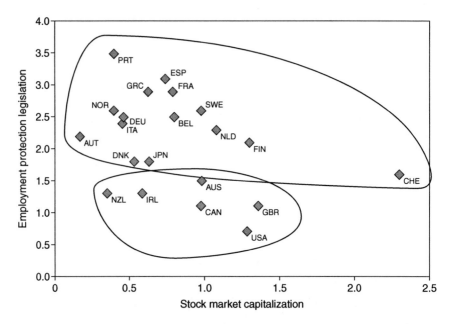

Figure 3.3 Stock market capitalization versus employment protection legislation in the
   early twenty-first century (sources: Beck *et al.* 2000; OECD 2004).

Note
Stock Market Capitalization: Stock Market Capitalization/GDP, averages for 2001–2004 Employ-
ment Protection Legislation: EPL ver2. in 2003.
Sample (21 countries): Australia (AUS), Austria (AUT), Belgium (BEL), Canada (CAN), Denmark
(DNK), Finland (FIN), France (FRA), Germany (DEU), Greece (GRC), Ireland (IRL), Italy (ITA),
Japan (JPN), Netherlands (NLD), New Zealand (NZL), Norway (NOR), Portugal (PRT), Spain
(ESP), Sweden (SWE), Switzerland (CHE), the UK (GBR), and the United States (USA)

national VoC (Hall and Soskice 2001; Gourevitch and Shinn 2005; Amable
2003). They suggest that policy stability in consensus democracies lowers
workers' risk of investment in sector- and firm-specific skills, which is a key
characteristic of the labor market of CME. In consensus democracies, coalition
governments and the existence of multiple veto players inhibit the adoption of
new policies and, even if they are successfully adopted, their change is difficult
to effect. With such policy stability, consensus democracies favor corporatist
coalition of large manufacturers and core workers at the expense of the interests
of minority shareholders. Protection of employment of core workers induces
them to invest in "specific" skills only useful for the industry or firm. In contrast,
because of quick and substantial swings of policy changes in majoritarian democracies, workers are reluctant to make expensive decisions to invest in these
skills, which is a feature of the labor market in LMEs.

However, in these studies, the type of democracy and the VoC are both
assumed to be fixed systems. In contrast, the central assumption of this chapter

is that the type of democracy and the VoC both experience important changes in today's globalized world. First, I suggest that globalization increases the pressure on advanced countries to modify, reshape, and update their national VoC. Although no case of a fundamental shift of VoC has been reported, a growing body of literature on the "hybridization" of VoC has argued that there are less radical modifications of VoC (i.e., changes within VoC), particularly within some of the domains of the VoC such as labor market and corporate governance (Campbell and Pedersen 2007; Deeg and Jackson 2007; Jackson 2005). These changes in the economies of advanced countries have blurred the distinction between LMEs and CMEs in today's globalized economy.

Then, I describe how the type of democracy is also variable. My contention in this chapter is that although the types of democracy remain the same in most countries, the strong pressure of globalization has led to its partial yet substantial modification in some countries. Unlike institutions that define types of democracy that do not change drastically during the time period that this study covers, such as federalism, unicameralism versus bicameralism, judicial review, and the independence of central banks, the party system is one of the few time-varying institutions that constitute the type of democracy. Indeed, the adoption of new electoral systems (e.g., the increased amount of majoritarian systems in Italy and Japan, the proportional representation [PR] system in New Zealand), the emergence of new right-wing parties (e.g., Vlaams Belang in Belgium, the Swiss People's Party in Switzerland, and Lijst Pim Fortuyn in the Netherlands), and their increasing importance in national politics have reshaped the party systems of these countries in the past two decades (Gallagher and Mitchell 2005; Katz 2005; D'Alimonte 2005; Reed 2005; Vowles 2005; Kriesi *et al.* 2008). I assert that in the countries that have undergone major party system changes (e.g., from multiparty to two-party systems or vice versa), the type of democracy experiences a partial yet consequential modification (i.e., from consensus toward majoritarian democracy or vice versa). An instance of this type of modification is the adoption of mixed electoral systems that are predominantly majoritarian in Italy and Japan, which have resulted in the emergence of new, more bipolar party systems in these countries (D'Alimonte 2005; Reed 2005). I expect that such major party system changes will in turn shift the country's political process in the direction of a more adversarial majoritarian type of democracy. I conjecture that the exact reverse will occur in New Zealand, which replaced the first-past-the-post electoral system with a proportional electoral system (Vowles 2005).

In accordance with the proposal of the dual transformation of VoC and type of democracy, this chapter emphasizes the important role of the type of democracy as a "catalyst" in the ongoing process of the transformation of VoC under strong pressure of globalization. As a key intervening variable, the type of democracy is expected to mediate the impact of globalization on the transformation of the VoC. This chapter suggests that by providing contrasting incentives to political and economic actors, majoritarian and consensus democracies largely shape the orientations of these actors' responses to globalization and hence the directions of the transformation of the VoC. In particular, this chapter asks whether different types of democracy across advanced countries have led to different fates in their VoC (either convergence to the single model or continuing divergence) despite the same globalization pressures. In order to identify a country's type of democracy and the type of change it has undergone, I will focus on one aspect of democracy: the party system.

Business parties in majoritarian and consensus democracies

What is the mechanism by which the type of democracy has an impact on change in the VoC? This section emphasizes the important role of parties promoted by businesses (hereafter business parties) in the political process of VoC change. In their study on the emergence of contrasting VoC in advanced countries in the early twentieth century, Martin and Swank (2008) offer a convincing explanation of a political mechanism that has contributed to a strong association between the types of democracy and the VoC: because coalition governments and multipartyism were a norm in PR countries, business parties needed to be accustomed to cooperating with the other parties in power. The cooperative attitudes of business parties in politics in turn translated into cooperation between business and labor in the economic sphere in these countries, and their market economies became CMEs. The business parties in consensus and majoritarian democracies hold contrasting preferences: business parties in consensus democracies pursue cooperation with labor in the economic sphere, whereas those in majoritarian democracies prefer confrontation with labor. In the contemporary environment of globalization, what repercussions do the contrasting preferences of business parties in consensus and majoritarian democracies have on the two key institutions of VoC, i.e., corporate governance and the labor market?

In LMEs' shareholder system of corporate governance, managers who are under intense pressure from the stock market pursue maximization of short-term profits with measures such as large-scale introduction of labor-saving technologies and outsourcing of production processes to cheap labor countries. In such circumstances, only secondary importance is paid to workers' employment and wages. In CMEs' blockholding system of corporate governance, managers who can rely on their main banks' financial support pursue the long-term goals of their businesses instead of short-term profits by securing the loyalty of their highly skilled workforce with stable employment and high wages. Social democratic parties naturally prefer the blockholding system. In consensus democracies, I assume that business parties consent to the maintenance of the blockholding system because they need the cooperation of these social democratic parties in their coalition governments. In majoritarian democracies, on the other hand, I expect that business parties, with their hostile attitude toward labor, promote the development of the stock market. Thus, I expect that business parties in multiparty coalition governments will take a friendly attitude toward the blockholding of shares by stakeholders, such as by trade unions, whereas business parties in two-party systems will oppose it. (When social democratic parties are in power, they protect the blockholding system of corporate governance.)

I now discuss the impact of the types of democracy on the labor market. One of the notable changes that advanced economies have experienced in the last two decades is a substantial increase in the share of an atypical workforce, such as the employment of temporary workers and part-time workers. In interpreting this important change in the labor market of advanced countries, the "insider labor" argument in recent political economy research is of great help. According to this theory, social democratic parties primarily represent the interests of "insider labor," i.e., workers with permanent employment (usually, male, regular workers), not the interests of all workers (Rueda 2005). With an increasingly competitive world market, the social democratic parties of advanced countries have been consenting to the wider use of part-time contracts and temporary employments (for "outsider labor") in order to protect permanent jobs of their constituency (i.e., "insider labor"). Thus, I expect that because they need the cooperation of their partners in coalition governments such as those of social democratic parties, business parties in consensus democracies would adopt policies that expand atypical labor. On the other hand, I expect that business parties in majoritarian democracies will not take such measures.

Party system changes in advanced countries

Several indices have been proposed for the measurement of the structure of party systems. In particular, the "effective number of parties" (ENP) created by Laakso and Taagepera (1979) is widely used to gauge the fragmentation of party systems. The ENP index can be computed with respect to votes as well as seats in legislatures. Because the fragmentation of party systems in legislatures has a direct bearing on a country's policy-making ability, and hence on the type of democracy, this section examines the ENP with respect to seats in advanced countries. A small ENP suggests that the countries are majoritarian democracies. For instance, the ENP for the UK and the United States in the early twenty-first century were at the low levels of 2.1 and 2.0, respectively. In contrast, the ENP for consensus democracies is usually greater than 2, for instance, the values for Germany and Sweden in the early twenty-first century were 3.3 and 4.3, respectively. In Figure 3.4, the mean ENP with respect to seats in the legislatures of 23 advanced countries for the period 1960–2005 confirms the general trend of increasing fragmentation of party systems in advanced countries (for similar findings, see Dalton *et al.* 2000).

However, the changes in party systems of advanced countries were not uniform. Table 3.1 reports the magnitude of changes in party systems across advanced countries from the early 1990s to the early 2000s. In most of the advanced countries, such as the UK, Australia, Denmark, and France, the type of democracy remained the same, with little change in the fragmentation of most of their party systems. However, the fragmentation of party systems increased in several of these countries, such as New Zealand – the country Lijphart (1999)

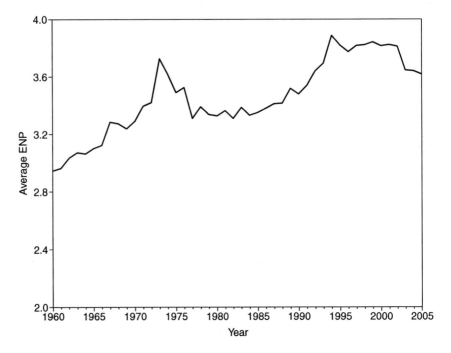

Figure 3.4 Average ENP with respect to seats in the 23 advanced democracies, 1960–2005.

Sample (23 countries): Australia, Austria, Belgium, Canada, Denmark, Finland, France, Germany, Greece, Iceland, Ireland, Italy, Japan, Luxembourg, Netherlands, New Zealand, Norway, Portugal, Spain, Sweden, Switzerland, the UK, and the United States.

once cited as the best example of a majoritarian democracy. Since the introduction of a PR electoral system and holding of the first election under this new system in 1996, New Zealand has been ruled by either multiparty coalition governments or minority governments with outside support of the opposition parties. The ENP for New Zealand doubled from 1.8 in the early 1990s to 3.6 in the early 2000s. At least at the electoral party level, New Zealand approached a consensus model of democracy. However, in other countries such as Italy, fragmentation of the party systems decreased, and they approached a majoritarian democracy. Italy adopted a new mixed electoral system and held its first election under this more majoritarian system in 1994. The ENP for Italy actually declined by half – from 4.1 in the early 1990s to 2.2 in the early 2000s.

Empirical analyses of relationship between party system changes and VoC transformation

In the preceding sections, I showed that the type of democracy in most advanced countries has remained the same, as measured by the fragmentation of party

Table 3.1 Party system changes in advanced countries

Country	ENP		
	Early 1990s*	*Early 2000s***	*Changes*
Australia	2.5	2.5	0.0
Austria	3.0	3.1	0.2
Belgium	8.2	8.8	0.6
Canada	2.4	2.5	0.2
Denmark	4.5	4.5	0.0
Finland	5.3	5.0	-0.3
France	3.0	3.0	0.0
FRG/Germany	3.2	3.3	0.2
Greece	2.3	2.2	0.1
Ireland	3.2	3.3	0.8
Italy	4.1	2.2	−2.0
Japan	3.0	3.0	0.0
Luxembourg	3.5	4.3	0.8
Netherlands	3.8	5.0	1.3
New Zealand	1.8	3.6	1.8
Norway	4.2	5.2	0.9
Portugal	2.3	2.6	0.3
Spain	2.8	2.5	−0.3
Sweden	4.1	4.3	0.2
Switzerland	6.3	4.6	−1.7
UK	2.2	2.1	−0.1
United States	1.9	2.0	0.1
Average	3.5	3.6	0.1

Notes
* Average ENP for 1991–1994.
** Average ENP for 2001–2004.

systems, whereas the type of democracy in some countries, such as Italy and New Zealand, has undergone significant modifications. Regarding VoC transformation, a general trend in advanced countries was the liberalization of labor market regulation and financial deregulation. Yet, there was a significant variation in the degree of liberalization in both aspects among advanced countries. The subject of empirical analyses in this section is whether such variations in the liberalization of labor market regulation and financial deregulation are caused by the type of party systems (two-party vs. multiparty systems) and the different pace of their changes across advanced countries. For this purpose, I will conduct panel analyses with cross-section dummies of advanced countries to examine the impact of party system changes on the size of stock market capitalization as well as on the share of part-time workers within each country.

Panel analysis of modifications in the domain of corporate governance

Next, I will examine the impact of party systems (as measured by their fragmentation) on modifications in the domain of the corporate governance of VoC, as measured by the size of stock markets, in a sample of 20 countries (Australia, Austria, Belgium, Canada, Denmark, Finland, France, Germany, Ireland, Italy, Japan, the Netherlands, New Zealand, Norway, Portugal, Spain, Sweden, Switzerland, the UK, and the United States) for the period 1983–2004. For the estimation of the models, I adopted a panel analysis with country-specific fixed effects. With this estimation method, I can control for likely unobservable country-specific factors and estimate the relationship between the dependent variable and the independent variables within countries. The results are presented in Table 3.2.

The dependent variable is stock market capitalization/GDP. The data is obtained from Beck *et al.*'s (2000) Financial Structure Dataset, which is compiled from Standard & Poor's Emerging Market Database and Emerging Stock Markets Factbook. Admittedly, stock market capitalization/GDP, which gauges the development of a stock market in a country, is not the sole indicator by which to measure corporate governance. Although it is undoubtedly important, the relative size of the stock market in the economy is only one key aspect of corporate governance. It neither assesses the scope of blockholding in a country, by calculating the proportion of shares under the control of large stockholders such as owning families, nor evaluates the national regulatory frameworks of corporate governance, such as the protection of small stockholders. However, other measures of key aspects of corporate governance, such as ownership concentration (La Porta *et al.* 1999) and national legal frameworks of corporate governance (La Porta *et al.* 1998) are only available in cross-sectional forms. Stock market capitalization/GDP is one of the few measures currently available that captures time-variations in corporate governance among advanced countries that can be used for a panel analysis (Barker 2010).

Of the independent variables, political variables are defined as follows:

EFFPAR_LEG: the ENP with respect to seats according to the Laakso and Taagepera's (1979) formula. Source: Armingeon *et al.*'s (2008) Comparative Political Data Set I, hereafter Comparative Political Dataset.

GOV_RIGHT: right-wing parties as a percentage of total cabinet posts, weighted by days (see Appendix 2 for a list of the right-wing parties in the 20 countries). Source: Comparative Political Dataset.

GOV_CENT: center parties as a percentage of total cabinet posts, weighted by days (see Appendix 2 for a list of the center parties). Source: Comparative Political Dataset.

Table 3.2 Party system and stock market capitalization/GDP in 20 advanced countries, 1983–2004 (panel analysis, cross-section fixed effects (dummy variables))

	(1)	(2)	(3)	(4)	(5)	(6)
Dependent variables	Stock market capitalization					
Fixed effects included	Country					
Independent variables						
Constant	−9.823028***	−9.730649***	−9.770038***	2.102010	10.10741***	−10.64751***
	(1.648446)	(1.658336)	(1.659635)	(3.869134)	(2.131507)	(2.140770)
Political variables						
ENP in legislature	−0.062763**					−0.067628**
	(0.029713)					(0.029875)
Right cabinets		−0.000455				−0.000748
		(0.000471)				(0.000508)
Center cabinets			−0.000377			−0.000744
			(0.000637)			(0.000666)
Left cabinets				0.000136		
				(0.000426)		
Voter turnout					0.001178	0.029875
					(0.004588)	(0.004711)
Controls						
LOG(GDPPC)	0.953748***	0.921986***	0.925301***	−0.195886	0.949757***	1.022633***
	(0.174888)	(0.175345)	(0.175533)	(0.386714)	(0.203011)	(0.204001)
OPENC	0.017986***	0.018041***	0.018016***	0.007278***	0.017984***	0.017726***
	(0.002308)	(0.002321)	(0.002325)	(0.002677)	(0.002340)	(0.002326)
R-squared	0.741247	0.738174	0.737657	0.797362	0.737405	0.743668
Adjusted R-squared	0.722015	0.718714	0.718158	0.765677	0.717888	0.721796
Observations	319	319	319	319	319	319

Notes
Standard errors in parentheses. *p < 0.1, **p < 0.05, ***p < 0.01.
Sample (20 countries)
Australia, Austria, Belgium, Canada, Denmark, Finland, France, Germany, Ireland, Italy, Japan, the Netherlands, New Zealand, Norway, Portugal, Spain, Sweden, Switzerland, the UK, and the United States.

GOV_LEFT: left-wing parties as a percentage of total cabinet posts, weighted by days (see Appendix 2 for a list of the left-wing parties). Source: Comparative Political Dataset.

VTURN: Voter turnout in election. Source: Comparative Political Dataset.

As discussed in the preceding section, Laasko and Taagepera's ENP index that gauges the fragmentation of party systems with respect to seats in legislature (EFFPAR_LEG) is the central independent variable of this chapter. I expect that low EFFPAR_LEG (indicating two-party systems and hence majoritarian democracies) is associated with stock market development, whereas high EFFPAR_ LEG (indicating multiparty systems and hence consensus democracies) is associated with the maintenance of blockholder systems of corporate governance and the stagnation of stock market development.

In the political economy literature, the ideologies of governing parties on a left–right scale have been emphasized as a political determinant of VoC, although the signs of their causal effects differ according to various authors (Swank 2002; Roe 2003; Cioffi and Höpner 2006). Roe (2003) argued that social democracy, by aligning managers with employees, has made diffuse shareholding difficult and that its corporate governance system tends to be characterized by less separation of ownership. Roe's study suggested that stock market development stagnates in left-wing cabinets, whereas it advances in right-wing cabinets. In contrast, Cioffi and Höpner (2006) suggested that right-wing and centrist parties oppose the development of stock markets on the basis that they represent the vested interests of large banks and large manufacturers that are the main beneficiaries of the closed domestic market, whereas left-wing parties – the outsiders in the established regimes – promote the development of stock markets (also see Gourevitch et al., n.d.). Although both these hypotheses made no distinction between right and centrist parties in terms of parties promoted by businesses, liberal parties can be expected to adopt an unambiguous promarket attitude and promote the development of the stock market and centrist parties to oppose it. Because centrist parties (most of which are Christian democratic parties) represent the interests of business as well as those of workers and other social strata (e.g., agricultural population), I expect them to adopt a less distinct, more ambiguous attitude in their economic policies (Esping-Andersen 1990; Iversen and Stephens 2008; Callaghan 2009).[4] Here, I tested whether the governments of right (GOV_RIGHT), center (GOV_CENT), and left-wing parties (GOV_LEFT) have a differential impact upon the speed of financial deregulation, as measured in the development of stock markets.

In the political science literature, people with lower incomes are considered to be nonvoters (Lijphart 1999). Because the main beneficiaries of highly developed stock markets are people with high incomes, I expect low voter turnout to result in the development of the stock market.

I also controlled for variables that have been reported to affect stock market development. These controls are as follows:

LOG(GDPPC): log of GDP per capita (in 2000 US$). Source: World Development Indicators (downloaded: June 19, 2008).

OPENC: openness of the economy in current prices, measured as total trade (the sum of imports and exports) as a percentage of GDP. Source: Comparative Political Dataset.

I now examine the impacts of political variables on stock market development. First, I found that multipartyism is negatively associated with stock market development (see the first column of Table 3.2), and it is also statistically significant. Thus, one of the main hypotheses of this chapter – that majoritarian democracies, as measured by less fragmented party systems, are associated with developed stock markets – is confirmed. Conversely, I found that the growth of stock markets stagnated in consensus democracies. This finding validates the argument of this chapter in which a mechanism linking the type of democracy and VoC is suggested. In consensus democracies, coalition governments protect the blockholding system of corporate governance and obstruct the development of stock markets. Social democratic parties prefer the blockholding system because it assures the stable employment of core workers, and business parties consent to the maintenance of the system to secure the social democrats' cooperation in governments.

In the countries that have moved in the direction of majoritarian democracies at the level of party systems (i.e., toward being two-party systems), the economic systems have made changes toward becoming LMEs, at least in the area of corporate governance (with the growth of stock markets). The cases of Italy and Switzerland, in which the fragmentation of their party systems decreased (with the ENP changes of –2.0 and –1.7, respectively; Table 3.1) and the growth in stock markets increased (Figure 3.2), appear to corroborate such a causal relationship. On the other hand, in the countries that have moved in the direction of consensus democracies at the level of party systems (i.e., toward being multiparty systems), the economic systems have made changes toward becoming CMEs in the corporate governance area (i.e., with the non-growth of stock markets). This seems to apply to the case of New Zealand, which increased the fragmentation of its party system (with an ENP change of 1.8; Table 3.1) and experienced stagnation in the growth of its stock market.

Second, I found that although none of the government party ideology variables (GOV_RIGHT, GOV_CENTER, and GOV_LEFT) are significantly correlated with the development of the stock market, their signs – negative signs for right and center cabinets and a positive sign for left cabinets – lend support to the arguments proposed by Cioffi and Höpner (2006) and Gourevitch *et al.* (n.d.) (see the second through fourth columns of Table 3.2). In support of the interests of large banks and large manufacturers, right and center parties were opposed to financial deregulation. In contrast, left-wing parties promoted the opening of the financial markets in their effort to form alternative coalitions.

The final finding is that the fifth column of Table 3.2 is contrary to my prediction: higher voter turnout is positively associated with the development of stock markets. However, it is not statistically significant.

With all political variables in the model, a fit between the model and data has improved (increased value of adjusted R-squared in the last column of Table 3.2).

Panel analysis of modifications in the domain of labor market

Using the same panel analysis method, I will examine the impact of party system changes on modifications in the domain of labor market, a key institution of VoC, as measured by the share of part-time workers in dependent employment, with a sample of 18 countries (Australia, Austria, Belgium, Canada, Denmark, Finland, France, Germany, Ireland, Italy, the Netherlands, New Zealand, Norway, Portugal, Spain, Sweden, Switzerland, and the UK) for the period 1983–2004. The results are presented in Table 3.3.

In order to measure the "liberalization" of labor markets, in this chapter I will examine the share of temporary workers in total employment in the OECD countries based on the availability of time series data for most of the OECD countries in the past few decades. The dependent variable is the percentage of part-time employment in dependent employment. It is calculated from annual labor market statistics in full-time and part-time employment based on a common definition of the standard 30-hour workweek in a person's main job. The source is OECD Employment and Labor Market Statistics (downloaded: July 10, 2008). I consider the expansion in the number of part-time workers as one of the key aspects of liberalization and increased flexibility of the labor market; hence, I interpret it as a move toward LME. The independent variables are the same as those used for estimating the impact of party system change on stock market capitalization (EFFPAR_LEG, GOV_RIGHT, GOV_CENT, GOV_LEFT, VTURN, LOG(GDPPC), and OPENC).

The first column of Table 3.3 indicates that multiparty systems are positively associated with the expansion of the share of part-time workers (the value for the ENP in legislature is 0.653611). This is statistically significant. As the number of the ENP in legislature increases, the share of part-time workers in total workers grows. In actuality, Denmark and the Netherlands – both consensus democracies – increased the share of part-time workers in dependent employment (a move toward LME in the domain of the labor market) while maintaining their generous welfare states and training programs, which are both traits of CMEs. As a result of these reforms, Denmark and the Netherlands have realized an institutional mix known as "flexicurity," with new "institutional complementarities" between their "liberalized" labor markets (an LME element) and their generous welfare states and training programs (CME elements). This move to a hybrid VoC among consensus democracies seems to corroborate the argument of this chapter: because social democratic parties supported the expansion of atypical workers to protect the interests of core male workers and other coalition

Table 3.3 Party system and part-time workers/total workers in 18 advanced countries, 1983–2004 (panel analysis, cross-section fixed effects (dummy variables))

	(1)	(2)	(3)	(4)	(5)	(6)
Dependent variable	Part-time workers/total workers					
Fixed effects included	Country					
Independent variables						
Constant	-68.22665*** (8.868408)	-73.47400*** (8.717014)	-70.23795*** (8.920770)	-74.44144*** (8.885599)	-94.53626*** (11.60485)	-81.88947*** (11.52695)
Political variables						
ENP in legislature	0.653611*** (0.181293)					0.645462*** (0.177260)
Right cabinets		0.011354*** (0.002861)				0.008344*** (0.003031)
Center cabinets			-0.010466** (0.004080)			-0.005639 (0.004082)
Left cabinets				-0.005538** (0.002759)		
Voter turnout					0.090465*** (0.032262)	0.065133** (0.032794)
Controls						
LOG(GDPPC)	8.017565*** (0.982632)	3.789241*** (0.953558)	8.514972*** (0.973623)	8.949138*** (0.972559)	10.26693*** (1.094815)	8.891580*** (1.089295)
OPENC	0.043954*** (0.013389)	0.040239*** (0.013312)	0.041968*** (0.013497)	0.040244*** (0.013549)	0.038637*** (0.013493)	0.042145*** (0.013046)
R-squared	0.929881	0.930445	0.928532	0.927982	0.928806	0.934316
Adjusted R-squared	0.925593	0.926191	0.924161	0.923577	0.924452	0.929654
Observations	348	343	348	348	348	348

Notes
Standard errors in parentheses. *p < 0.1, **p < 0.05, ***p < 0.01.
Sample (18 countries)
Australia, Austria, Belgium, Canada, Denmark, Finland, France, Germany, Ireland, Italy, Netherlands, New Zealand, Norway, Portugal, Spain, Sweden, Switzerland, and the UK.

partners including business parties supported them, atypical labor was expanded in consensus democracies.

Next, the positive value in the second column of Table 3.3 shows that right-wing cabinets support the expansion of part-time workers. The negative value of the estimate of center cabinets in the third column of Table 3.3 lends support to the hypothesis that centrist parties oppose increase in flexibility of the labor market. The negative value for left cabinets in the fourth column indicates that such cabinets oppose the expansion of part-time workers.[5]

Last, I found that higher turnout is positively associated with an expansion of the share of part-time workers (see the fifth column of Table 3.3). This finding is contrary to the original expectation. Since nonvoters are known to be concentrated among lower income people, I expected that lower turnout would reinforce the political influence of the main beneficiaries of expansion of a flexible workforce, i.e., people with high incomes. Thus, I expected that low voter turnout would result in expansion in the share of part-time workers. This unexpected finding might be explained by the following mechanism: the mobilization of "insider workers" – other important beneficiaries of expansion of atypical workers – that contributes to high voter turnout is the main culprit of expansion of the share of part-time workers.

In all political variables in the model, the fit between the model and data has improved (see increased value of adjusted R-squared in the sixth column of Table 3.3). However, the variable of center parties in the cabinets is statistically insignificant.

Implications and discussion

This chapter finds the following contrasting developments of VoC in the domains of corporate governance and labor markets in majoritarian and consensus democracies, at least as measured by the degree of fragmentation of party systems: majoritarian democracies have reinforced the LME nature of their economies in the domain of corporate governance. In the past two decades, majoritarian democracies have seen a substantial increase in the relative sizes of their stock markets in their financial systems. In contrast to the "liberalization" of the systems of corporate governance, majoritarian democracies (e.g., the UK) have maintained their already flexible labor markets. In contrast, consensus democracies, in which the VoC is CME, have introduced substantial elements of LME into their "rigid" labor markets. In the same period, consensus democracies have expanded part-time employment in their labor markets substantially. In contrast to the liberalization of their rigid labor markets (e.g., the "flexicurity" of Denmark), consensus democracies have largely maintained their bank-based financial markets and the growth of their stock markets have stagnated.

The results of this study also suggest a connection between changes in the political sphere and modifications in VoC for the countries that have recently undergone party system changes, such as Italy, Japan, and New Zealand. In Italy, where the party system has become less fragmented in the move toward a majoritarian democracy, the share of the stock market in its financial system has increased sharply, which represents a move toward LME in the domain of corporate governance. (Japan has also experienced a comparable party system change. However, the exceptional event involving the collapse of the "bubble economy" that crashed Japan's stock market makes the evaluation of the impact of its political change on the adjustment of its VoC extremely difficult.) On the other hand, in New Zealand, where the party system has become more fragmented in a move toward a consensus democracy, the growth of the stock market has stagnated, which represents a move toward CME in the domain of corporate governance.

These associations of party system changes and adjustment of VoC are not accidental. Political reforms of Italy and Japan that sought to alternate the governing parties in two-party systems started with national movements to deregulate these economies as a response to globalization. In the case of New Zealand, the 1996 adoption of a highly proportional mixed-member proportional electoral system was a result of popular campaigns by ordinary citizens who were indignant about the extensive privatization and deregulation that had taken place in the country's economy since the 1980s. It is clear that political entrepreneurs and the general public perceived the importance of changing political frameworks for effecting critical changes in economic systems. This chapter explains the importance of political factors in understanding the VoC change and globalization. In addition, it contributes to unraveling the political processes involved in the transformations of VoC by offering a party-centered explanation that assumes differing preferences of business parties in majoritarian and consensus democracies.

Appendix 1

Table 3.4 Correlation matrix of independent variables

	GOV_RIGHT	GOV_CENT	GOV_LEFT	EFFPAR_LEG	GDPPC	OPENC	VTURN
GOV_RIGHT	1						
GOV_CENT	−0.44576	1					
GOV_LEFT	−0.65114	−0.35988	1				
EFFPAR_LEG	−0.19221	0.14248	0.065559	1			
GDPPC	0.01017	0.032953	0.000882	0.272193	1		
OPENC	−0.1363	0.168211	0.026552	0.384563	0.295705	1	
VTURN	−0.15998	−0.01927	0.186925	0.123213	−0.35546	0.246693	1

Appendix 2: classification of political parties

In statistical examinations, I followed the following classifications of political parties by ideologies (Armingeon *et al.* 2008). "Left-wing parties" are social democratic parties and political parties left of social democracy. "Right-wing parties" are liberal and conservative parties. "Center parties" are center parties, in particular Christian democratic or Catholic parties.

"Left-wing parties" are Australian Labour Party (ALP) [Australia], Socialist Party (SPÖ) and Communist Party (KPÖ) [Austria], Social Progressive Alternative/SPIRIT (SP.a/SPIRIT) (until 2001: Flemish Socialist Party), Communist Party (KPB/PCB), Francophone Socialist Party (PS), AGALEV, and ECOLO [Belgium], Social Democrats (SD), Left Socialist Party (LSP), Socialist People's Party (SPP), and Communist Party (COM) [Denmark], Social Democrats (SDP), Finnish People's Democratic Union (SKDL), Social Democratic League (TPSL), Left-Wing Alliance (VAS), and Green League (VIHR) [Finland], Socialist Party (PS), Communist Party (PCF), Greens, Movement for Citizens (MDC), Generation Ecology, Left Radicals (PRG) (formerly Mouvement des radicaux de gauche (MRG), and Radical Socialist Party (RSP)) [France], Social Democrats (SDP), and Bündnis 90/Die Grünen [Germany], Labour Party (LAB) and Democratic Left (DL) [Ireland], Socialist Party of Proletarian Unity (PSIU), Communist Party (PCI), Socialist Party (PSI), United Socialist Party (PSU), Social Democratic Party (PSDI), Greens, Party of the Democratic Left (PDS) and The Democrats (DEM) [Italy], Social Democratic Party (SDP), Japan Communist Party (JCP), Democratic Socialist Party (DSP), and United Democratic Socialists (UDS) [Japan], Labour Party (PvdA) and Political Party of the Radicals (PPR) [The Netherlands], Labour Party (LAB), Alliance and Progressive Coalition [New Zealand], Labour Party (DNA, AP), Socialist Left (SV), and Socialist People's Party [Norway], Socialist Party (PS) [Portugal], Socialist Party (PSOE) and Communist Party, United Left (PCE/PSUC/IU) [Spain], Social Democrats (S), Communist Party, Left Party (V) [Sweden], Social Democrats (PSS/SPS) [Switzerland], Labour Party (LAB) [UK].

"Center parties" are People's Party (ÖVP) [Austria], Christian Democrat & Flemish (CD & V) (until 2001: Christian People's Party (CVP)), Democrat Humanist Centre (CDH) (until 2002: Christian Social Party (PSC)), Francophone Democratic Front (FDF), New Flemish Alliance (N-VA) (former: Flemish/People's Union (VU)), Democratic Union (DU), and Wallon Rally (RW) [Belgium], Liberal Party (LIB) [Canada], Centre Democrats (CDM) and Christian People's Party (CPP) [Denmark], Centre Party (KESK), Liberal People's Party (LKP), Christian League (SKL) and Finnish Rural Party (SMP) [Finland], Centre of Social Democrats (CDS), Democratic Force (FD), Popular Republican Movement (MRP), Centre of Progress and Modern Democracy (PDM), Union for French Democracy (UDF), Reformers' Movement (REF, Reformer's Movement), and Republican Party (PR) [France], Christian Democratic Union (CDU) and Christian Social Union (CSU)

[Germany], Republican Party (Clann na Poblachta) (CNP) and Fine Gael (FG) [Ireland], Christian Democratic Party (DC), Republican Party (PRI), Italian Popular Party (PPI), Union of the Centre (UDC), Dini List–Italian Renewal (RI), Democratic Union (UD), Union of Republican Democrats (UDR), since 1999 known as UDEUR (Union of Democrats for Europe), Christian Democratic Centre, United Christian Democrats (CCD, CDU) [Italy], Komei Party, Komeito (CGP), and (New) Sakigake Party [Japan], Catholic People's Party (KVP), Christian Democratic Appeal (CDA), Democratic Socialists' 70 (DS'70), and Democrats' 66 (D66) [The Netherlands], Centre Party (SP) and Farmers' Party, Christian People's Party (KRF, CPP) [Norway], Popular Alliance, Popular Party (AP/PP) and Union of the Democratic Centre (UCD) [Spain], Agrarian Party, Center Party (C), Christian Democratic Union (KDS) [Sweden], Christian Democrats (PDC/ CVP) [Switzerland], Democratic Party [United States].

"Right-wing parties" are Liberal Party (LIB) and Country National Party (CNT) [Australia], Freedom Party (FPÖ) [Austria], Liberal Party (LP), Flemish Liberals & Democrats (VLD) (former: Party of Liberty and Progress (PVV)), and Reform Movement (MR) (former: Francophone Liberal Reform Party (PRL)) [Belgium], Progressive Conservative Party (PC) [Canada], Liberals (Venstre) (LIB), Conservative People's Party (Hoyre) (CON), Justice Party (JP), and Radical Party (Social Liberal Party) (RV) [Denmark], National Coalition (KOK) and Swedish People's Party (SFP/RKP) [Finland], Gaullistes (GAUL), Centre National des Indépendants (IND), Centre Democracy and Progress (CDP), Gaullists, Rally for the Rebublic (RPR) (formerly Union pour la Nouvelle, République (UNR) and Union des Démocrates pour la République (UDR), in 2002: Union for a Presidential Majority (UMP)), and Radical Party (RAD) [France], German Party (DP) and Free Democrats (FDP) [Germany], Party of the Land (Clann na Talmhan) (CNT), Progressive Democrats (PD) and Fianna Fail (FF) [Ireland], Liberal Party (PLI), Forza Italia (FI), Lombard League, Northern League (LN), and National Alliance (NA) [Italy], Liberal Democratic Party (LDP), Japan Renewal Party (JRP), Japan New Party (JNP), New Conservative Party (NCP), and Liberal Party (LP) [Japan], People's Party for Freedom and Democracy (VVD), Christian Historical Union (CHU), Anti Revolutionary Party (ARP), and List Pim Fortuyn (LPF) [The Netherlands], National Party (NP), New Zealand First (NZF), United Party [New Zealand], Conservatives (Hoyre) (CON, H) and Liberals (Venstre) (LIB, V) [Norway], Social Democrats, Popular Democrats (PPD/PSD), Centre Social Democrats, Popular Party (CDS-PP), and Popular Monarchist Party (PPM) [Portugal], Convergence and Unity (CiU) [Spain], Conservatives, Moderate Unity Party (M), and People's Party (The Liberals) (FP) [Sweden], Radical Democrats (PRD/FDP) and Swiss People's Party (UDC/SVP) [Switzerland], Conservative Party (CON) [UK], Republican Party [United States].

Notes

* In writing this chapter, I have greatly benefited from comments on "Party System Change and the Transformation of Production Regime" in 2006, 2007, and 2008 by Philippe C. Schmitter, T.J. Pempel, Helen Callaghan, Carlo Trigilia, Laszlo Bruszt, Christopher McNally, Takashi Oshimura, Hideko Magara, and other participants of the first, second, and third international conferences. I am also grateful for the contributions of my research assistant Masaaki Higashijima. This research project was financed by the Japan Society for the Promotion of Science, Grant-in-Aid for Scientific Research (B) (18330028) (Project Leader: Masanobu Ido).

1 Regarding types of democracy, in this chapter I adopt Lijphart's (1999) classic distinction of majoritarian vs. consensus democracies. The term "majoritarian democracies" largely describes the Anglo-Saxon model of politics that has two-party systems and pluralist interest groups systems as its key features. The term "consensus democracies" largely describes the continental European model of politics that has multiparty systems and corporatist interest group systems as its key features.

2 This measure was devised by researchers at the Organization for Economic Cooperation and Development (OECD) to gauge the strictness of employment protection legislation in terms of regular as well as atypical workers, such as temporary workers in its member countries (OECD 1999, 2004).There are two versions of overall EPL. The former does not consider collective dismissals of workers and is available from the late 1980s. The latter does consider collective dismissals and has data only for the late 1990s and for 2003. In this chapter, I compare the values of the overall EPL of the first version in the late 1980s and in 2003.

3 Along with Luxembourg, Japan constitutes an exception to this trend. In this period, the value of stock market capitalization in Japan actually dropped. It is clear that this decrease is a result of the collapse of the country's "bubble economy" in the early 1990s and its succeeding long economic slump. Figure 3.2 excludes these two cases from its sample.

4 For the classification of ideologies of governing parties, this chapter utilizes Armingeon *et al.*'s (2008) Comparative Political Dataset. In this dataset, political parties are classified into right-wing, center, and left-wing parties. In particular, left-wing parties include social democratic parties and political parties left of social democracy, right parties include liberal and conservative parties, and center parties are typically Christian Democratic or Catholic parties (see Appendix 2). Thus, the right and center parties in the Comparative Political Dataset are almost identical to liberal and Christian Democratic parties, respectively, as mentioned in Esping-Andersen (1990).

5 This finding appears to contradict one of the main presumptions of this chapter, which is that social democratic parties, as the representative of "insider labor," support deregulation of labor markets. However, the negative value for "left cabinets" is likely to be a consequence of the inclusion of social democrats as well as communists and other radical left parties that oppose increasing the flexibility of labor markets under the single "left cabinets" variable in the panel analysis. In future research, it will be desirable to split the "left cabinets" variable into "social democrats cabinets" and "communist cabinets" variables and to separately estimate their effects on the expansion of atypical labor.

References

Amable, B. (2003). *The Diversity of Modern Capitalism*, Oxford: Oxford University Press.

Barker, R. M. (2010). *Corporate Governance, Competition, and Political Parties*, Oxford: Oxford University Press.

Callaghan, H. (2009). "Insiders, Outsiders and the Politics of Corporate Governance: How Ownership Structure Shapes Party Positions in Britain, Germany, and France," *Comparative Political Studies*, 42(6), 733–762.

Campbell, J. L. and O. K. Pedersen (2007). "The Varieties of Capitalism and Hybrid Success: Denmark in the Global Economy," *Comparative Political Studies*, 40(3), 307–332.

Cioffi, J. W. and M. Höpner (2006). "The Political Paradox of Finance Capitalism: Interests, Preferences, and Center-Left Party Politics in Corporate Governance Reform," *Politics & Society*, 34(4), 463–502.

D'Alimonte, R. (2005). "Italy: A Case of Fragmented Bipolarism," in M. Gallagher and P. Mitchell (eds.), *The Politics of Electoral Systems*, Oxford: Oxford University Press, pp. 253–276.

Dalton, R., I. McAllister, and M. Wattenberg (2000). "The Consequences of Partisan Dealignmnet," in R. J. Dalton and M. Wattenberg (eds.), *Parties Without Partisans*, Oxford: Oxford University Press, pp. 37–63.

Deeg, R. and G. Jackson (2007). "The State of the Art: Towards a More Dynamic Theory of Capitalist Variety," *Socio-Economic Review*, 5, 149–179.

Esping-Andersen, G. (1990). *The Three Worlds of Welfare Capitalism*, Cambridge: Polity Press.

Gallagher, M. and P. Mitchell (2005). "Appendix B," in M. Gallagher and P. Mitchell (eds.), *The Politics of Electoral Systems*, Oxford: Oxford University Press, pp. 598–606.

Gourevitch, P. and J. Shinn (2005). *Political Power and Corporate Control*, Princeton: Princeton University Press.

Gourevitch, P., P. M. Pinto, and S. Weymouth (n.d.). *The Politics of Stock Market Development*. Available at: http://ssrn.com/abstract=1144069.

Hall, P. and D. Soskice (eds.) (2001). *Varieties of Capitalism*, Oxford: Oxford University Press.

Iversen, T. and J. D. Stephens (2008). "Partisan Politics, the Welfare State, and Three Worlds of Human Capital Formation," *Comparative Political Studies*, 41(4–5), 600–637.

Jackson, G. (2005). "Stakeholders under Pressure: Corporate Governance and Labour Management in Germany and Japan," *Corporate Governance*, 13(3), 419–428.

Katz, R. (2005). "Why are There so Many (or so Few) Electoral Reforms?" in M. Gallagher and P. Mitchell (eds.), *The Politics of Electoral Systems*, Oxford: Oxford University Press, pp. 57–76.

Kriesi, H., E. Grande, R. Lachat, M. Dolezal, S. Bornschier and T. Frey (2008). *West European Politics in the Age of Globalization*, Cambridge: Cambridge University Press.

Laakso, M. and R. Taagepera (1979). "'Effective' Number of Parties: A Measure with Application to West Europe," *Comparative Political Studies*, 12(1), 3–27.

La Porta, R., F. Lopez-de-Silanes, and A. Shleifer (1999). "Corporate Ownership Around the World," *Journal of Finance*, 54(2), 471–518.

La Porta, R., F. Lopez-de-Silanes, A. Shleifer, and R. W. Vishny (1998). "Law and Finance," *Journal of Political Economy*, 106(4), 1113–1155.

Lijphart, A. (1999). *Patterns of Democracy*, New Haven: Yale University Press.

Martin, C. J. and D. Swank (2008). "The Political Origins of Coordinated Capitalism: Business Organizations, Party Systems, and State Structure in the Age of Innocence," *American Political Science Review*, 102(2), 181–198.

OECD (1999). *Employment Outlook*, OECD.
OECD (2004). *Employment Outlook*, OECD.
OECD (2006). *Employment Outlook*, OECD.
Reed, S. (2005). "Japan: Haltingly Toward a Two-Party System," in M. Gallagher and P. Mitchell (eds.), *The Politics of Electoral Systems*, Oxford: Oxford University Press, pp. 277–295.
Roe, M. J. (2003). *Political Determinants of Corporate Governance*, Oxford: Oxford University Press.
Rueda, D. (2005). "Insider-Outsider Politics in Industrial Democracies: The Challenge to Social Democratice Parties," *American Political Science Review*, 99(1), 1–14.
Swank, D. (2002). *Global Capital, Political Institutions, Policy Change in Developed Welfare States*, Cambridge: Cambridge University Press.
Vowles, J. (2005). "New Zealand: The Consolidation of Reform?" in M. Gallagher and P. Mitchell (eds.), *The Politics of Electoral Systems*, Oxford: Oxford University Press.

Data sources

Armingeon, K., M. Gerber, P. Leimgruber, M. Beyeler, and S. Menegale (2008). *Comparative Political Data Set I, 1960–2005*, Institute of Political Science, University of Berne. Available at: www.ipw.unibe.ch/content/team/klaus_armingeon/comparative_political_data_sets/index_ger.html.
Beck, T., A. Demirgüç-Kunt, and R. Levine (2000). "A New Database on Financial Development and Structure," *World Bank Economic Review*, 14, 597–605.
Beck, T., G. Clarke, A. Groff, P. Keefer, and P. Walsh (2001). "New Tools in Comparative Political Economy: The Database of Political Institutions," *World Bank Economic Review*, 15(1), 165–176.
OECD (1999). *Employment Outlook*, OECD.
OECD (2004). *Employment Outlook*, OECD.
OECD (2008). *Employment and Labor Market Statistics*. Available at: www.oecd.org/employment/databse.

4 Reversing the causal arrow

How ownership structure shapes party positions in Britain, Germany and France[1]

Helen Callaghan

Introduction

According to conventional wisdom, parties on the left favor the interests of stakeholders over shareholders. In Mark Roe's (2003) influential argument, 'social democracy' – through its presumed negative effect on shareholder rights – is the main determinant of cross-national differences in ownership dispersion. Roe assumes that minority shareholders in countries where social democratic values prevail have more reason to fear that their interests will be trampled on, inducing owners to hold larger blocks of shares. This widespread view stems from the impression that traditional leftist ideology and commitments to working-class and low-income constituencies are incompatible with the distributional consequences of increased shareholder orientation.

Recent empirical evidence challenges the conventional wisdom. Cioffi and Höpner (2006; Höpner 2007) find that recent shareholder-friendly reforms in Germany, Italy, France and the United States were promoted by left-leaning parties, against resistance from the right. To explain their findings, Cioffi and Höpner focus mainly on factors affecting the electoral strategies of parties on the left, including a need to attract middle-class voters and the growing number of individuals owning shares. Höpner (2007) adds that transparency gains from some shareholder-oriented reforms can benefit workers as well as shareholders, leading these two groups to unite against company managers. Parties on the right receive less attention but are depicted as reluctant to embrace shareholder oriented reforms because of ties to corporate elites, supposedly leading "politicians on the right to value managerial autonomy as matters of political expedience, personal economic interest, and ideological conviction" (Cioffi and Höpner 2006: 487).

This chapter takes the enquiry one step further to systematically examine when and why left-leaning parties promote the interests of shareholders, and to look more closely at the electoral strategies of parties on the right. By mapping German, French and British party positions on takeover regulation from the 1950s onward, I show that the pattern identified by Cioffi and Höpner does not obtain everywhere. Instead, I find significant variation along three dimensions. First, left/right competition differs across countries. In Britain, from the 1950s until the arrival of Tony Blair it was a straightforward battle between capital and labor. In Germany, left/right positions are reversed, with Social Democrats, Greens and Socialists all joining the Liberal Party to promote outside shareholder interests against Christian Democrat resistance. In France, left and right are barely distinguishable due to equal ambivalence on both sides. Second, the timing of debate varies considerably. In Britain, takeover regulation first entered the political agenda in the early 1950s. In Germany, it was a non-issue until the mid-1990s. In France, it received little attention until the mid-1980s, then provoked passionate reactions before vanishing from the agenda, only to resurface again ten years later. Third, over time, parties everywhere have become more supportive of outsider-friendly takeover rules.

My explanation links party positions to the structure of corporate ownership. The theoretical reasoning behind this argument is laid out in the second section. The third section maps British, French and German corporate ownership structures and political debates over takeover regulation from the 1950s onward to demonstrate that the values of the dependent and independent variable differ across these countries and co-vary over time. The fourth section spells out the implications of my argument for research on party politics, corporate governance, varieties of capitalism and institutional change. I conclude with suggestions for further research.

The argument: how ownership structure affects party positions

To explain the variation documented below, my argument links party positions on takeover regulation to the structure of corporate ownership by focusing on the party–voter nexus. I assume that party positions reflect the preferences of their core voters and argue that the preferences of both upscale socioeconomic groups and working-class clienteles are shaped by ownership patterns. Upscale groups are affected because they are split into 'insider' and 'outsider' factions, and the relative size of these factions depends on the degree of ownership dispersion. Workers are affected because ownership structure determines the frequency of job-threatening hostile bids and defines the target group for anti-capitalist sentiments. (Where banks and large blockholders can be plausibly cast as the main villains, left-leaning parties can better afford to support outside shareholders without alienating their base.) The following paragraphs discuss the assumptions that underlie this argument.

The assumption that voters care about an issue as seemingly technical as takeover regulation rests on four observations. First, it does not amount to assuming that all voters are mobilized on the issue. Many voters do not know or care about corporate governance matters. I only expect parties to cater to those who do. Second, the proportion of voters owning shares, while still small, is by no means negligible in all advanced industrialized democracies. In the UK, it reached 21 percent of the population after Thatcher's privatization initiatives (see Table 4.6). Third, voters are affected by takeover rules not only as shareholders, but also as employees. (As shareholders, they are likely to support rules that facilitate hostile bids because these are widely regarded as a means of encouraging shareholder value maximization. As employees, they are likely to oppose such rules because hostile takeovers are commonly associated with job loss and restructuring.) Fourth, while takeover regulation is not typically foremost on the mind of most voters, it does rise to prominence in the wake of controversial bids, when it is catapulted to the front pages of newspapers and generates the heated political debates documented below.

The assumption that parties are both office-seeking and loyal to their core clienteles draws on two theories of party behavior that are distinct but often regarded as complementary. Vote-seeking theories assume that "[p]arties formulate policies in order to win elections, rather than win elections in order to formulate policies" (Downs 1957: 25, 28). Policy-promoting theories assume that parties have electoral ambitions because they want to implement policies favoring their core constituencies (e.g., Hibbs 1977). My argument is based on the compromise view that both motivations operate jointly, i.e., that "parties are organizations of political entrepreneurs who make strategic calculations even while implementing policies that are in the interest of their supporters" (Alt 1985: 1037; see also Frey and Schneider 1982; Korpi 1985: 1037; Strøm 1990).

To understand why upscale socioeconomic groups are divided into insiders and outsiders, one needs to know that a major purpose of corporate governance is to address the principal–agent problems that arise in companies run by managers on behalf of shareholders. Which solutions are available depends on the structure of corporate ownership. Large blockholders can supervise from the inside by threatening to use their seats on the supervisory board and/or their majority of voting rights in the shareholders' assembly to replace badly performing managers. Minority shareholders have fewer means of exercising voice because they suffer from collective action problems and lack individual incentives to spend resources on monitoring management. Instead, dispersed shareholders exercise arm's length control by threatening exit from companies that perform badly.

Regarding takeover regulation, the interests of insiders and outsiders are almost diametrically opposed. Outside shareholders like takeover rules that spur managers to maximize shareholder value. One such rule is the requirement that managers obtain authorization from shareholders before implementing so-called 'poison pills' which may deter hostile bidders. Managers dislike such rules because the increased supervision constrains their scope for acting as they see fit. Large blockholders have little reason to care one way or the other, because they have more direct means of keeping managers in check, and because companies with concentrated ownership are rarely subject to hostile bids.

The relative size of the insider and outsider factions depends on the structure of corporate ownership for at least three reasons. First, more dispersed ownership usually, though not always, implies more outside shareholders favouring active markets for corporate control. (In principle, increased dispersion can also result from the same number of investors spreading their capital over a larger number of firms. Moreover, an increase in the number of individuals owning shares need not imply a larger constituency in favour of hostile bids. Where employees acquire shares in their own company, this is not the case.) Second, dispersed ownership is a precondition for hostile bids, and more active markets for corporate control imply more lawyers, investment bankers, stock market analysts *et al.* whose jobs depend on outsider-friendly takeover rules. Third, ownership structure defines the target group for anti-capitalist sentiments. Where ownership is widely dispersed, the typical class enemy is a 'casino capitalist' with a diversified and mobile portfolio. In countries like with concentrated capital ownership, 'bosses, banks and blockholders' are the preferred villains for the left.

Based on these assumptions and observations, I argue that ownership structure affects party positions both on the right and on the left. Right-leaning parties respond to changes in the relative size of the insider and outsider factions among their core upscale socioeconomic clientele. A larger outsider faction implies deeper divisions on the right of the political spectrum and increases the likelihood that outsiders prevail. Left-leaning parties respond to changes in companies' vulnerability to hostile bids and to the spread of share ownership among their core clientele. On the one hand, more dispersed ownership and the associated increase in potentially job-threatening hostile bids makes it harder for parties on the left to support outsider-friendly takeover rules. On the other hand, a larger number of individuals owning shares makes it easier for parties on the left to support outsider-friendly takeover rules as a means favoring small shareholders over bosses, banks, and blockholders. Where both developments coincide, left-leaning parties face a dilemma, but, as explained above, this is not always the case. Beyond that, variation in ownership structure also contributes to explaining cross-national differences in the timing of debate. Two separate mechanisms are at work here. First, a pro-outsider constituency must emerge before politicians will advance its cause. Where minority shareholders are rare, their concerns are less likely to attract political attention. Second, public interest in takeover regulation tends to peak in the wake of high-profile bids, and a minimal degree of ownership dispersion is a necessary precondition for such bids. The following section presents my empirical evidence.

The evidence: party positions and corporate ownership patterns in Britain, Germany and France

A large-N study of whether ownership has a significant influence on party positions is beyond the scope of this chapter and may be impossible to conduct. In theory, the argument could be falsified by showing the lack of a significant correlation between the dependent and independent variable. In practice, many other variables besides ownership – including voting rules, number of parties, economic structure, political climate, historical legacies, etc. – are likely to affect party positions on corporate governance issues. Given the limited number of advanced industrial democracies, it is impossible to control for all of them. Moreover, mapping party positions over time for a large number of countries is a time-consuming endeavor, and measurement on a numeric scale is fraught with difficulties. Corporate governance issues, which are too technical in nature to regularly appear in party manifestos, are not covered by the manifestos project dataset (Budge *et al.* 2001).

Instead, the following section presents historical evidence for the three cases from which the argument was inductively derived. It maps British, French and German political debates on takeover regulation from the 1950s onward to show that differences in party positions across countries and over time broadly correspond to differences in the structure and evolution of corporate ownership. Comparison across countries shows that ownership has always been far more dispersed in the UK, with hostile bids far more frequent, and this is broadly reflected in party positions. On the right, British Conservatives were more deeply divided than French Gaullists and the German Liberals and Christian Democrats, and the outsider faction was more vocal. On the left, pre-Blair Labour was more passionately opposed to outsider-friendly takeover rules than the French Socialists and all German left-of-center parties, including the post-communist PDS.

Over time, ownership concentration has declined everywhere, the frequency of hostile bids has fluctuated, and the number of individuals owning shares has increased abruptly after large-scale privatization of previously state-owned companies. These developments are reflected both in changing party positions and in the timing of debate. In all three countries, sudden growth in the number of individuals owning shares was followed by left party efforts to champion the interests of small shareholders. In Germany, where the spread of shares coincided with an increased vulnerability to hostile bids, the Social Democrats belatedly noticed the double-edged nature of shareholder capitalism and made a U-turn on takeover regulation with their spectacular last-minute withdrawal of support for the outsider-friendly EU takeover directive. Moreover, in all three countries, debate was sparked off by controversial takeover battles following increased ownership dispersion. In Britain, takeover regulation first entered the political agenda in the early 1950s. In Germany, it was a non-issue until the mid-1990s. In France, it received little attention until the mid-1980s, then provoked passionate reactions before vanishing from the agenda, only to resurface again ten years later. Before turning to the political debates, the following paragraphs present details on the variation in corporate ownership structures across countries and over time.

Corporate ownership structure in Britain, Germany and France

The stark contrast between British, French and German levels of ownership concentration is captured by several indicators. First, listed companies in the UK account for a larger fraction of total national corporate activity than in Germany or France (see Table 4.1). This matters for the purposes of my argument because only companies listed on the stock market are potential targets for hostile bids. In Britain, since 1963, the number of domestic companies listed on the stock exchange has ranged from 4,400 to 1,900, out of a total population of around

500,000 firms. In Germany, it never exceeded 750. In France, the number of domestic listed companies peaked at around 1,000 in 1950 and again at the turn of the millennium. The total value of companies listed on the stock market was also much higher in Britain, rising from close to 77 percent of GDP in 1950 to more than 200 percent in 1999. In Germany and France, market capitalization throughout most of the period was well below one-third of the British level (see Table 4.2).

Second, ownership concentration of listed companies is lower in Britain than Germany or France (see Table 4.3). This matters because listed companies are less vulnerable to hostile takeovers if their ownership is concentrated. In all the years for which data are available, more than 50 percent of French and German companies had a blockholder owning more than 50 percent of shares, and 70 percent of companies had at least one blockholder owning more than 25 percent of shares. In Britain, the proportion of companies with a majority blockholder was always well below 10 percent, and the proportion of companies with at least one blockholder owning more than 20 percent of shares never exceeded 16 percent.

Third, cross-shareholdings are less common in Britain than in Germany or France (see Table 4.4). This matters because differences in the degree of cross-shareholdership are a further source of divergence in companies' vulnerability to hostile bids. Where companies have significant ownership stakes in each other, mutual dependencies increase the incentives for corporate shareholders to shield managers against raiders. From 1970 to the late 1990s, non-financial enterprises held around 40 percent of all German shares, compared to 5 percent in the UK. Despite a recent decline, German corporate cross-shareholdership remains very high by international standards. In France, the privatization process of the late 1980s was designed to deliberately strengthen France's cross-ownership network, through the sale of large stakes to a limited number of interlocked shareholders (see Schmidt 1996: 369–392). These *noyaux durs* remain strong despite some recent erosion. In 2002, 30 directors enjoyed between them 160 seats on the boards of major French firms (Clift 2007: 552, fn 1).

Fourth, until recently, the role of banks in corporate ownership was more pronounced in Germany than elsewhere. Under the system of bank proxy voting (*Depotstimmrecht*), private shareholders could authorize the banks where their shares were deposited to vote on their behalf at companies' annual shareholder meetings. This means that even dispersed ownership need not imply dispersed control because the controlling influence of banks is far greater than their equity holdings suggest. As dominant shareholders, mainly by proxy, banks were until recently represented on the supervisory boards of most German companies, acting as a shield against hostile bids. A study on the role of banks in 24 of the top 100 listed Germany companies showed that, in 1992, banks on average controlled 84 percent of voting rights – 13 percent by virtue of their own shareholdings; 10 percent by virtues of their own subsidiary investment funds; and no less than 61 percent by virtue of proxy votes (Jürgens *et al.* 2000: 59). In 1996, the supervisory boards of 29 of the 100 largest firms were chaired by representatives of Deutsche Bank (Beyer and Höpner 2003).

Over time, ownership concentration has declined everywhere. The German network of inter-company shareholdings started displaying signs of dissolution in the late 1990s, with share ownership by non-financial enterprises dropping below 30 percent for the first time in 1999. The number of capital ties between the 100 biggest German companies declined from 169 to 80 between 1996 and 2000. At the same time, German banks began loosening their ties to industrial companies, partly to avoid conflicts of interests with their increasingly lucrative investment banking activities, partly in response to a new law limiting proxy voting (Beyer and Höpner 2003). In France, cross-ownership networks have also begun unraveling since the late 1990s, and the number of foreign institutional investors has grown (Goyer 2007; Morin 2000: 39). The British decline, starting from lower levels of concentration, was more gradual and less significant, with industrial cross-shareholdings dropping from 5 percent in 1963 to 0.7 percent in 2003.

The number of individuals owning shares increased abruptly in all three countries following large-scale privatization of previously state-owned companies (see Table 4.5). In the UK, largely due to share offerings carried out by companies privatized under Thatcher, the number of individual shareholders rose from less than three million, or 5 percent of the population, in 1980 to more than 11 million, or 21 percent of the population, in 1991. British Gas shares alone gained 2.4 million shareholders, British Telecom gained 800,000. Around 1.6 million people acquired shares in the company for which they worked (Florio 2002: 21). In France, the privatization initiatives of the 1980s raised the proportion of individuals owning shareholders from 4.4 percent of the population in 1980 to 16 percent in 1991. In Germany, where privatization was initiated later and on a smaller scale, the proportion of shareholders among the population peaked at 9.7 percent in 2000 after public offerings by Deutsche Telecom.

The frequency of hostile bids has fluctuated over time (see Table 4.6). Unfortunately, systematic comparative data on the number of hostile bids is available only from 1988 onwards. It is, however, well documented that hostile bids in the UK first started occurring during the early 1950s and that the mid-1980s were a period of intense takeover activity. Franks and Mayer (cited in Goergen and Renneborg (1997: 185)) report 80 hostile takeovers in the UK for 1985–1986 alone. In Germany, the first hostile offer was made in 1988, and the total number of hostile bids, both successful and unsuccessful, can be counted on two hands. In France, hostile takeovers were unknown until the late 1960s, when three hostile bids were launched, all of them unsuccessful (see von Kapff 1975: 162–166). The next 15 years saw very little takeover activity. According to Daigre (1990: 92):

> between 1965 and 1975, less than a hundred takeovers occurred, and all were friendly. In the years 1976, 1977 and 1978 about twenty takeovers a year occurred, most of them friendly. From 1979 to 1986 takeovers steadily declined in number.

However, this figure increased sharply from 1986 on, sparking off the political reactions documented below. While the actual number of takeovers remained low by Anglo-American standards, the rise was sufficient to inspire headlines such as "Paris gripped by takeover fever" (*Financial Times*, April 2, 1986) and to render the French acronym for takeover bid (*OPA*) "a cult word to use in every context from political commentaries to illicit love-affairs" (*Financial Times*, April 11, 1988). The following narratives show how this variation in ownership structure across countries and over time is reflected in British, French and German party positions from the 1950s onwards.

British, French and German party political debate over takeover regulation, 1953–2003

In Britain, takeover regulation first entered the political agenda in the early 1950s, in response to the previously unknown phenomenon of hostile bids. Heated debate during the 1959 election campaign followed controversial bids for British Aluminium and the brewing company Watney Mann and a major City scandal involving takeover malpractice. As Roberts (1992: 137) explains, "[t]he City had long been a *bête noire* of some Labour politicians, and take-overs provided a 'live issue on which to arraign the government.'" The *Financial Times* reckoned that "the average person ... is so offended by the trappings of some bids and mergers that he tends to be sickened by the whole process," making takeovers "just about the only issue on which the Socialists could win an election these days" (*Financial Times*, July 7, 1959, cited in Roberts 1992). A second peak of political interest, during the late 1980s, occurred in the wake of high-profile controversial takeover battles for British Leyland, Pilkington and Rowntree and an insider trading scandal at Guinness.

Labour conformed to the conventional image of a leftist, anti-shareholder party for most of the period under consideration. In 1953–1954, Labour Party spokesmen, including Hugh Gaitskell, Roy Jenkins and Harold Wilson, complained about the asset stripping and large tax-free profits associated with hostile bids (Johnston 1980: 10–12). During a heated Commons debate in June 1959, Labour MPs condemned takeovers as "economic gang warfare." Harold Wilson, then shadow chancellor, accused the Conservative government of serving shareholders at the expense of the national interest:

> Just as shareholders are becoming more and more avid for quick gains, so the Government regard any quick capital gains as good business, to be encouraged whatever the production realities. Of course, the capitalist international knows no national frontiers. In the presence of a quick profit the patriotism of the government melts like snow in the summer sun.
>
> (Commons Hansard 1959: 36–37)

Evoking the image of class struggle, Wilson calculated how long it would take a "coal miner in the most profitable mine in the country" or a "Lancashire mule spinner, after thirty years in the industry" to earn the sums associated with take-overs. He asked the government how it could

> appeal for wage restraint in the payment of a job honestly and well done, while millions of pounds can be made in this effortless manner by a section which does no work at all? [...] These people "toil not, neither do they spin" yet their gains are out of all proportion to any services they render to that industry.
>
> (Commons Hansard 1959: 39–42)

Thirty years later, the same rhetoric was still in use. In 1986 and 1987, Roy Hattersley, shadow chancellor, branded the Thatcher administration as a "government of the City, for the City, and by far too large an extent by the City" that would not address the problems created by takeovers (*Guardian*, March 13, 1986). Labour's campaign coordinator Bryan Gould complained on TV about

> the sort of society which the present government has tried to bring about. It's a get rich, something for nothing sort of society where people can get enormous rewards not related in any way to the real contribution they make to our economy.
>
> (Newswire, February 18, 1987)

Tony Blair, at that time Labour's industry spokesman, questioned whether 30 or 40 fund managers were the right people to decide the future of key industrial sectors (*Financial Times*, May 28, 1988). From 1991 onward, the Labour Party toned down its confrontational rhetoric. Mo Mowlam, Labour's spokeswoman for the City, announced that "[u]p until now there has been a natural antagonism between the City and Labour. That has now passed." But at the same time, Mowlam declared that industry was "pig-sick" of its vulnerability to predators (*Financial Times*, April 26, 1991: 13).

The desire to control the takeover process was also reflected in Labour's policy initiatives. Harold Wilson's Labour government, elected in 1964, brought large mergers within the ambit of the monopolies legislation, thereby increasing the scope for government intervention in takeovers (Johnston 1980: 165). Labour's proposals while in opposition included incorporating the Takeover Code and Takeover Panel into a statutory framework of City regulation; asking companies to prove that industrial or commercial gains would come from a proposed merger; replacing the "Tebbit doctrine" – which made competition the main test for barring takeovers – with other public interest tests, including research and development; lowering the threshold triggering mandatory bids; assuring employee consultation on takeovers; and changing the tax treatment of share ownership to produce a bias in favor of long-term holdings (see Callaghan 2006: 78–79).

Labour's stance on takeover regulation changed shortly before Tony Blair's 1997 election victory. In February 1997, a commission established by the left-leaning Institute of Public Policy Research pronounced that "[t]here should be no new administrative restraints on takeovers." Since its election in May 1997, the Labour government has followed this advice. In June 2000, Stephen Byers, trade and industry spokesman, told a conference organized by the Trades Union Congress that reforms intended to make companies pay more attention to stake-holders were not on the government's agenda (*Financial Times*, June 8, 2000: 8). In May 2001, Tony Blair promised a shake-up of business merger law to facilitate takeovers, proud to be

> right in the centre of the City of London, one of the main financial institu-
> tions, launching our business manifesto with the support of many successful
> business people and able, credibly, to claim after four years the mantle of
> economic confidence and economic stability in our country. I don't suppose
> there is a greater indication of the change in British politics than that and
> certainly there is nothing that we have done over the past four years that I
> am prouder of than that.
>
> (*Guardian*, May 30, 2001: 16)

Britain's Conservatives throughout the period provided the counter-rhetoric to Labour's traditional leftist stance, branding their opponent as anti-capitalist and depicting themselves as the saviors of free markets and private property. During a Commons debate in 1959, Derick Heathcoat Amory, Chancellor of the Exchequer, countered Harold Wilson's complaint about takeovers by arguing that

> the [Labour] Government of which he [Wilson] was a member did quite a
> bit of taking-over, and it seems that the Opposition are planning to thrust
> more down the throats of the people if they ever again get the chance. There
> is, however, one vital dis-qualification. The take-overs of the right hon.
> Gentleman and his colleagues were compulsory ones, with no choice to the
> owners. What the right hon. Gentleman today has been inveighing against
> are take-overs with the collective approval of the owners of the businesses
> concerned. That is a significant distinction.
>
> (Commons Hansard 1959: 63)

In the same vein, Cecil Parkinson, a former secretary for trade and industry, sug-gested, three decades later, that City concern with short-term interests was partly Labour's fault:

> One of the reasons why our investors shorten their thinking is because of the
> uncertainty that could arise if we have a change of government. Unlike other
> successful capitalist countries, we have an Opposition which basically
> doesn't believe in private enterprise and does not support the system.
>
> (*Guardian*, January 29, 1987)

The Conservatives defended shareholder-value orientation both for its own sake and as a means to better overall economic performance. In 1959, Heathcoat

Amory insisted that "we have to accept that the control of a business is vested in its shareholders" and that, on balance, takeovers to date had been "beneficial rather than harmful from the point of view of the efficiency of industry, of the interests of the employees concerned and of the economy at large" (Commons Hansard 1959: 65–67).

Similarly, Kenneth Clarke, then minister for trade and industry, declared, in 1987, that

> [t]he Conservative party believes that the greatest national public interest lies in allowing such things [as takeovers] to take place within the market place. [...] It is contrary to all experience to believe that an industrial strategy, as managed by Labour Ministers, is in the interests of employees, compared with the decisions of shareholders in the free market economy that we are now operating.
>
> (Commons Hansard 1988: 333)

The argument that takeover threats could help keep managers in check was also regularly invoked, especially by Thatcher's supporters, who regarded barriers to hostile bids as incompatible with government efforts to bring in "the refreshing winds of competition." Lord Young, then secretary for trade and industry, dismissed calls for better protection against bids as "ingenious schemes to protect sitting directors" (*Times*, March 1, 1989). Determined to promote the best interests of business even against the express wishes of the peak employer federation, he explained that "[i]f we were to follow the sort of policy it [the CBI] advocates, the economy would soon lose its competitive edge" (*Financial Times*, November 9, 1998: 11).

Unlike their French and German counterparts, British Conservatives were deeply divided over takeover regulation, with a sizeable faction resenting the pro-shareholder stance of their party leaders. In 1959, the *Financial Times* suspected that, on a free vote, a motion condemning hostile takeovers brought by the Labour opposition would have been carried by a majority of two to one. During a Commons debate in January 1987, Edward Heath, the former Conservative prime minister, condemned predators moving into long-established family firms which had set aside money for long-term investment (Commons Hansard 1987: 792–795). Sir Anthony Grant, "as traditional a Tory MP as one could find," regretted that the energy spent on takeover deals was not invested into building up productive business (*Times*, January 18, 1987). In 1988, *Crossbow*, the publication of the Conservative Bow Group, called for a change of rules to ensure "that takeover activity is not undertaken at a frenetic pace at the behest of City interests" (*Times*, August 8, 1988). Peter Lilley, trade and industry secretary under Thatcher and Major, said in October 1990 that deal-making in London's capital market had gone "beyond the economically justifiable to become almost an end in itself" and that shareholder-value pressure could not be dismissed as a factor feeding short-termism (*Financial Times*, October 25, 1990). Less than two weeks after Thatcher's resignation, even John Redwood, former head of the prime minister's policy unit, with a reputation as a free-marketeer, joined the chorus by referring to evidence that,

> except in the very short term, takeovers can all too often damage the wealth of shareholders of the bidding company rather than improve it. Only a limited number of British companies have been adept at taking over others and taking the business on to better success.
>
> (*Independent*, December 8, 1990)

Many Conservatives also criticized the Thatcher government's non-interference with foreign takeovers. In the context of the 1986 bid for British Leyland (BL), Tory MPs supporting the "Keep BL British" campaign pressed the government to cease talks with General Motors and concentrate on negotiating with UK organizations (*Financial Times*, February 17, 1986). In June 1988, more than 60 Conservative MPs signed a Commons motion brought by the Labour Party against the government decision not to refer Nestlé's bid for Rowntree to the Monopolies and Mergers Commission (*Toronto Star*, June 2, 1988: 28). *Crossbow* accused Lord Young of "blatantly and shamelessly" ignoring the regional dimension in merger policy (*Financial Times*, August 8, 1988).

However, the pro-shareholder faction always maintained the upper hand in the Conservative Party. Conservative governments never yielded to calls for legislative or political intervention that were advanced not just by the Labour opposition but also from within their own ranks. In 1984, Norman Tebbit, then secretary for trade and industry, renounced the main instrument of intervention available to British governments by announcing that, henceforth, takeovers would only be referred to the Monopolies and Mergers Commission if there were reason to fear significant adverse effects on competition. During the years that followed, the government resisted pressure to prevent foreign takeovers of British "crown jewels" including British Leyland, Pilkington and Rowntree (*Financial Times*, May 16, 1988: 1). The change in Conservative rhetoric after Thatcher's departure was not matched by any significant change in policy. An all-party parliamentary select committee on trade and industry recommended wide-ranging changes to takeover law in 1991 and again in 1994, but these recommendations were not implemented (*Financial Times*, December 20, 1991; *Independent*, April 29, 1994). Instead, the Major government sought to address the problem of market myopia by promoting private coordination. Tax breaks to encourage long-term shareholdings were ruled out in favor of attempts to improve communication between investors and managers over business aims and investment plans (*Financial Times*, October 25, 1990: 8). In the same spirit, the 1995 Myners Report *Developing a Winning Partnership* "described what institutional investors should do but did nothing to ensure they would do so" (Howard 2005: 180).

In Germany, takeover regulation was a non-issue until the mid-1990s. The country lacked not just binding rules regarding the conduct of takeovers but also the political will to create them, despite periodic attempts by the European

Commission from 1974 onward to promote takeover law harmonization (see Callaghan 2006). Both chambers of the German parliament unanimously rejected the 1989 draft of the EU takeover directive on the grounds that there was "no need for regulation" (Deutscher Bundesrat 1989; Deutscher Bundestag 1990). A complete absence of hostile takeovers until the 1990s provides the backdrop to this lack of political interest in takeover regulation until after unification, when more German firms started turning to the stock market to finance their investments. As in Britain and France, political passions were first aroused by large-scale hostile bids. The 1997 battle between Krupp and Thyssen brought 35,000 steelworkers to the streets in protest (see Ziegler 2000: 210). Two years later, 62 percent of Germans surveyed thought that Vodaphone's takeover of Mannesmann would be bad for their country, while only 19 percent welcomed the idea of German companies being taken over by foreigners (Associated Press Worldstream, February 9, 2000).

When takeover battles in the late 1990s brought the issue to the forefront of the political agenda, all parties condemned hostile bids. In response to Krupp's hostile bid for Thyssen AG in 1997, "[p]oliticians from left to right, from state government to federal government, union leaders, the media, all protested against the Krupp move and clamored to have the tender offer withdrawn" (Hellwig 2000: 122). Vodaphone's bid for Mannesmann two years later met with similar cross-party condemnation (for details, see Callaghan 2006: 104–106).

However, outside the spotlight of public attention cast on the issue by these unpopular bids, party positions were more nuanced and, by contrast to pre-Blair UK, a conventional left–right framework does not capture the main cleavage line. During the late 1990s, the Social Democrats, Greens and Socialists (PDS) all joined the Liberals to support the dismantling of two major structural barriers to takeover bids in Germany, namely the system of proxy voting by banks and the tight network of cross-ownership, while the Christian Democrats defended these characteristic features of "Germany Inc" (see Cioffi 2002; Cioffi and Höpner 2006; Höpner 2007).

The FDP, consistent with its ideological commitment to economic liberalism, strongly supported active markets for corporate control. The Liberals were a driving force behind the 1998 Control and Transparency Act (KonTraG) which stripped German firms of important takeover defenses by placing limits on proxy voting and abolishing unequal voting rights, voting caps and the voting of cross-shareholding stakes above 25 percent in supervisory board elections. When the KonTraG was debated in the Bundestag in 1997, Otto Graf Lambsdorff called Germany a rent-seeking society and insisted that German companies would benefit from increased exposure to capital market pressures (Höpner 2007). During a debate on the German takeover law in 2001, FDP member Rainer Funke complained that the chancellor had caved in to trade unions and managers instead of facing international competition (Deutscher Bundestag 2001a).

More surprisingly, the center-left SPD during the late 1990s also supported the dismantling of takeover barriers, before suddenly reversing its stance in 2001. In 1997, while still in opposition, the SPD took the initiative of presenting the draft for a German takeover law, which, like the EU takeover directive, contained a neutrality rule and mandatory bid rule. The Control and Transparency Act, presented by the FDP/CDU coalition government in 1997, was criticized by the SPD as insufficiently shareholder-oriented. During a 1998 Bundestag debate on the proposal, Hans-Martin Bury (SPD) called the KonTraG a "placebo law designed to appease the public without introducing any real change, a law to protect managers and banks against shareholders." He argued that the German corporate sector was stifled by the power of banks, interlocking directorates, lack of transparency and underdeveloped markets for corporate control and demanded a ban on bank ownership of industrial shares (Deutscher Bundestag 1998: 20354). Eckhard Pick added that the protection of shareholders and the development of the capital market were important goals for the SPD (Deutscher Bundestag 1998: 20365). Four years later, during a Bundestag debate on the German takeover law, Nina Hauer insisted that "the shareholders own the corporation and should have the final say" (Deutscher Bundestag 2001b: 19829). Upon coming to power in 1998, the Social Democrats, in coalition with the Green Party, immediately passed the KonTraG, which stripped German firms of important defenses against hostile bids. Two years later, they abolished capital gains tax on the sale of large share blocks, to unwind the web of cross-shareholdings which had traditionally made takeovers difficult (Cioffi 2002: 38). Initially, the Schröder administration also lent its support to the EU takeover directive. However, following heavy lobbying from both business associations and trade unions, Schröder changed his stance in 2001. On April 28, weeks before the final vote in the European Parliament, Schröder withdrew his support from the European Council's common position on the directive. In May, the government announced its intention to redraft the German takeover law to allow management and supervisory boards to obtain shareholder authorization for the use of poison pills prior to an actual bid. This law, allowing pre-authorization of poison pills, was passed in November 2001.

Left of the SPD, the Green and Socialist parties during the late 1990s also supported the removal of takeover barriers. As Ziegler explains, the Greens used the issue of corporate governance

> to criticize established concentrations of economic power as obstacles to desirable types of change. Much like the Social Democrats, the Greens attacked the multiple sources of influence that the large universal banks exercised over German firms. Much like the liberals, they argued ever more pointedly through the 1990s that Germany needed a modern equity market to support entrepreneurs in the small and medium-sized sector.

The Socialists shared the desire to curb the power of banks and interlocking capital. During a Bundestag debate on the KonTraG, Uwe-Ernst Heuer for the PDS explained that more active markets for corporate control would democratize and revitalize the economy (Ziegler 2000: 205).

This left the Christian Democrats as the main defenders of Germany's structural barriers to hostile bids. During a Bundestag debate on SPD proposals for a

German takeover law in 1997, members of the CDU rejected the draft as "too early and too wide-ranging" and maintained that, to date, the absence of a takeover law had not done any harm (*FAZ*, October 4, 1997). Instead, they favored a self-regulatory system based on the voluntary takeover code introduced in 1995. During a Bundestag debate on the KonTraG in 1998, Joachim Gres (CSU) said that a change of direction in German corporate governance was neither intended nor necessary. "Constancy," he said, "is important in economic policy ... Please don't think that the job of economic policy makers is to permanently introduce new ideas." Gres also insisted that the image of a 'Germany Inc.' built upon quasi-cartels did not reflect reality. Hartmut Schauerte (CDU) dismissed calls for curbing the power of banks as "pure ideology" (Deutscher Bundestag 2001a). Klaus-Heiner Lehne (CDU), rapporteur for the directive in the European Parliament, played a key role in mobilizing his fellow MEPs against the neutrality rule and proudly claimed credit when the European Parliament rejected the directive in 2001.

In France, political interest was sporadic. Hostile takeovers were unknown until the late 1960s, when three hostile bids, although unsuccessful, occasioned a brief spell of debate resulting in France's first takeover code (see von Kapff 1975: 162–166). The following decade of silence on the issue was a period of low takeover activity. Political interest returned during the mid-1980s in response to increased activity on the market for corporate control. As in Britain, takeover battles and scandals over controversial bidding practices heated up the political atmosphere (for details, see Callaghan 2006: 112). The subsequent period of relative calm was one of low takeover activity. Political interest only returned in October 1996 when French employer federations AFEP and "Entreprise et Cité" launched papers demanding reforms of French takeover law to make takeovers more difficult (*Le Monde*, October 15, 1996). One observer explains the sudden mobilization after years of complacency by pointing to changes in corporate ownership structures:

> [Until recently], few French companies considered themselves attractive to foreign investors. [...] But they now find themselves in a state of weakness that is cause for concern. [...] French companies see themselves as potential victims of takeovers, all the more because the "hard core" *(noyau dur)* system of cross-shareholdings put in place ten years ago is dissolving.
>
> (*Le Monde*, October 15, 1996: 19)

As in Germany and Britain, and in line with populist sentiment, the immediate political response to hostile bids was passionately hostile. During his presidential re-election campaign in April 1988, Mitterrand called for regulatory intervention to tame "financial anarchy and savage takeovers," deeming it "time for the triumph of an economy of short-termist speculation to come to an end" (Mitterrand 1988). A year later, during a TV interview shortly before the French municipal elections, he warned his audience "against takeover mania, against the gangsterism and the rule of the strongest" and promised to defend French producers, company managers, French entrepreneurs, against this wandering money, these birds of prey, who grab all this [...] without having taken part in the daily effort. That's too easy! So I say that the role of the state, in this area, is a major role. The state can prevent things.

(*Le Monde*, February 14, 1989)

However, the accumulated words and actions of French politicians both on the left and right send a less clear-cut message. Edouard Balladur, Gaullist finance minister under prime minister Jacques Chirac, explained in 1988 that, regarding takeovers,

[t]wo things need to be taken into account. First, protecting the continuity of companies and the interests of their shareholders and employees. Second, ensuring that the companies do not seal themselves off, blocking all evolution, all alliance formation, all restructuring. Where is the good measure between these contradictory aims? It clearly depends on the circumstances.

(*Le Monde*, March 1, 1988)

Balladur's successor Pierre Bérégovoy, Socialist finance minister under prime minister Michel Rocard, opened a parliamentary debate in 1989 by declaring that "[t]he government wants to neither prevent nor encourage takeovers, but the role of the legislator and of the market authorities is to guarantee the clarity and legality of the rules of the game" (*Le Monde*, April 21, 1989: 44). Gaullist prime minister Jacques Chirac announced in 1996 that "[w]e do not want to return to protectionism, but we don't want to sell out either" (*Le Monde*, October 15, 1996: 19). These ambivalent attitudes are also reflected in legislative measures. The Gaullists in 1986 embarked on the privatization of French industry, but not without creating golden shares and interlocking capital structures to protect the previously state-owned enterprises against hostile bids (see *Le Monde*, June 13, 1987: 4). Foreign ownership of privatized companies was initially limited to a maximum of 20 percent (*Financial Times*, June 15, 1987: IV). In March 1988, following takeover battles over Prouvost, Télémécanique, Rhin-Rhône and Compagnie de Midi, Balladur suggested that

the recent takeover developments should lead us to consider whether it would not be useful, in certain cases, to increase the stabilized portion of capital of companies that are particularly threatened, and to reduce the number of candidates so that the hard core becomes less fragile.

(*Le Monde*, March 4, 1988: 27)

Balladur also asked the French stock market authorities to reinforce companies' defense options against hostile bids. The stock market authorities turned down his request, but three less radical rules designed to reduce the number of hostile bids were adopted in April 1988 (*Vie Française*, May 14, 1988). In 1995, Alain Madelin, then economics minister, abolished the legal requirement for all foreign takeovers to be registered with and formally approved by the government (*Financial Times*, June 20, 1996). However, one year later, Jacques Chirac felt that, "by comparison to our main competitors, we are too open at times" (*Le Monde*, October 5, 1996: 31) and initiated three changes to the French takeover code to make hostile bids more difficult (*Le Monde*, October 11, 1996; *Le Monde*, March 21, 1997).

Socialist policies were similarly ambivalent. Between 1984 and 1986, during his first term in office under the Socialist government of Laurent Fabius, economics minister Bérégovoy launched France on its path of financial modernization by pruning credit and exchange controls and creating new markets for commercial paper and financial futures. In 1986, he gave up his ministry's right to veto all French takeovers. However, as takeover activity increased, Bérégovoy stepped on the brakes. In the spring of 1988, while still in opposition, he proposed creating a special investment fund to intervene in takeover battles on behalf of a besieged management. Back in office, he responded to a series of takeover scandals in the spring of 1989 by passing a bill on the 'Safety and Transparency of the Financial Markets,' which strengthened the disciplinary powers of the Commission des Opérations de Bourse (COB), the French stock market watchdog. The bill also strengthened employee information rights in the context of takeover bids, allowed target companies to augment capital in order to dilute the proportion of shares held by bidders, required the CEO to inform the comité d'entreprise (works council) of takeovers in progress and introduced transparency requirements regarding the crossing of thresholds and the revelation of shareholder pacts (*Le Monde*, April 21, 1989: 44). The Nouvelles Régulations Économiques (NRE), passed by the Socialist government of Lionel Jospin, strengthened employee information by depriving bidders of all voting rights acquired during an offer until they would comply with the obligation of discussing their intentions with the works council. The NRE also broadened the scope for state intervention by requiring potential bidders for a bank or insurance company to inform either the economics minister or the president of the committee of banks and investment companies in advance of an offer. However, they also suspended shareholder pacts involving more than 0.5 percent of capital for the duration of the offer period, thereby facilitating hostile bids (*Echos*, May 14, 2001: 67).

Implications

In sum, my chapter illustrates how "political feedback effects from the structure of the political economy sustain distinctive VoCs" (Hall 2007: 81). I show that British, French and German political debates over takeover regulation since the 1950s differ along several dimensions, including the pattern of left/right competition and the timing of debate, and that these differences broadly correspond to differences in the structure of corporate ownership. To explain the observed correlation, I focus on the party–voter nexus, by assuming that parties cater to their core constituents and providing reasons for why ownership structure should affect the preferences of both upscale socioeconomic groups and working-class clienteles.

The chapter challenges existing work on the relationship between ownership patterns – an element of the VoC – and minority shareholder protections – a product of party politics via the legislative process, by reversing the arrow of causation. Most authors explain correlations between ownership dispersion and various political factors by treating ownership as the dependent variable. Roe (2003) argues that 'social democracy' discourages ownership dispersion by making it more difficult for outside shareholders to claim primacy vis-à-vis other stakeholders, including workers. Gourevitch and Shinn (2005) suggest that the larger number of veto players in consensus-oriented as opposed to majoritarian political systems favors concentrated ownership by encouraging corporatist coalitions between managers, workers and blockholders against outside owners. La Porta *et al.* (2000) claim that the degree of dispersion depends on the quality of corporate law, including minority shareholder protection. I argue that a causal arrow runs in the opposite direction, from ownership structures to politics and corporate law. Outside shareholders must first emerge as a sizeable constituency before a political party will advance their cause. Unlike the arguments discussed above, mine is compatible with Coffee's (2001: 66) observation that, historically, political and legal efforts to protect shareholders have tended to follow, rather than precede, the appearance of securities markets.

The chapter contributes to growing evidence that different patterns of party competition correspond to different varieties of capitalism by showing that Britain and Germany – the closest real-world examples of a liberal and a coordinated market economy respectively – display strikingly different patterns of party competition on a policy issue that is considered central to generating the comparative institutional advantages of these national production regimes.

It advances the literatures on varieties of capitalism and institutional change by suggesting that political support for shareholder capitalism is greater in Britain than in Germany *not* because actors in both countries know about and seek to defend the comparative institutional advantage of their production regimes, but simply because Britain has more shareholders. The assumption implicit in parts of the varieties of capitalism literature that interest groups and governments care mainly about preserving the comparative institutional advantage of their national production regime (see Fioretos 2001: 255) makes it difficult to explain moves away from equilibrium. Widespread recent growth in support for shareholder-oriented corporate governance is easier to explain once ownership structure is recognized as a determinant of preferences and party positions. My argument implies that increased ownership dispersion due to privatization, tax changes or the like may undermine political support for stakeholder-friendly corporate governance rules regardless of their contribution to the comparative institutional advantage of coordinated market economies.

Beyond that, my chapter opens up several agendas for further research. First, more nuanced descriptions of ownership patterns and their relationship to political preferences would be desirable. The present chapter takes only one of many necessary steps toward disaggregating capital. While the insider–outsider distinction is reasonably informative on the issue of takeover regulation, it may not be the most relevant cleavage on other corporate governance issues. Among the insiders, one could distinguish further between managers and owners of listed and unlisted, small and large companies of different sectors, between family owners, banks, the state as blockholder in nationalized enterprises, etc. Among the outsiders, individual shareholders differ from various types of institutional investors, including pension funds, hedge funds and mutual funds. Who wants what on any particular issue is impossible to ascertain analytically because no model is better than its assumptions, and standard assumptions such as the idea that material interests can be inferred from material positions remain controversial. A systematic empirical study of lobbying efforts by groups representing different segments of capital would alleviate some of these concerns.

Second, while the present chapter focuses on the party–voter nexus, electoral pressures are clearly not the only conceivable channel through which ownership structure might affect party positions. Alternative channels include a structurally privileged position of business in capitalist economies (see e.g., Lindblom 1979), or the role of bureaucrats in the policy-making process (see e.g., Tiberghien 2007). Arguments along these lines require different assumptions from the ones I make regarding the motivations and autonomy of politicians, but they are compatible with my claim that party positions depend on the structure of corporate ownership, to the extent that business preferences and expert recommendations depend on the structure of corporate ownership. There are good reasons for believing that this is the case. The varieties of capitalism literature has long argued that companies in coordinated market economies, where concentrated ownership prevails, have different corporate governance requirements than companies in liberal market economies more exposed to stock market pressures (e.g., Vitols 2001), and recent empirical research confirms that these differences are reflected in employer preferences (Callaghan 2011). Ascertaining whether politicians are swayed more by electoral pressures or interest group demands is ultimately impossible, but careful process-tracing of lobbying efforts and political responses might go some way toward answering this question.

Third, the effect of factors other than ownership structure on the politics of corporate governance merits further exploration. Institutional variables, while insufficient by themselves, surely play a role. Apart from the above-mentioned effect of electoral systems on coalition behavior, differences between federal and unitary systems seem likely to be relevant. So far, research into the effect of federalism on corporate governance has focused on policy outcomes (Bebchuk and Ferrell 1999: 1176–1177; Miller 1998: 70–73; Roe 1993: 332–333). It seems worth exploring how multilevel governance affects party competition. More so than the United States, the European Union would be a promising terrain for such studies.

Fourth, the consequences of the timing and sequencing of debate for the content of debate remain to be examined. As shown above, British parties started arguing over takeover regulation almost four decades before the issue entered the German political agenda. Timing is likely to affect the content of debate not only because economic ideas *en vogue* in one period may be less fashionable decades later. The order in which countries liberalize their markets for corporate control is also likely to matter because latecomers suffer disadvantages of backwardness. Britain removed barriers to hostile bids at a time when cross-border capital mobility was limited, and British firms had decades to adapt to the British Takeover Code before it was proposed as a blueprint for regulation throughout the European Union. Partly as a result, German firms found themselves in a position of asymmetric vulnerability, which helps explain why German members of the European parliament from all political parties voted against the outsider-friendly 2001 version of the EU takeover directive (Callaghan and Höpner 2005). The advantageous position of British companies in an increasingly transnational market for corporate control may also help explain why British parties on the right and left, bitterly divided over takeover regulation until the 1990s, have since converged to endorse the absence of barriers to hostile bids.

Finally, it will be interesting to see how German, French and British parties respond to future changes in the structure of corporate ownership. But this is a question which only time can answer.

Appendix

Table 4.1 Number of listed companies

	1950	1960	1963	1970	1980	1986	1990	1995	2000	2003
UK			4,409	3,418	2,747	2,173	2,111	1,971	2,371	2,311
Germany	670	628		550	460	492	649	678	744	684
France	1,095	836		812	749	598	873	710	1,013	

Sources: 1986–2003 data: DAI Factbook 2004 table 02–3; UK data 1963–1980: Franks and Mayer (2004: 27), table 1B; French and German data 1950–1980: author's calculation based on Rajan and Zingales (2003: 17), table 5 and the US Census Bureau International Database, September 2004 version.

Table 4.2 Market capitalization of domestic companies as a percentage of GDP

	1950	1960	1970	1980	1990	1999
UK	77	106	163	38	81	225
Germany	15	35	16	9	20	67
France	8	28	16	9	24	117

Source: Rajan and Zingales (2003: 15), table 3.

Table 4.3 Proportion of listed companies where largest blockholder owns more than 50 [25] percent of shares

	1951	1976	1984	1986	1990	2000
UK	>10 [>10]		5		6 [16]	2 [10]
Germany				59	50 [85]	50 [70]
France		55			50 [80]	50 [70]

Sources: 1990 data: Becht and Mayer (2001: 2); 2000 data: Van der Elst (2004); 1976–1986 data: Berglöf (1990: 126); UK 1951 data: Florence (1961: 69).

Table 4.4 Percentage of shares owned by non-financial companies

	1953	1963	1969	1975	1981	1989	1991	1993	1995	1997	1999	2001	2003
UK		5.1	5.4	3	5.1	3.8	3.3	1.5	–	1.2	2.2	1	0.7
G	39.86	39.14	38.8	42.1	46.5	37.2	46.3	44.4	46.0	40.2	34.9	36.8	32.5
F									25.7	19.2	23.8	23.7	23.7

Sources: UK: Office of National Statistics (ONS); Germany: DAI Factbook 2004, tables 08.1–2 and 08.1–3: France 1995–2003: Banque de France.

Table 4.5 Proportion of individuals owning shares, as a percentage of the population

	1980	1981	1984	1987	1988	1990	1991	1992	1994	1996	1999	2000	2001	2003
UK	5		7	15		19	21	17						
G		5.3			6.8	5.8		6.4	6.3	6	7.8	9.7	8.9	7.8
F	4.4			10.9			16			10.1		12.7		16

Source: DAI Factbook 2004, table 08.6–2. France 1987: author's calculation based on Goldstein (1996: 1314).

Table 4.6 Number of hostile bid announcements

	1950–1964	1965–1975	1988	1989	1990	1991	1992	1993	1994	1995	1996	1997	1998	1999
UK			41	35	24	31	16	11	9	16	14	11	12	24
G	0	0	1	0	2	1	0	0	0	0	0	1	0	1
F	0	3	6	5	0	0	2	1	0	1	1	4	0	6

Source: 1988–1999 data: Thomson Financial SDC Platinum Database 1950–1975 data: von Kapff (1975: 162–165), Daigre (1990: 92).

Note

1 Based on an article published in *Comparative Political Studies* 2009, Vol. 42, No. 6, pp. 307–332, entitled "Insiders, Outsiders and the Politics of Corporate Governance."

References

Alt, J. E. (1985). Political Parties, World Demand, and Unemployment. Domestic and International Sources of Economic Activity. *American Political Science Review*, 79(4), 1016–1040.

Bebchuk, L. A. and Ferrell, A. (1999). Federalism and Corporate Law: The Race to Protect Managers from Takeovers. *Columbia Law Review*, 99(5), 1168–1199.

Becht, M. and Mayer, C. (2001). Introduction. In F. Barca and M. Becht (eds.), *The Control of Corporate Europe* (pp. 1–46). Oxford: Oxford University Press.

Berglöf, E. (1990). *Corporate Governance and Capital Structure – Essays on Property Rights and Financial Contracts*. Stockholm: Institute of International Business.

Beyer, J. and Höpner, M. (2003). The Disintegration of Organised Capitalism: German Corporate Governance in the 1990s. *West European Politics*, 26(4), 179–198.

Budge, I., Klingemann, H.-D., Volkens, A., Bara, J. and Tanenbaum, E. (2001). *Mapping Policy Preferences: Estimates for Parties, Electors, and Governments 1945–1998*. Oxford: Oxford University Press.

Callaghan, H. (2006). European Integration and the Clash of Capitalisms – British, French and German Disagreements over Corporate Governance, 1970–2003. Unpublished doctoral dissertation, Northwestern University, Evanston, IL, USA.

Callaghan, H. (2011). Constrain-thy-neighbor effects as a determinant of transnational interest group cohesion. *Comparative Political Studies*, 44(8), 910–931.

Callaghan, H. and Höpner, M. (2005). European Integration and the Clash of Capitalisms: Political Cleavages over Takeover Liberalization. *Comparative European Politics*, 3, 307–332.

Cioffi, J. (2002). Restructuring "Germany, Inc.": The Corporate Governance Debate and the Politics of Company Law Reform. *Law and Policy*, 24(4), 355–402.

Cioffi, J. and Höpner, M. (2006). The Political Paradox of Finance Capitalism: Interests, Preferences, and Center-Left Party Politics in Corporate Governance Reform. *Politics and Society*, 34(4), 463–502.

Clift, B. (2007). French Corporate Governance in the New Global Economy: Mechanisms of Change and Hybridisation within Models of Capitalism. *Political Studies*, 55(3), 546–567.

Coffee, J. (2001). The Rise of Dispersed Ownership: The Roles of Law and the State in the Separation of Ownership and Control. *Yale Law Journal*, 111(1), 1–82.

Commons Hansard (1959). Parliamentary debate on the condition of private industry (pp. 35–173).

Commons Hansard (1987). Parliamentary debate on government economic policies (pp. 763–802).

Commons Hansard (1988). Parliamentary debate on Rowntree plc. (pp. 327–338).

Daigre, J.-J. (1990). The Regulation of Public Takeover Bids and Offers of Exchange and Anti-P.T.B. and O.O.E. Mechanisms in France. In J. J. M. Maeijer and K. Geens (eds.), *Defensive Measures Against Hostile Takeovers in the Common Market* (pp. 91–112). Dordrecht: Martinus Nijhoff.

Deutscher Bundesrat (1989). Drucksache 136/1/89.

Deutscher Bundestag (1990). Drucksache 11/6612.

Deutscher Bundestag (1998). Plenarprotokoll 13/222.

Deutscher Bundestag (2001a). Plenarprotokoll 14/192.

Deutscher Bundestag (2001b). Plenarprotokoll 14/201.

Downs, A. (1957). *An Economic Theory of Democracy*. New York: Harper & Row.

Fioretos, K.-O. (2001). The Domestic Sources of Multilateral Preferences: Varieties of Capitalism in the European Community. In P. Hall and D. Soskice (eds.), *Varieties of Capitalism* (pp. 213–244). Oxford: Oxford University Press.

Florence, S. (1961). *Ownership, Control and Success of Large Companies: An Analysis of English Industrial Structure and Policy, 1936–1951*. London: Sweet & Maxwell.

Florio, M. (2002). A State without Ownership: the Welfare Impact of British Privatisations 1979–1997. *Working Paper No. 2002–24*, Universita degli Studi di Milano.

Franks, J. and Mayer, C. (2004). Spending Less Time with the Family: The Decline of Family Ownership in the UK, *NBER Working Paper*. Cambridge, MA: National Bureau of Economic Research.

Frey, B. and Schneider, F. (1982). Politico-economic Models in Competition with Alternative Models: Which Predict Better? *European Journal of Political Research*, 10(3), 241–254.

Goergen, M. and Renneborg, L. (1997). United Kingdom. In K. Gugler (ed.), *Corporate Governance and Economic Performance* (pp. 184–200). Oxford: Oxford University Press.

Goldstein, A. (1996). Privatisations et contrôle des entreprises en France. *Revue économique*, 47(6), 1309–1332.

Gourevitch, P. and Shinn, J. (2005). *Political Power and Corporate Control: The New Global Politics of Corporate Governance*. Princeton: Princeton University Press.

Goyer, M. (2007). The Transformation of Corporate Governance in France. In P. Culpepper, P. Hall and B. Palier (eds.), *Changing France: The Politics that Markets Make* (pp. 80–104). Houndmills: Palgrave.

Hall, Peter (2007). The Evolution of Varieties of Capitalism in Europe. In Bob Hancké, Martin Rhodes and Mark Thatcher (eds.), *Beyond Varieties of Capitalism Conflict, Contradiction and Complementarities in the European Economy* (pp. 39–85). Oxford: Oxford University Press.

Hellwig, M. (2000). On the Economics and Politics of Corporate Finance and Control. In X. Vives (ed.), *Corporate Governance* (pp. 95–134). Cambridge: Cambridge University Press.

Hibbs, D. (1977). Political Parties and Macroeconomic Policies. *American Political Science Review*, 71, 467–487.

Höpner, M. (2007). Corporate Governance Reform and the German Party Paradox. *Comparative Politics*, 401–420.

Howard, A. (2005). The Governance of Flexibility: Contemporary Politics and the British Company. Unpublished doctoral dissertation, George Washington University, Washington, DC.

Johnston, A. (1980). *The City Takeover Code*. Oxford: Oxford University Press.

Jürgens, U., Naumann, K. and Rupp, J. (2000). Shareholder Value in an Adverse Environment: The German Case. *Economy and Society*, 29(1), 54–79.

Korpi, W. (1985). Power Resources Approach vs. Action and Conflict: On Causal and Intentional Explanations in the Study of Power. *Sociological Theory*, 3(2), 31–45.

La Porta, R., Lopez-de-Silanes, F., Shleifer, A. and Vishny, R. (2000). Investor Protection and Corporate Governance. *Journal of Financial Economics*, 58(1), 3–27.

Lindblom, C. E. (1979). *Politics and Markets: The World's Political-Economic Systems.* New York: Basic Books.

Miller, G. (1998). Political Structure and Corporate Governance: Some Points of Contrast Between the United States and England. *Columbia Business Law Review,* 1998(1), 51–78.

Mitterrand, F. (1988, April). Lettre à tous les Français. Available at: www.psinfo.net/.

Morin, F. (2000). A Transformation in the French Model of Shareholding and Management. *Economy and Society,* 29(1), 36–53.

Rajan, R. G. and Zingales, L. (2003). The Great Reversals: The Politics of Financial Development in the Twentieth Century. *Journal of Financial Economics,* 69(1), 5–50.

Roberts, R. (1992). Regulatory Responses to the Rise of the Market for Corporate Control in Britain in the 1950s. *Business History,* 34(1), 183–200.

Roe, M. J. (1993). Takeover Politics. In M. Blair (ed.), *The Deal Decade* (pp. 321–380). Washington, DC: Brookings.

Roe, M. J. (2003). *Political Determinants of Corporate Governance – Political Context, Corporate Impact.* Oxford and New York: Oxford University Press.

Schmidt, V. A. (1996). *From State to Market? The Transformation of Business in France.* Cambridge: Cambridge University Press.

Strøm, K. (1990). A Behavioural Theory of Competitive Political Parties. *American Journal of Political Science,* 34, 565–598.

Tiberghien, Y. (2007). *Entrepreneurial States: Reforming Corporate Governance in France, Japan, and Korea.* Ithaca: Cornell University Press.

Van der Elst, C. (2004). Industry-specificities and Size of Corporations: Determinants of Ownership Structures. *International Review of Law and Economics,* 24(4), 425–446.

Vitols, S. (2001). Varieties of Corporate Governance: Comparing Germany and the UK. In P. Hall and D. Soskice (eds.), *Varieties of Capitalism* (pp. 337–360). Oxford: Oxford University Press.

von Kapff, K. (1975). Übernahmeangebote (take-over bids und offres publiques d'achat) in England und Frankreich. Unpublished doctoral dissertation, Universität Mannheim (Wirtschaftshochschule).

Ziegler, J. N. (2000). Corporate Governance and the Politics of Property Rights in Germany. *Politics and Society,* 28(2), 195–222.

5 Politics against market

The hard way of Italian capitalism

Luigi Burroni and Carlo Trigilia

Introduction

Since the 1990s advanced economies had to face the new challenges brought about by globalization. Comparative studies have focused on different paths of development followed by various countries to deal with these tensions. One of the most important theoretical and empirical contributions in this field was provided by the "Varieties of Capitalism" (VoC) approach (Hall and Soskice 2001; Hall and Gingerich 2004). As is well-known, this strand of literature has its main focus on the national dimension: a coherent set of national institutions shapes the organizational architecture of firms and the governance of the economy. Peter Hall and David Soskice (2001) identified two ideal types of capitalism: the Coordinated Market Economies (CMEs) (Austria, Germany, Japan and Nordic European countries) and the Liberal Market Economies (LMEs) (including Anglo-Saxon capitalism). As Hall and Soskice acknowledge, this typology is less effective in classifying countries such as Italy, Spain and France and for this reason more recent empirical and theoretical contributions have focused on the so-called "Mixed-Market Economies" model (MMEs), including cases of Mediterranean capitalism and of Central and Eastern Europe (Hancké *et al.* 2007).

According to these authors, the Mediterranean variety of capitalism has hybrid features and combines market and non-market forms of coordination with an important role played by the state. Molina and Rhodes (2007) underline that MMEs are characterized by limited social protection and high employment protection for some social groups (public employees and workers in large firms). As for the production regime, "lower competitive pressures due to high levels of product-market regulation and state intervention help maintain stable bank-industry relations and contain the growth of financial market" (p. 226). These two features promote an industrial specialization based on small-scale firms that – according to these authors – compete mainly on low price, low quality goods. Other contributions underline that these mixed models lack the institutional architecture able to support their competitiveness. Amable (2003), for example, showed that MMEs do not have a coherent system that triggers the emergence of valuable and effective "institutional complementarities." Hall and Gingerich emphasized that pure systems – such as LMEs or CMEs – perform better than mixed cases (Hall and Gingerich 2004). Moreover, in MMEs this suboptimal competitive architecture will be retained by the action of strong actors – including the state – interested in maintaining the status quo (Hancké *et al.* 2007).

However, this literature focuses on mixed models with idiosyncratic institutional features, but it is not able to give a satisfactory explanation of some national cases, such as Italy or Spain for three main reasons. First of all, mixed models – as the Hall and Soskice's original contribution – refer to the national level and therefore are not well equipped to take account of deep internal diversities in economic organization. Second, they strongly rely on the idea of institutional complementarities that may lead to overlook tensions and contradictions between different institutions at the national level, but also between center and periphery. These tensions and lack of integration can hinder the overall economic performance, but can also open up chances for adjustment and change. In the case of Italy, for instance, an analytical frame strongly based on the national level and on the assumption of institutional complementarities would face difficulties in explaining the remarkable and long-standing performance of some Italian industrial districts and local productive systems, and their contribution to economic growth. Third, the role of the state and politics has usually been overlooked by the VoC approach (see Hancké *et al.* 2007), with a consequent lack of research on the relationships between types of political regimes and types of capitalism. From this point of view, Italy represents an interesting case: since the beginning of the 1990s many reforms modified the Italian electoral system and at the same time, other reforms changed some of the pillars of Italian capitalism. Thus, looking at the Italian case can help to shed light on the complex link between politics and mode of capitalism.

We will start by focusing on the main features of Italian variety of capitalism before the 1990s. Then we will point to changes that modified both the electoral and political system and influenced a series of economic and social reforms affecting the structure and performance of the Italian economy. Our main hypotheses are the following.

First, changes in the electoral rules and in the party system were not able to trigger a coherent set of economic and social reforms. The Italian polity came closer to a bipolar and competitive system with the formation of two coalitions (center-left and center-right) and their alternation in power. However, both coalitions were very fragmented. A high degree of internal political contentiousness affected their action. This may explain why the major economic and social reforms were carried out by "technical" governments[1] at the beginning of the 1990s in a period of strong economic and political crisis (the old party system was in disarray). In the ensuing period, the new political coalitions were formed. But governments were not able to pursue ambitious policies: only incremental changes took place (with two major exceptions: labor market regulations and the decision to join the euro). This led to what can be defined as "incomplete reformism," which was not able to promote institutional complementarities.

Second, these reforms introduced significant changes in the Italian model of political economy but they were not able to shift the Italian VoC toward either a liberal or a coordinated model. The Italian case continues to show a hybrid set of national institutions, with some similarities with the CME model (such as the high level of labor market rigidities or the weak role of the stock market), and other features that are closer to the LME model (such as the pluralist system of interests representation with many fragmented collective organizations). In addition, regional differences both in institutional and productive organization continue to play a strong role.

Third, the "incomplete reformism" had both positive and negative outcomes: for example governments promoted the reduction of inflation and unemployment and fostered financial stability; but at the same time, the "incomplete reformism" exacerbated some of the weaknesses of the Italian systems, such as the inefficiency of the public administration or the high costs for services. However we will also show that despite these constraints, private firms and their networks started a process of restructuring that led to a partial but encouraging economic recovery.

Fourth, by relying on the Italian case we will underline strengths and weaknesses of the VoC approach in explaining economic performance. In particular, we will show how the Italian case has been characterized by a "divergent" performance between the macro and the micro level: on the one hand, during the 1980s and the 1990s Italy performed badly in term of labor market, GDP, financial stability and inflation; this can be related to the absence of institutional complementarity that endangered the functioning of macro political economy. But on the other hand, some Italian regions performed particularly well during the 1980s and interesting signs of regional and local development can be found also in the last years, despite the widespread economic crisis. Therefore, the Italian case suggests that relying only on national institutions, and on their contribution to the operation and performance of firms, can be too restrictive. Failures of the national governance can be offset – to some extent – by local and regional adjustments, especially in some cases with strong regional diversities. This, in turn, may reduce the rigidity of the VoC model and may allow to recognize more sources of change and adjustment (see for example Crouch *et al.* 2001, 2004).

National politics and the Italian variety of capitalism

The Italian variety of capitalism before of the 1990s

The VoC literature classifies countries and their modes of capitalism adopting a methodological frame based on the comparative analysis of some important institutional arena: the financial system and corporate governance, education and training, labor market regulation, industrial relations and welfare, social networks. Adopting this approach it is also possible to identify the main features of the Italian variety of capitalism and to understand if it resembles to one of the two ideal types proposed by Hall and Soskice. We decided carry out this analysis focusing on two periods, before of and after the 1990s: the decision to identify this cleavage is related to the series of important reforms that started during this period, reforms that modified the peculiar relationship between politics and the economy in the Italian case.

The Italian institutional settings and the national political economy before the 1990s were characterized by a series of peculiar features (Regini 1995; Salvati 2000; Trigilia 1997) (Table 5.1). First of all, as for the financial system and corporate governance, the large part of manufacturing firms were of very small scale and mainly family-owned. The role of the stock exchange was particularly limited and private firms financed their activity and investments mainly with family resources or via local banks. These small- and medium-scale firms mainly specialized in so-called "Made in Italy" products (leather, textile and clothing, jewellery) and in machine tools and were territorially concentrated in a specific kind of local system, the industrial districts of central and north-eastern regions (Becattini 1990, 2001; Bagnasco 1977, 1988; Trigilia 1986). This system of small scale firms went hand in hand with a completely different type of organizational architecture, specialized in "heavy" industries such as chemical production, energy, steel industry, etc. This second mode of organization was based on very large scale state-owned firms that operated in a protected market; they were completely dependent on state funds and aids and this weakened their efficiency and competitiveness in the long run: since the second half of the 1980s with the rise of international competition many of these firms had to face radical processes of restructuring.

As for the education and training system, training was mainly conceived as a collective and public good and for this reason the state was one of the main providers. Central state and decentralized public authorities organized and offered both general and technical skills with schools and universities targeted at the entire population. This public-led educational system coexisted with less formal and private system of training based on the process of learning by doing that characterized the small-scale firms above mentioned.

As for the labor market, the Italian case was often identified as a case of persistent rigidity because of the strict regulation of the labor market based on a strong and durable protection for large firms' dependent employment, with high level of employment protection legislation. But at the same time, this mode of regulation coexisted with a susbstantial and "informal" flexibility: practices of work organization especially in SMEs were based on functional flexibility, flexible distribution of pay, and external forms of flexibility were massively implemented. At the same time, another form of flexibility was given by the so-called shadow economy, namely activities that are in some form illegal, monetary and private, but which could be legal if they were carried out in accordance with prevailing regulations, such as in the case of firms that only employ workers illegally, or in cases where there are both regular and irregular workers; in others again all workers have a regular contract, but they are required to work overtime or receive a salary lower than the amount agreed. The shadow economy offered an important source of flexibility especially in industrial districts and in some sectors such as construction and in some local systems of the southern part of the country.

Table 5.1 The Italian varieties of capitalism

	1980–1990	*1990–2009*
Financial system and corporate governance	*State-owned large firms* *Family-owned SMEs* *Limited role of stock exchange*	*Privatization with limited liberalization* *Limited role of public company* *Still limited role of stock exchange* *Important role of family and pyramidal control*
Education and training	*Training as collective good and role of public institutions and technical schools* *Informal learning by doing* *Limited efficiency of education and training*	*Training continues to be a collective good* *Limited efficiency of education and training*
Labor market regulation	*Well protected standard employment* *Rigidity in the LM but…* *Informal functional flexibility in SMEs* *Large role of hidden economy*	*Flexibilization without security* *Segmentation of the labor market between protected and non-protected group*
Industrial relations and welfare	*Unstable neo-corporatism* *Fragmented system of interest representation* *occupational model with a large role of family in care activities* *High protection for stable workers employed in large firms and in the public sector but not for SMEs and shadow economy*	*Rise and decline of trilateral negotiation* *Important role of collective bargaining* *Re-organization of welfare system but aimed at promoting its financial sustainability* *Absence of new guarantees for flexible workers*
Social networks	*Importance of relational capacities, social capital and local associations* *Socially embedded SMEs systems (industrial districts)* *Territorial dimension of economic competitiveness*	*High importance of relational capacities and social capital* *Socially embedded SMEs systems (industrial districts)* *Territorial dimension of economic competitiveness*

Specific features characterized also the industrial relations arena. The system of interest representation was characterized by a very high fragmentation, both on unions and employers' associations; at the end of the 1990s the so-called autonomous unions – small and antagonistic trade unions – emerged mainly in the public sector adding further fragmentation to the complex the Italian IR system. Almost paradoxically, the very high fragmentation among interests' representation did not hinder some corporatist experiments that were experienced in the first part of the 1980s, but it should be noted that they failed without producing a final agreement or pact, such as the so-called *Lodo Scotti* in 1984. Collective bargaining was strong and able to reinforce the security of workers employed in large firms, especially in the industrial and labor-intensive sectors, while, as we have already said, workers in SMEs were less protected; obviously, a low level of protection also characterized workers in the shadow economy. A more universalistic protection prevailed in the welfare system, even if informal mechanisms of care such as the family played a very important role especially in managing care services.

Last but not least, relational capacities were among the main pillars of competitiveness in all the sectors of the "Made in Italy" production: interpersonal trust and social capital reduced transaction costs and promoted the production of local collective competition goods able to foster the performance of SMEs. Looking at this phenomenon some authors adopted the definition of "social construction of the market," emphasizing the social embeddedness of private manufacturing firms (Bagnasco 1988). This embeddness emerged in specific kinds of local systems, such as in the industrial districts of the so-called Third Italy (Bagnasco 1977; Trigilia 1986). The importance of the local level of regulation emphasized territorial differences in the Italian case, that was not simply characterized by a peculiar set of *national institutions*: the political economy was more and more influenced by *local formal and informal institutions*. From this point of view, the Italian model can be defined as *"regionalized capitalism,"* and was characterized by two main features. First, most innovative and competitive firms, open to international competition, relied on non-market coordination mechanisms: their competitiveness was based on cooperative structures based on informal social ties (individual social capital) involving both entrepreneurs and entrepreneurs and their employees; and also on more formal relationships (collective social capital) between collective organizations, local and regional governments aimed at producing and allocating local collective competition goods. Thus, it is possible to define this model as a *networked economy based on relational capacities*. A second important feature of the Italian model as regionalized capitalism is related to the strong and persistent territorial differences in terms of organizational architecture of firms (large firms, industrial districts and clusters of small firms) and regulatory mechanisms of local economies. Therefore, before of the beginning of the 1990s the Italian case was characterized by remarkable intra-national differences (Burroni and Trigilia 2001; Trigilia and Burroni 2009).

Thus, the Italian mode of capitalism before the 1990s was a hybrid model, with some features that are more typical of liberal market economies and others that characterized coordinated market economies. For this reason, according to the VoC literature, the Italian case should have performed worse than "pure" cases belonging to LME or CME groups. This was true if we consider data on employment and GDP aggregated at national level. But if we consider data at subnational level we note an interesting point. Northern and central regions performed well during this decade: at the beginning of the 1990s the national unemployment rate was around 10 percent while unemployment in northern regions was around 4.4 percent; a similar difference can be found in per-capita GDP. We will see that this trend also characterizes the Italian case during recent years.

This shows that the hybridity of the Italian model was not simply an institutional constraint. On the contrary it went hand in hand with a sort of twofold performance: focusing on data aggregated at national level on GDP, inflation and employment we note a situation of crisis and difficulty both for production and for the labor market.[2] But at the same time, if we take into account data at territorial level we note that some local systems experienced economic growth during these years. Thus, during the 1980s and at the beginning of the 1990s Italy was characterized by high unemployment rate, low employment rate, high inflation, low level of GDP per-capita, massive process of restructuring of large firms, but all this coexisted with the good performance of some territories, especially those characterized by "flexible specialization" and industrial districts.

This led to the paradox of a national economy characterized by a remarkable level of productive dynamism, together with inflation and a public deficit and an increasing public debt and these two phenomena were strongly interlinked. The growth of SMEs in the Third Italy was triggered by some policies at a central level. In particular, the policy of devaluation pursued by the Bank of Italy had relevant positive effects, triggering export for the kind of goods produced by industrial districts and a sort of fiscal protection favored small firms. In other words, the private dynamism at the micro level benefits from the "positive and indirect effects" of inefficiency at the macro level. At the same time, small-firm dynamism, by easing the impact of the economic crisis, reduced the pressure for a change in macroeconomic management (Trigilia 1997).

Summing up, the Italian variety of capitalism before of the 1990s was a hybrid system that combined market and non-market forms of coordination with an important role played by the state, limited social protection and high employment protection for some groups of workers, an important role played by informal mechanism of regulation (family and communitarian networks), and with relevant territorial differences due to a high concentration of manufacturing activities in specific local systems. The absence of complementarity and coherence between national policies weakened the performance of the whole system and contributed to the bad macroeconomic performance. During these years the political system was not able to reduce the inefficiency at the macro level because there was a strong search for electoral consensus that prevented the reduction of some inefficiencies of the system at the macro level: the coalition between Democrazia Cristiana and Partito Socialista was inadequate to promote radical reforms because on the one hand it was weakened by the opposition of a strong and growing Communist Party and on the other hand the coalition's consensus was related to social groups hostile to a massive process of reforms (Trigilia 1997).

At the same time, the regional dimension of the Italian capitalism favored effective processes of readjustment and the reinforcing of a mode of development based on local systems of small and medium firms concentrated in the so-called "Third Italy." As a consequence, the assumption that "pure cases perform better" is not fully confirmed by the analysis of the Italian case, and at the same time this case study shows that it is important to combine the national dimension of analysis – typical of the VoC approach – with the regional and local one: focusing the analysis only on the macro level it is not possible to explain the dynamism at the micro level.

Continuity and change in the Italian political economy after the "end of the First Republic"

At the beginning of the 1990s a series of profound transformations modified the political system that was behind this mode of capitalism. First of all, the fall of the Berlin Wall had a relevant impact on left parties, promoting a process of restructuring that led to the end of the Italian Communist Party (Partito Comunista Italiano – PCI) in 1991, with the division between the more radical part of the party (Partito della Rifondazione Comunista – RC) and the more social-democratic part (Partito Democratico di Sinistra – PDS). In 1992 the legitimacy of the political system was strongly lowered by a series of scandals of corruption (*Tangentopoli* – Bribeville) that involved many of the most important parties and political leaders. Partly related to this scandal the Christian Democracts (Democrazia Cristiana – DC) and the Socialist Party (Partito Socialista Italiano – PSI) were radically restructured and lost a lot of political consensus: the Christian Democrats split in three, the Partito Popolare Italiano (PPI), the Movimento Cristiano Sociali and the Centro Cristiani Democratici (CCD). In the emerging quasi-bipolar systems, segments of former Christian Democrats (CCD) sustained the center-right coalition while others supported the center-left (PPI). During the same period there was the rise of new autonomist parties, especially in the north-eastern part of the country, such as the Lega Nord. These parties were strongly embedded at local level and gained a lot of consensus especially in area previously dominated by the Christian Democrats (Diamanti, Riccamboni); as we will see, the rise of this kind of party was also influenced by the economic crisis that affected north-eastern regions at the beginning of the 1990s.

The reorganization of the political system was also promoted by the 1993 electoral referendum that contributed to a shift from a proportional system to a partially compensatory mixed-member system in which 75 percent of seats were filled by simple plurality in single-member districts and 25 percent from lists. But the new system, largely a product of accident combined with narrow partisan interests, satisfied no one (D'Alimonte 2005). The system was not a pure bipolar one: both center-right and center-left coalitions were strongly influenced by some of their parts, such as the Lega Nord for the center-right and the radical left for the center-left. As we will see, this influence directly hindered the set up of efficient reforms able to overcome the traditional weaknesses of the Italian mode of capitalism.

This complex ensemble of changes led to what was defined as the Second Republic, characterized by a progressive trend toward a bipolar system with a high degree of competition, with a very high level of internal heterogeneity among the two coalitions and with a high instability: in the period 1994–2008 there were eight different governments.[3] At the same time, since 1992 to 1995 there were three *technical governments* run by Giuliano Amato in 1992, Carlo Azeglio Ciampi in 1993 and Lamberto Dini in 1995.

The political crisis went hand in hand with a very serious economic crisis, that affected the country both at macro and micro level. At macro level, employment and GDP levels continued to be lower than other European countries while the public deficit was among the highest in Europe; there was also a serious financial crisis with a massive devaluation of the Lira and with the exit from the European Monetary System (EMS) (1992). As for the micro level, we underlined that a crucial condition for keeping the export market shares was devaluation and this triggered the dynamism of SME local systems during the 1980s. With the exit from the EMS devaluation was no longer possible and this contributed to endanger the performance of local systems of the Third Italy; at the same time, the growing international competition in consumption goods led to processes of restructuring among SME firms. Thus, conversely to what happened during the 1980s when there was a divergence between the micro and the macro level – with the above-mentioned good performance of industrial districts and the crisis of the national political economy – in the first part of the 1990s there was a convergence between macro and micro levels toward a serious economic crisis.

This complex and changing situation led to important transformation in the Italian model of political economy. The economic crisis and the consequent emergence of the system at the macro and micro level and the above-mentioned technical governments were two variables that favored the set up of important reforms aimed at facing this situation of crisis. There were four main pillars of these reforms: the control of inflation and wage moderation, the reorganization of the industrial relations system, the reform of the pensions system and the privatization of large public-owned firms.

As for the first pillar, *the control of inflation*, in 1992 a national trilateral pact was signed to definitively put an end to the so-called *"scala mobile,"* an automatic mechanism of indexation of wages that triggered inflation and after a period of intense trilateral negotiation led to the 1993 agreement that set up a new system of income policy. This agreement reformed the method of wage increases, introducing a new system based on the so-called *inflazione programmata* (planned inflation) that led to a very long period of wage moderation. The agreement established that in industry-wide agreement wage increases have to be related to the planned inflation rate, which is established through the process of income policy's social negotiation, and must guarantee the purchasing power of workers; the inflation rate is planned within trilateral negotiations in two sessions: the first one – in May–June – in which the government and social partners discuss the measures of political economy to be provided by the Economic and Financial Plan (*Documento di programmazione economica e finanziaria*) and the second one – in September – in which social partners will approve the final draft of the Plan. In this new system the negative spiral between inflation and wage rise was solved, with a consequent reduction of inflation and with a long-standing wage moderation.

Second, the 1993 agreement also established new important rules for the *industrial relations system*, especially for the representation of economic interest (such as the introduction of the RSU – Rappresentanza Sindacali Unitarie – elected works councils at plant level which directly participate in company level collective bargaining). Moreover, the agreement regulated the relationship between the central (general and industry-wide) levels of collective bargaining and the decentralized ones (territorial and plant level), recognizing the national industry-wide level of bargaining (*Contratto Collettivo Nazionale di Lavoro – CCNL*) as the most important one, defining also its duration and the procedures for wage setting. Moreover, the agreement entrusts to industry-wide agreements the power of regulating decentralized collective bargaining. Finally, it is also important to stress that the 1993 agreement provides also a system of incentives and sanctions for social partners responsible for the delay of renewal of agreements. Such a violation entails economic consequences, in terms of a particular bonus (*indennità di vacanza contrattuale*).

Third, as for the *welfare reform*, the center-right government of Berlusconi made a first attempt at reform in 1994, with the attempt to bypass social partners' consultation on this issue, imposing some new measures without the consensus of trade unions. This strategy triggered an intense social conflict and the government had to remove these measures from the Financial Plan. This conflict also contributed to the rise of a major political crisis. On the contrary, in 1995 Dini's technical government opened a deep negotiation with social partners (especially with trade unions) that made it possible to launch a negotiated law on welfare, providing for a gradual saving of social expenditure for pensions (Regini 1995). It is worth noting that the logic behind Dini's actions and the following reforms was that of promoting the financial sustainability of the system and not to introduce new forms of social security for flexible workers.

Fourth, during this period a massive process of *privatization of state-owned firms* started, with the privatization of many large firms in the energy, transport and communication sectors (such as Ferrovie dello Stato, IRI, ENI, INA, ENEL).

As we have already said, many of these reforms were promoted by governments that had a technical and not political legitimization: for this reason, these governments were probably less influenced by political parties and less exposed to political pressures that could have hindered radical reforms. At the same time, the relevant economic and financial crisis reinforced in the center-left and center-right electorate the idea that these reforms were absolutely indispensable for the recovery of the country.

After this period of massive reformism, however, a period in which actors experienced relevant difficulties in promoting coherent and effective reforms followed, with many incremental changes that followed the path traced by technical governments. The only other two "radical" reforms were on the labor market and on the joining of the euro – the new European currency. As for the labor market, in 1996 with the first Prodi government the so-called Legge Treu/Law n. 196/97 promoted a massive flexibilization of the labor market setting up new instruments and forms of labor market regulation, introducing in particular the temporary work, previously forbidden in Italy. Moreover, the Legge Treu restructured vocational training (*Contratti di formazione e lavoro*), as well as defined-term contracts, part-time work, apprenticeships and social works, making them more flexible. As for the joining of the euro, this was a bold political choice with far-reaching consequences. Joining the euro brought significant advantages to the Italian economy. The cost of public debt was lowered by a remarkable reduction of interest rates and the two-digit inflation rate declined to 3 percent. In addition, the risks of attacks against the Italian currency were avoided. However, it was no longer possible to devalue.

What was the impact of this strand of reforms on the Italian variety of capitalism? Did they push the Italian system toward LMEs or CMEs?

As we can see in Table 5.1, effectively the above-mentioned reforms introduced some changes. As for the corporate governance, the process of privatization changed the propriety structure of many former state-owned large firms, but the absence of a process of liberalization did not entail a real market competition in the production and supply of this kind of services, and the role of both public company and of the stock exchange remains limited. Moreover, looking at the manufacturing sector it is possible to note that the role of the family in terms of ownership and financial support is still crucial.

Training continues to be considered as a collective good and public institutions are the most important providers of this strategic good. Many of these institutions organize specific training activities funded by European programs. Since the mid-1990s the higher education system experienced a long series of reforms, but their effectiveness is strongly controversial and the public character of the higher education system continues to be predominant. At the same time, learning by doing in small-scale firms is still important, especially in manufacturing activities.

The labor market faced relevant changes: the already mentioned massive process of flexibilization introduced new forms of "atypical" contracts – especially time determined contracts. These new forms were aimed at disadvantaged groups like young people and women. At the same time, this rise in flexibility was not balanced by new forms of security for flexible workers: the large part of welfare reforms were aimed at promoting the financial sustainability of the system but not to introduce new forms of social protection. For this reason, the segmentation between protected and non-protected groups increased during recent years.

In the industrial relations arena, the role of trilateral negotiations rose and declined: "*concertazione*" practices successfully promoted important reforms like the social pacts of 1992 and 1993 on the general framework of industrial relations and on the definitive end of the "Scala Mobile" but some other trilateral reforms had a very limited impact (such as the 1998 Christmas Pact). After 1998, the importance of social trilateral negotiation varied, with a center-right government that mainly referred to social dialogue to emphasize the decline of importance of trilateral negotiations and with a center-left government that re-established the *concertazione* as the ideal policy tool for reforms, such as the 2007 agreement on the labor market, welfare and competitiveness. A major instability can be found also in the relationships between unions, that in some case were characterized by inter-union cooperation but in others by strong conflicts, especially between CGIL on the one hand and CISL, UGL and UIL on the other.

Finally, relational capacities and social capital continue to play a very important role, both in small-scale firms local systems (like industrial districts) and in areas characterized by medium- and large-scale firms. Even if local inter-firm relationships have been endangered by massive processes of delocalization and many of the most dynamic Italian SMEs have been defined as "small multinationals" for their international networks, the role of local and regional institutions in the provision of competition goods continues to be particularly important in promoting firms' competitiveness. For this reason, not only manufacturing activities but also high-tech industry continue to cluster in some specific Italian regions.

Summing up, even if the above-mentioned reforms entailed some changes the Italian mode of capitalism is still a hybrid one. On the one hand some features are similar to LMEs (fragmentation in interest representation, radical flexibilization of labor market, etc.), on the other hand many features are similar to CMEs (trilateral negotiations on reforms, the idea of training as public good), some are peculiar (role of family, of local community and governments, etc.). Among these peculiarities, the role of territorial differences in terms of institutional settings and productive organization are particularly important. Thus, the incremental change did not entail a coherent shift of the Italian political economy toward one of the two ideal types of capitalism, but reinforced its "hybridness."

New opportunities and constraints for the Italian mode of capitalism

Looking at the outcomes of the above-mentioned reforms it is possible to note a twofold impact. On the one hand, they were able to improve the efficiency of the Italian institutional setting: collective bargaining improved, inflation diminished radically, the sustainability of welfare system increased, there was a relevant reduction of unemployment. On the other hand, the incomplete character of these reforms entailed the emergence of important constraints. For instance, the process of privatization of many state-owned companies without a parallel process of liberalization promoted the rise of different forms of oligopoly. Another example is given by the joining of the euro, a very important reform that paradoxically risked becoming a constraint and not an opportunity if not accompanied by a series of complementary reforms. However, notwithstanding these constraints, at the end of the decade there was a re-emergence of dynamism in some private sectors; once again the divergence of performance between macro and micro levels regained importance.

This "incomplete reformism" was due to the heterogeneous character of political coalitions that hindered the set up of a wide and coherent framework of reforms and for this reason the Italian productive system faced some problems, two of them particularly important, namely the high costs and inefficiencies of the service sector not open to international competition and the increased competition brought about by globalization in the traditional productions of "Made in Italy."

As far as the service sector is concerned, the costs of energy, legal and professional services, insurance and financial services are higher in Italy in comparison to other European countries (in some cases, as for energy, by around 30 percent). The high costs in services went hand on hand with the high costs produced by the massive bureaucratization of public administration: Italy has the highest cost to start a new business among all the European countries except Poland. Finally, according to the World Bank the level of efficiency of public administration is very low. This low level of efficiency is also due to the fact that both coalitions (center-left and center-right) are divided and the radical wings strongly influence their policies: weak governments are less able to undertake difficult reforms such as the reorganization of public administration and of public services.

This cost of inefficiency of the service sector and of public administration exacerbated the growing impact of globalization in the Italian model with the increase of international competition in the sectors of the "Made in Italy." As a result the Italian economy experienced serious difficulties in the 2000s: slow growth, low increase in productivity and a decline in exports.

These shortcomings massively endanger the competitiveness of the Italian mode of capitalism. However, it is interesting to note that despite these disadvantages private firms and their networks started a process of restructuring that led to a partial, but encouraging, economic recovery. This recovery is based on three main pillars: the territorial concentration of manufacturing activities rose in industrial districts and local production systems; there has been a remarkable growth of medium-sized firms in many local production systems; the emergence of local systems specialized in high-tech industry and in high added value activities.

The rise of territorial concentration emerges looking at trends in employment in manufacturing, where employment activities declined by 7 percent at the national level during the period 1991–2001. At the same time, however, manufacturing employment in industrial districts and local productions systems declined only by 0.4 percent, and total employment in these areas rose by 10 percent. This trend has continued in more recent years, and is associated with the widespread provision of well-developed collective goods and resources (ISTAT 2007; see also Viesti 2000). The result of these changes is the growing territorial concentration of manufacturing activities that tend to cluster in areas with high levels of specialization in such activities. Together with the rise of manufacturing employment, these areas experienced a notable increase in business services:

during the period 1991–2001 more than half of the total employment growth in local production systems was due to employment in services to private firms, which grew by 59 percent.

This leads to a second change to which we wish to draw attention. The majority of the local systems that registered a growth in manufacturing employment consists of those with a stronger presence of medium-sized firms (+45 percent). During the period 1996–2003 medium firms experienced a growth in revenues (+42.8 percent versus +26.4 percent for large firms), in exports (+51.7 per cent, +31 percent for large firms), in added value (+33.3 percent, +11.9 percent for large firms) and in employment (+18 percent, –10.2 percent for large firms) (Unioncamere and Mediobanca 2006). The emergence of medium-sized firms with a role of leadership is a particularly important change for the Italian model of regionalized capitalism (Berta 2004; Rullani 2004; Rullani and Romano 2004). These firms are specialized in mechanical engineering and machine tools but also have more traditional specializations in the so-called "Made in Italy" goods, such as textiles, clothing, footwear, furniture etc. The management structure is still based on family control, but professional managers are increasingly used. The network of suppliers, especially those with a strong influence on the quality of goods and services for the final market, is often located in the same local system as the client firm. At the same time, these medium-sized firms intensify the relationships with foreign sub-suppliers, offshoring some stages of the productive process or the making of specific components, while more strategic stages, such as design, development of new products, marketing, manufacturing of components that are crucial for quality, continue to cluster near to lead firms. As a consequence, there is a decline in the volume of production in Italian industrial districts and local production systems, while the employment in services to firms grows. The intensity of this process of restructuring varies from one region to another, but it tends to increase its influence together with the growing attempts of firms to follow the "high road" for development based on quality. The sectors in which SMEs are mostly specialized are light industry (textiles and clothing, footwear, furniture decorating products, jewelery) but also machine tools and mechanical engineering. During the last two decades, the firms producing the so-called "Made in Italy" goods, together with the machinery sector, exported about 40 percent of the total national value and they employed more than 40 percent of total manufacturing employment.

Third, another interesting trend is the rise in competitiveness in some high-tech activities (software and biotech). These activities registered a relevant growth since the mid-1990s, especially in urban and metropolitan areas of the center and north of the country. It is a sector with a high prevalence of small firms (at the beginning of 2000 48 percent of all firms in this sector employed less than ten employees, and only 17 percent of the number of jobs provided in this sector are in firms with more than 250 employees) but there is also a quite large group of very dynamic medium- and large-scale firms. Like in manufacturing, the territorial dimension of high-tech activities is very important in Italy, contrary to what one might expect for a sector based on the use and production of new communications technologies: looking at software production, for example, it is possible to note that more than 70 percent of all workers engaged in software production are placed in only 2 percent of all local software systems in Italy. The local institutional setting is importance in explaining the reasons for clustering in this sector: unlike manufacturing enterprises, high-tech firms tend to be concentrated in medium to large metropolitan areas together with other services for firms. These areas also tend to be characterized by the presence of universities and vocational institutions specializing in the informatics sector, by elevated numbers of young people and college graduates, and finally, by a lower concentration of manufacturing activities. Thus, universities and training centers have supported – sometimes unintentionally – the development and competitiveness of local firms. Most important are their contributions in terms of the human resources development and expertise necessary for the development of high-tech activity, and the dissemination of these specialists. At the same time, the universities have also favored the realization of more intangible local collective competition goods, such as the development of informal networks.

These three trends show that despite the above-mentioned institutional constraints, the Italian regionalized capitalism is still characterized by individual and collective resources at the local level able to trigger economic competiveness in some sectors and for some types of firms. In other words, national level constraints hindered the performance of some institutional arena at national level but did not prevent processes of adjustment at regional and local level. Once again the divergence of performance between macro and micro level is confirmed to be one of the main features of the Italian mode of capitalism.

Summing up, looking at recent transformations in the Italian mode of capitalism a peculiar situation emerges. On the one hand, the series of important reforms started during the 1990s at national level produced relevant changes in the institutional setting of Italian capitalism, but they were not able to shift it toward a more "pure model": thus, the "hybridness" of the Italian system persists. At the same time, these reforms were able to create some collective goods – such as the control of inflation – but they were not able to solve other problems related, for example, to the high costs of services or to the inefficiency of the public administration. But on the other hand, even if these constraints represented a serious obstacle for the competitiveness of the Italian system, some forms of dynamism of private firms emerged especially for some kind of productive organization (medium firms), territories (industrial districts) or specialization (high-tech local systems).

Thus, looking at complementarities at the macro level is important and can contribute to explain some of the features of the Italian mode of capitalism but this strategy of research is not able to explain processes of dynamism at the micro level. We showed how this dynamism is based not only on endogenous resources but also on the capability of the micro level of "exploiting" macro inefficiency. At the same time, changing the national electoral system does not automatically produce changes in the national variety of capitalism: cleavages and political practices influenced – and hindered – change in the Italian mode that is still a hybrid model.

Conclusions

During the last 15 years many changes modified the electoral rules and the party system; as a result of these changes, the Italian polity came closer to a bipolar system with the rise of two coalitions but both characterized by a very high degree of fragmentation and internal conflicts. This fragmentation affected the action of governments, hindering their capability of setting up effective reforms. Major economic and social reforms were carried out by "technical" governments – less affected by fragmentation, less exposed to political pressures and less influenced from political parties – at the beginning of the 1990s in a period of strong economic and political crisis. In the ensuing period new political coalitions were formed, but they continued to be characterized by an internal fragmentation and promoted mainly incremental changes (with two major exceptions: labor market regulations and the decision to join the euro). This led to what can be defined as "incomplete reformism," which was not able to promote effective institutional complementarities and exacerbated some of the weaknesses of the Italian systems, such as the inefficiency of the public administration or the high costs for services.

The reforms of electoral rules and changes in the party system introduced significant changes in the Italian polity but without modifying the model of political economy. The Italian case continues to show a hybrid set of national institutions, with some similarities with the CME model and other features that are closer to the LME model; in addition, regional differences both in institutional and productive organization continue to play a strong role. However, despite the hybrid character of Italian capitalism and its inefficiencies, private firms and their networks have been able to start a process of restructuring that led to a partial but encouraging recovery, mainly driven by medium-sized firms.

The above-mentioned trends and changes show the possibility of a divergence between the macro and the micro level: on the one hand, during the 1980s and the 1990s the absence of institutional complementarity endangered the functioning of the macro political economy. But on the other hand, some Italian regions performed particularly well during the 1980s and interesting signs of regional and local development can be found also in recent years. Therefore, the Italian case suggests that it is important to adopt a "broader" approach than the Varieties of Capitalism, focusing not only on national institutions and on their contribution to the performance of firms, but also on the combinations of national and regional processes and adjustments, especially in some cases with strong regional diversities. This kind of approach may reduce the rigidity of the VoC model and may allow to recognize more sources of change and adjustment.

Notes

1 By technical governments we mean governments run by prime ministers and ministers without party attachment and a clear-cut majority in parliament.
2 It is important to note that official statistics do not consider the shadow economy that played a very important role during these years.

3 1994 (Berlusconi – center-right), 1996 (Prodi), 1998 (D'Alema I), 1999 (D'Alema II), 2000 (Amato – center-left), 2001 (Berlusconi – center-right), 2006 (Prodi – center-left); 2008 (Berlusconi – center-right).

References

Amable, B. (2003) *The Diversity of Modern Capitalism*, Oxford: Oxford University Press.

Bagnasco, A. (1977) *Le tre Italie*, Bologna: Il Mulino.

Bagnasco, A. (1988) *La costruzione sociale del mercato*, Bologna: Il Mulino.

Becattini, G. (1990) "The Marshallian Industrial District As a Socio-Economic Notion," in F. Pyke, G. Becattini and W. Sengenberger (eds.) *Industrial Districts and Inter-Firm Co-operation in Italy*, Genève: ILO, 37–51.

Becattini, G. (2001) *The Caterpillar and the Butterfly: An Exemplary Case of Development in the Italy of the Industrial Districts*, Florence: Le Monnier.

Berta, G. (2004) *Metamorfosi. L'industria italiana tra declino trasformazione*, Milan: Egea.

Burroni, L. and Trigilia, C. (2001) "Italy: Economic Development Through Local Economies," in C. Crouch, P. Le Galès, C. Trigilia and H. Voelzkow (eds.) *Local Production Systems in Europe. Rise or Demise?*, Oxford: Oxford University Press, 46–78.

Crouch, C., Le Galès, P., Trigilia, C. and Voelzkow, H. (eds.) (2001) *Local Production Systems in Europe. Rise or Demise?*, Oxford: Oxford University Press.

Crouch, C., Le Galès, P., Trigilia, C. and Voelzkow, H. (2004) *Changing Governance of Local Economies. Responses of European Local Production Systems*, Oxford: Oxford University Press.

D'Alimonte R. (2005) "Italy. A Case of Fragmented Bipolarism," in M. Gallagher and P. Mitchell (eds.) *The Politics of Electoral Systems*, Oxford: Oxford University Press.

Hall, P. A. and Gingerich, D. (2004) "Varieties of Capitalism and Institutional Complementarities in the Macroeconomy: An Empirical Analysis." Discussion Paper 04/05, Max-Planck-Institut fürGesellschaftsforschung, Köln.

Hall, P. and Soskice, D. (2001) *Varieties of Capitalism: The Institutional Foundation of Comparative Advantage*, Oxford: Oxford University Press.

Hancké, B., Rhodes, M. and Thatcher, M. (eds.) (2007) *Beyond Varieties of Capitalism Conflict, Contradictions, and Complementarities in the European Economy*, Oxford: Oxford University Press.

ISTAT (2007) *Rapporto Annuale. La situazione del paese nel 2006*, Rome: Istat.

Molina, O. and Rhodes, M. (2007) "The Political Economy Of Adjustment In Mixed Market Economies: A Study Of Spain And Italy," in B. Hancké, M. Rhodes and M. Thatcher (eds.) *Beyond Varieties of Capitalism Conflict, Contradictions, and Complementarities in the European Economy*, Oxford: Oxford University Press, 223–253.

Regini, M. (1995) *Uncertain Boundaries: The Social and Political Construction of European Economies*, Cambridge: Cambridge University Press.

Rullani, E. (2004) *Economia della conoscenza. Creatività e valore nel capitalismo delle reti*, Rome: Carocci.

Rullani, E. and Romano, L. (2004) *Il Postfordismo. Idee per il capitalismo prossimo venturo*, Milan: Etas.

Salvati, M. (2000) *Le occasioni mancate. Economia e politica in Italia dagli anni '60 a oggi*, Rome/Bari: Laterza.

Trigilia, C. (1986) *Grandi partiti e piccole imprese*, Bologna: Il Mulino.

Trigilia, C. (1997) "The Political Economy Of A Regionalized Capitalism," *South European Society and Politics*, 2(3): 52–79.

Trigilia, C. and Burroni, L. (2009) "Italy: Rise, Decline and Restructuring of a Regionalized Capitalism," *Economy and Society*, 38(4): 630–653.

Unioncamere and Mediobanca (2006) *Le medie imprese industriali italiane*, Milan and Rome: Ufficio Studi Mediobanca and Ufficio Studi Unioncamere.

Viesti, G. (2000) *Come nascono i distretti industriali*, Rome/Bari: Laterza.

6 Between pork and productivity

Upending the Japanese model of capitalism

T. J. Pempel

From 1955 when the Liberal Democratic Party was formed until 1993 when it split, Japan was perhaps the most extreme example of the industrial world's limited number of "uncommon democracies" (Pempel 1990). Analogous to Sweden under the SAP, Italy under DC and Israel under Labor, but with even greater electoral dominance by the LDP, Japan had all the formal institutions of democracy, yet a single political party enjoyed decades of uninterrupted and relatively unchallenged control over government offices and public policy-making. For 38 years the LDP sustained roughly 2:1 majorities over the largest opposition party, allowing it to control virtually all cabinet posts and giving it virtually unprecedented influence in shaping national and most local policies. Conservative political power was effectively unshakable. Such long-term dominance was unusual to say the least in comparison to most other industrial democracies. But it was accompanied by, and inexorably aligned to, the fact that over the same period, Japan enjoyed exceptional levels of economic productivity. Japan's GNP grew at rates that were typically double that of the other OECD countries. This fusion of conservative political dominance and high levels of economic productivity put in place a powerful and unusual productivity regime which continued unabated until the economic downturn that started in 1990–1991.

The political economy that prevailed from roughly 1955 until 1990 was mutually reinforcing – political control by the LDP fostered socioeconomic policies beneficial to growth and productivity (as opposed to consumption and social programs). Sustained economic growth in turn bolstered the electoral fortunes of the LDP. It was a rather distinctive Japanese combination of politics and capitalism when seen in light of the systems in place within other industrial democracies. Most critically, the socioeconomic coalition undergirding the system provided a historically unusual alliance among big business, small business and agriculture, while simultaneously excluding organized labor. Most other industrial democracies saw some overt collaboration or tacit accommodation at the macro-level between big business and organized labor that led to a substantial liberalization of trade and, in the words of Ron Rogowski (1989: 99) "even while providing generous death benefits, presided over agriculture's demise." The major exceptions to this pattern were the Scandinavian democracies built on long-standing alliances between labor and agriculture and the few land-rich countries such as Australia, Canada, the United States or New Zealand where export-oriented farmers frequently aligned themselves with globally oriented business (e.g., Albert 1993; Dore 2000; Esping-Andersen 1999; Gourevitch 1986; Pempel and Tsunekawa 1979; Rogowski 1989; Yamamura and Streeck 2002). Japan's unusual political economy however proved a stunning and reinforcing success for roughly four decades.

The country's positive sum fusion of economic growth and conservative political control came to a crushing end with the sudden bursting of Japan's economic bubble in 1990 and the subsequent fracturing within the LDP in 1993. Since then the Japanese political economy has been incapable of returning to, or to reconstituting, the previous productivity regime with its reinforcing mixture of conservative political power and economic productivity. Particularly problematic has been the return to decent levels of economic productivity.

The LDP did manage to regain political power, first in coalition with its long-time *bête noire*, the Social Democratic Party of Japan (previously the Japan Socialist Party), and later in collaboration with New Komeito (Clean Government Party). It was the pre-eminent party in government from 1994 to 2009 although always with more fetters than during the period of its unchallenged dominance from 1955–1993. However, with its stunning Lower House electoral victory in September, 2005, coming as it did in a wave of economic reforms, the party gained a more dominant Lower House majority than it ever enjoyed during its earlier reign of power and seemed as if it could oversee a return to a highly productive economy. Yet, the LDP's crushing defeat in the 2007 Upper House elections again realigned the political balance by giving the opposition the power to block legislation and to hold hearings that could challenge government actions while the brief glimmer of economic productivity flickered and faded. Lower House elections in spring 2009 saw the LDP forced out of government completely.

Throughout the decade of the 1990s, Japan's GNP grew at an anemic 0 to 1 percent for most years. Since the turn of the century, there have been hints of a return to productivity, and indeed starting in February 2002 Japan began its longest postwar period of economic growth; it continued until late in 2007. That expansion beat past booms in length though hardly in underlying momentum: growth averaged about 2.4 percent per year, far below the 11.5 percent seen from November 1965 until July 1970 or the 5.4 percent from December 1986 until February 1991 (*Nikkei Weekly*, November 29, 2006: 1). And the current global economic depression has sucked Japan along with most other countries into its vortex leaving current economic projections ranging between dismal and despairing.

This mixture of substantial but constrained political control plus limited economic productivity poses the central puzzle of this chapter: how were political power and economic productivity linked during the so-called "1955 system?"

And how has that linkage changed in the period since that regime's collapse? Equally important going forward, does the current DPJ pre-eminence presage a return to the prior productivity regime along with some fresh burst of economic productivity, or have the two forces – politics and economics – that were once so intricately connected – begun to move independently of one another? And if so, what does that portend for the future of Japan's political economy and the model of capitalism that it long represented?

The Japanese pattern of capitalism under the "1955 system"

Elsewhere I have described Japan's one-party dominant regime as involving a mutually supportive mixture of institutions, a socioeconomic coalition and public policies (Pempel 1998). In essence, Japan's political economy represented a balanced equilibrium among institutions, policies and socioeconomic blocs that provided a "positive cycle of reinforcing dominance." As noted above, for most of the period from 1955 until roughly 1990, this reinforcing interplay kept the LDP in office for longer, and with fewer coalitional or oppositional constraints, than any other democracy in the industrialized world, even as it oversaw exceptionally high levels of national economic productivity.

Japan's political economy during this period was complicated and has been described in great detail in various studies (Pempel 1998). But for our purposes the following points are most salient. When it was formed in 1955, a period in Japan that Samuels (2003: 230) astutely characterizes as one of "fluid ideological borders and political desperation," the Liberal Democratic Party (LDP) was a cobbled together byproduct of highly diverse constituencies united less by an agreed upon policy agenda and more by two separate elements: first, a common ideological and economic opposition to the newly unified Japan Socialist Party (JSP) and second, a not-too-subtle predisposition to divvy up the spoils of office (Ôtake 1996). Formally and institutionally united, the newly merged conservatives remained internally cleft by numerous issues. On economics, however, several important tensions among the party's competing constituencies were resolved by particularly fortuitous compromises. Economic nationalism remained an overarching umbrella – improving the national economy's competitive standing was a sweepingly accepted goal – but there were sharp divisions over the specific mechanisms by which to do so. This intra-conservative tension can best be understood as that between "pork" and "productivity."

Consider the productivity segment first. Big business had been a major catalyst to the party's formation; also supporting the new party were many bureaucrats-turned-politicians such as Ikeda, Kishi, Fukuda and Sato. Generally speaking, these interests leaned heavily toward bureaucratically-led industrial policies, tightly balanced budgets, and rapid technological improvement of large-scale firms, domestic oligopolization, and the aggressive pursuit of export markets. The principal economic goal of this contingent was national productivity.

Equally importantly, however, many of the new party's most powerful politicians represented districts where small businesses and farming were the strongest economic voices in the constituent choir. As such, they were less hospitable to the policy predilections of the first group, instead pursuing local protection from both urban Japanese businesses and from overseas imports. Such constituent interests drove these politicians to embrace pork over productivity. Classic pork barrel politics, intra-national redistribution of governmental tax revenues, and the maintenance of a social safety net that would prevent market forces from undercutting the businesses and employment bases in their districts were the key concerns of such politicians (Estevez-Abe 2008). If pork and constituent services demanded less attention to tightly balanced budgets, so be it. Rapid economic growth and high levels of productivity were far less important to this latter group than was ensuring the economic viability of their district's farms and small businesses (Ôtake 1996: 110–146). Schlesinger (1997: 109) captures the resulting inclusiveness of the LDP by suggesting that the party was a vehicle for both "the bagmen and the statesmen." My focus on the underlying socioeconomics of this regime leads me to prefer treating the two groups as representing an alliance between pork and productivity.

Conspicuously excluded from any major role in governance was organized labor. For the most part labor divided its support among three parties – the Japan Socialist Party (JSP), the Democratic Socialist Party (DSP), and the Japan Communist Party (JCP). With the exception of a brief few months during the early years of the American Occupation, and a few months following the LDP's split in 1993, none of these parties were included in the government. In essence, Japanese labor never acquired the political muscle or the control of office to allow it to give serious shape to the national economic agenda in areas such as social welfare, or to provide a powerful counterweight to management's control over events at the firm level. Low unemployment, plant level welfare and low levels of family inequality softened many of the class consequences of this exclusion. But in broad-brush terms, Japan stood as a striking exception to the patterns of capitalism and political economy that prevailed in most of Western Europe or in the more conservative capitalisms of the United States or Britain.

The ingenuity of Japan's ruling conservatives lay in their capacity to accommodate the competing socioeconomic and political predilections of its disparate support groups through a mixture of high growth and local protection. As is well established, various government policies and considerable corporate creativity generated an exceptionally productive economy for Japan, with sky-high growth rates from the early 1950s until at least 1990. This chapter is concerned primarily with the political conditions underlying Japan's production regime rather than with the production regime itself. On the broader political economy the literature stressing Japan's role as a particularistic capitalist models is however considerable (e.g., Albert 1993; Berger and Dore 1996; Yamamura and Streeck 2003; Streeck and Yamamura 2005; Hall and Soskice 2001).

Yet central to the mix of politics and economics is the fact that Japanese capitalism was by no means modeled on the "free market" and "laissez-faire" principles undergirding US or British versions of capitalism. Although selling in global markets became a major goal for large segments of Japanese manufacturing, domestic markets were kept highly oligopolistic and largely closed to non-Japanese investments and imports. Well into the 2000s, Japan had a stunningly lower lever of incoming FDI/capita than any other OECD country. Equally vital to the LDP's longevity was control over the public purse and the regulatory powers that came with its hold over the reins of government.

Additionally and less fully addressed in the comparative capitalism literature, the highly visible productivity in Japan was fused with the country's much less publicized pork, building into the national political economy a strong "welfare" component, albeit one that was radically different from the welfare state model prevalent in much of Western Europe (Esping-Andersen 1990, 1999; Estevez-Abe 2008). The Japanese safety net provided public assistance less for disadvantaged individuals and more for economically distressed or slow growing geographical areas and economic sectors – or at least for those segments of industry and those geographical areas that had powerful political patrons. In theory, such assistance allowed these lagging areas and sectors the time cushion needed to make difficult transitions; in fact just as many individual social welfare recipients in other countries became increasingly dependent on public subsidization for their livelihood, so numerous Japanese regions, economic sectors and individual corporations were transformed into semi-permanent wards of the Japanese treasury with their LDP parliamentarians serving as welfare officers in exchange for large blocs of votes delivered in return.

The shotgun marriage of these two broadly different constituencies – pork and productivity – rested on continued conservative control over governmental offices, high economic growth and the consequently expanding budgetary resources available to the Japanese government. Numerous front and back channels displaying varying degrees of legality enriched party coffers, financed party leaders, and kept potential opponents at an impoverished distance from the ever-more-lucrative public money spigots. Mutual recognition by all party members of the incalculable political benefits that accrued from the perennial LDP hold over public office, combined with the actual financial and regulatory powers attendant on such control, facilitated the resolution of most intra-party disputes over economic policy. In essence, sufficient cash was always sloshing through the system to permit a variety of side payments to various potential losers in any economic policy battle making exit from the party an increasingly unpalatable alternative for virtually all intra-party disputants.

The LDP's diverse constituencies were represented by relatively comprehensive and sector specific corporatist networks that included exceptionally high proportions of their potential members (Pempel and Tsunekawa 1979). Numerous sector specific, and often regionally-comprehensive, associations existed for agriculture; different types of businesses; associations of professionals such as doctors, dentists, lawyers and the like. Most such associations were thus able to articulate relatively cohesive voices in national interest group politics; some even enjoyed direct representation in the Upper House of parliament; the most important were virtually guaranteed a seat at bureaucratic investigations of policy initiatives that affected them. Meanwhile, virtually all national bureaucratic agencies enjoyed tightly delimited spheres of regulatory control over, and regularized interactions with, these competing socioeconomic constituencies. Thus, the Ministry of Finance had virtually sole responsibility for the country's banks and financial institutions and consequently for monetary policy; the Ministries of Agriculture and Construction provided powerful links to the rural areas as well as being a guarantor of high subsidies and extensive market protection; MITI was the agency most actively promoting big firms and oligopoly, but with an Agency for Small Business also being under its purview holding an explicitly different representational mandate.

The LDP exercised political oversight of these networks largely through the functionally-specific committees on its Policy Affairs Research Council (PARC). PARC's committees were organized in parallel to the country's various cabinet offices and bureaucratic agencies. The vertical separateness of these policy-making nodes (e.g., Yamamoto 1972: 115) dominated policy-making while horizontal coordination and integration of separate spheres of economic activity was far less in evidence. Essentially, policy oversight and any tentative proposals for change involved a number of isolated and independently operating "iron triangles" each composed of a bureaucratic agency, one or more interest groups and self-selected groups of LDP politicians (*zoku giin*). Only after agreement was reached within these functionally-specific triangles would new proposals be submitted for approval to the cabinet and to parliament. The system thus provided only minimal opportunity for independent cabinet initiation of bills or for extensive horizontal coordination among agencies or affected interests. Vertically-organized networks represented, but in separate and isolated "silos," this multitude of mutually-insulated economic interests within the country. Over time, such corporatized networks became ever more deeply entrenched and difficult to dislodge. And with time many became rent-seeking impediments to sustained economic productivity.

Elsewhere (Pempel 1998, 1999) I have characterized the mix of economic policies pursued by Japan under the 1955 system as "embedded mercantilism." Japan's domestic markets were effectively closed to most foreign products and investments that might challenge the competitive positions of Japan's domestic industries. This went a long way toward protecting the LDP's pork constituency; buffered from both domestic and global competition, a host of minimally unproductive firms, sectors and geographical areas were preserved over time as if insulated in amber. The system also provided, in its earliest phases, a nurturing soil within which Japan's globally competitive firms could grow as they moved simultaneously to enhance the nation's productivity. With the home market largely closed to outside penetration, such firms gained dominance in the home market after which the most competitive moved on to export their best products globally. Along with their smaller domestic subcontractors and distributors, such firms were the major engines of Japan's high growth economy for the first 35 to 40 years following the end of World War II. Meanwhile, firms and sectors lacking such global competitiveness and whose primary markets remained domestic nevertheless survived by virtue of the entrenched system of politically enhanced protection and oligopolistic privileges at home. The resultant "national economy" was in fact an oil and water combination with some parts that were highly sophisticated, productive and closely integrated with the rest of the world (essentially the productivity component) while other parts remained predominantly dependent on protected national markets and almost totally buffered from global challenges and competition (Japan's pork component).

Long-term LDP rule depended on, and in turn was critical to the fusion of, these two dramatically different streams. It allowed a succession of LDP-run governments to pursue economic politics that avoided the need to make zero sum choices between its two potentially competing constituencies. High growth by large globally competitive Japanese firms generated sufficient revenues for the national treasury to permit the ruling politicians to ladle out huge dollops of pork and protection, both for smaller businesses and for the rural areas. The party and its members grew accustomed to – indeed it thrived on – economic policies driven by the erstwhile antagonistic logics of growth and redistribution.

Blisteringly hot GNP growth rates from the 1950s until 1990–1991 ensured that government revenues would spiral continually and automatically upward. Such revenues in turn allowed officials to undertake new policy initiatives with far less need to make offsetting cutbacks in older policies or to cut off the financial air supply for the country's inefficient sectors, firms or regions. Although doing so became progressively more costly over time, economic protection of Japan's least competitive sectors – including, for example, construction, distribution, financial services, air transport, road freight, food, agriculture, and small business generally – could be sustained without automatically undercutting the broader competitiveness of firms in areas such as automobiles, consumer electronics and machine tools.

Electorally, Japan's multi-member district system plus extensive gerrymandering that favored rural areas kept politicians in office whose *raison d'être* was keeping Japan's least productive sectors on permanent political life support. In numerous ways, Japan's political system privileged many of the country's least economically viable geographical areas and economic sectors. Control of government office, internal oligopoly, protectionism and high growth by the country's globally competitive firms and sectors, in turn, buffered such areas and sectors from the extremes of market competition.

The overall success of Japan's productivity segment however eventually caused the entire bargain to come unglued. Following two big waves of a strengthening yen (following the breakdown of Bretton Woods in 1971 and the Plaza Accord of 1985) many of Japan's most productive companies moved production facilities abroad. Previously national companies were transformed into multinational juggernauts with extensive production facilities and distribution outlets across the globe. No longer were they as dependent on, or as contributory to, the political and bureaucratic decisions made in Tokyo.

Such globalization of many of Japan's best firms was hardly the only major socioeconomic change that undercut the old regime. The regime's very economic success also meant that Japan's population became richer, older, more urban and more consumerist than earlier generations. As a result the most successful segments of the economy were also less automatically predisposed to support the LDP than their parents and grandparents.

Finally at least two important structural changes must be noted. First, the long-standing multi-member district system was replaced in 1994 by a mixture of single-seat constituencies (300 seats) and proportional representation (180 seats). There have been many consequences to this change but among the most salient has been the fact that the single member seats make it impossible for two or more LDP members to be returned from the same constituency as was relatively easy to do under the prior system (Reed 2002). Greater intra-party competitiveness has been spawned and a higher premium has been placed on the ability of individual candidates to generate broad electoral appeal than was true under the previous system. The second big change has been the "presidentialization" (Krauss 2007) of the Japanese prime minister's office as a consequence of a variety of administrative reforms that have strengthened the initiating power of both the prime minister and the cabinet at the expense of the LDP and the Diet.

The summary consequence is that the once successful blend of pork and productivity began to sow the seeds of the system's own demise. The splintering of the LDP and the declines in economic productivity were the most immediate manifestations that the old model could no longer generate the same outputs that it once did. The result was most apparent in the splintering of the LDP and its loss of power in 1993 and the decade of economic torpor that began in 1990–1991 (Pempel 2006).

Pork and productivity since the early 1990s

For much of the 1990s, LDP power and national productivity seemed to be inversely linked. Although the LDP regained and held power despite the absence of the dominant parliamentary majorities it once held, economic growth did not return to its prior sizzling pace. Instead, the LDP retained political power precisely as a consequence of economic policies that favored the party's least productive supporters through explicit dollops of pork. This helped the LDP electorally but at the expense of a return to national economic productivity where Japan languished well behind most industrialized economies and lagged behind its levels from 1976–1991 (see Figure 6.1). Not insignificantly, it benefited at the polls not just from its economic distributions to powerful voting constituencies but also from the fact that no opposition party was able to provide a viable challenge to the economically devastating policies it pursued (on the problems of the opposition during this period see Weiner 2002; Scheiner 2006).

This inverse linkage between political power and economic productivity was most evident for the first seven or eight years after the LDP returned to power in 1994. From the time the LDP returned to office, the ruling conservatives relied on a series of Keynesian fiscal stimulation packages of increasing magnitude to lard out publicly-funded pork to the party's valued (though

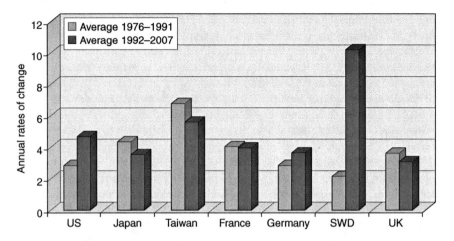

Figure 6.1 Output/hr in manufacturing – annual rates of change (1976–2007).

typically low-productivity) constituents. *The Economist* (April 23, 1998: 107) showed that between 1994 and 1998 public spending as a percentage of GDP shrunk in almost all the world's rich democracies. The biggest drop came in Sweden where it fell from 68 percent to 59 percent of GDP, an 11.9 percent drop. Britain saw a large 6.1 percent drop. In contrast, the only country where public spending increased during this period was Japan. Figure 6.2 shows the mounting public deficit in Japan.

Until at least 1998, Japan's ruling conservatives continued to pursue pork over productivity – despite the fact that national productivity plummeted

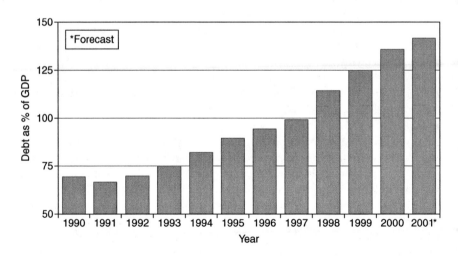

Figure 6.2 Japanese gross government debt as percentage of GDP.

(Muramatsu and Yanagizawa 2002). Retaining political power at the expense of national economic productivity was epitomized by the fact that Japanese public investments shrank in potentially high payoff technologies, new firms or innovative manufacturing procedures. With little public money going into projects likely to generate enhanced labor or capital productivity or likely to exert a strong multiplier effect throughout the economy, government debt levels soared to 140–160 percent of GDP, by far the highest levels in the industrial world. Public debt service in Japan gobbled up nearly one-quarter of the annual national budget in 2004. At that time, Japan was the only major country running a bigger budget deficit than it had four years earlier.

Such spending patterns exacerbated Japan's economic difficulties even as they provided undeniable political life support to the party in power. They were a key to the LDP's retention of power, in effect retaining contemporary constituent loyalty at the expense of future generations. Moreover, conservative control of the budget meant that the opposition, lacking the ability to control the national treasury, entered all electoral battles armed with a metaphoric slingshot against incumbents wielding howitzers.

LDP members were hardly in total agreement over the economic choices that were being made. For a good part of the latter years of the 1990s, ongoing skirmishes took place within the LDP between parliamentarians reluctant to make radical changes in Japan's long-standing economic structures and those convinced that substantial overhaul was essential to both Japan's and the LDP's long run success. That battle was eventually resolved (at least temporarily) in favor of the reform group with the ascension of Koizumi Junichiro to the prime ministership.

When Koizumi assumed his executive post the LDP's national popularity was tottering, and the opposition parties were gaining strength. But Koizumi boldly promised "reforms with no sanctuaries" and laid down an explicit challenge to those segments of the old regime that he identified as blocking political and economic change. With Koizumi controlling the prime ministership, the main axis of debate concerning economic and political reform moved squarely into the LDP where Koizumi and his allies enjoyed the advantage.

Koizumi's critics would argue that he was quicker to generate slogans and promises than to deliver comprehensive reforms. They suggest that the underlying structures of power remain largely unchallenged by his actions (Mulgan 2002).

Yet he presided over numerous changes in structures and policies, most put in place by his administration, others in place before he took office (Krauss 2007; Nonaka 2007; Vogel 2006). With his pithy aphorisms and personal charm, Koizumi proved a master at manipulating the media and of appealing to citizens more likely to benefit from productivity than pork. The combination created a reconfigured policy-making process that was far more "presidential" and that allowed the prime minister and his cabinet to take direct aim at the stranglehold of the old "iron triangles." Koizumi and his supporters pushed through changes in policy that weighed heavily against the rural and small business components of the party and that tackled the country's long draining non-performing loan problem head on. They also forced substantial changes over the internal structures of the LDP, reducing seriously the previous powers of many politicians whose careers rested more heavily on pork than on productivity.

In January 2001, Japan's 20-plus ministries were recombined into 14, with an important redistribution of functions and powers in many of the most important. Many of the previously tight links between agency and constituent interest group were broken and the long-standing system of vertical administration was challenged. Previous powers of bureaucratic officials to testify before the parliament were checked. The number of political appointees in each ministry, which had previously been limited to only the top two posts, was more than tripled for most agencies, providing additional layers of executive political control over earlier agency autonomy.

Perhaps most importantly, a new and well-staffed Cabinet Office, plus a bolstered Cabinet Secretariat, gained substantial strength to initiate and coordinate policies. At the end of 1999 the Prime Minister's Office had a staff of only 582 and the Cabinet Secretariat had 184. By the end of 2001, the new Cabinet Office had nearly 2,200 staff and the Secretariat had more than tripled to 487 (www. kantei.go.jp/jp/tokino-ugoki/9909/pdf9_18.pdf). Under 1999 legislation, the prime minister was also given explicit authority to engage in policy planning and to initiate legislation. A new Council on Economic and Fiscal Policy (CEFP) gained considerable leeway to generate a mixture of policies aimed at addressing the country's extensive economic and financial problems.

Collectively, these changes altered the previous balance of power between elected officials and senior bureaucrats as well as the balance within the LDP. Agency autonomy declined while the power of elected politicians, and particularly politicians in the executive branch, rose. Relatedly, the power of individual LDP leaders, including once formidable faction leaders, was reduced allowing the prime minister and the cabinet enhanced autonomy in policy-making. Koizumi was particularly flagrant in his refusal to follow the party's longstanding custom of consulting with LDP faction leaders over cabinet appointments; instead he appointed many non-parliamentarians or back benchers, undercutting one of the previously vital tools available to faction leaders.

Most notably, Koizumi utilized the new Council on Economic and Fiscal Policy in an attempt to begin various economic reforms, particularly concerning the non-performing loans so much at the heart of Japan's financial troubles. The Council proposed sweeping changes in a host of areas politically sensitive to the old guard pork oriented conservatives. In addition to efforts to address the NPL problem CEFP efforts were directed at road construction, the privatization of various public sector corporations and caps on the issuance of new bonds for public works (Amyx 2004). The Koizumi administration also cut back significantly on the budgetary outflow for public works projects while at the same time enhancing Japanese spending for IT and broadband access, among other things (see Figure 6.3). At least on the surface the balance of internal conservative power was shifting from pork to productivity.

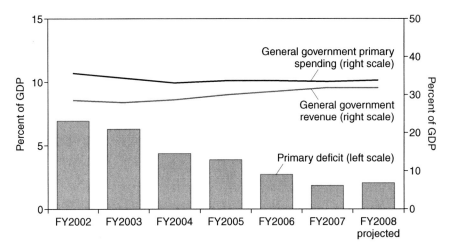

Figure 6.3 Sharp reduction: strong tax collections and cuts in public works have enabled Japan to sharply reduce its primary budget deficit.

By far his most successful battle, however, involved radical alterations to the postal savings system. Japan's extensive network of nearly 25,000 post offices and their well-organized postmasters were for a long time important vote-mobilizing machines for LDP candidates, particularly in the rural areas (Maclachlan 2004; Nonaka 2007). Moreover, the postal savings system has been Japan's, indeed the world's, largest single savings bank, as well as being a huge insurance company. Premiums collected from thousands of Japanese customers flowed into Japan's Fiscal Investment and Loan Program, essentially a "second budget," that was long used, among other things, to support politically favored public works and construction projects (e.g., Noguchi 1995; Park 2011). Koizumi and his allies proposed a dramatic overhaul that would privatize the postal system, a proposal that struck, even in its modified form, at the heart of a vital LDP vote-getting organization and one of the party's major slush funds. Importantly, certain LDP members, particularly in the rural areas, would be far more negatively affected than those LDP members in urban or suburban districts.

Koizumi's postal reform proposals exacerbated the intra-party opposition long simmering against his general economic reform efforts. Koizumi faced substantial opposition on many of his specific policy proposals – and often on his entire agenda – from well-entrenched party leaders, most heavily, though not exclusively, those tied to rural, construction and small business interests. Still, by relying heavily on his media savvy and the ability to paint opponents to his specific reform proposals as impediments to national economic recovery, he remained in office much longer than any of his ten immediate predecessors, all the while bypassing faction leaders in his cabinet choices and in many of his policy proposals, little-by-little undercutting their long-standing power, while strengthening his own.

A key source of Koizumi's strength lay outside the party, largely with a public grown frustrated with the decade plus of glacial political reform, slow economic growth, and with a media savvy that allowed him to bypass traditional internal party channels and intra-party consensus building, in favor of direct populist appeals. Much of the Koizumi rhetoric resonated with a voting public anxious to see a return to a nationally productive economy and for much of his tenure the party's old guard, despite their unhappiness with large segments of his threatening policy agenda, were resistant to replacing him because to do so would almost certainly risk massive electoral retribution. Koizumi was the beneficiary of a classic catch-22 faced by his LDP opponents.

Despite the fact that the LDP enjoyed a clear majority in the Lower House of parliament as well as a functioning majority in the Upper House as a result of its coalition with the small New Komeito, the prime minister's proposed postal reform bill only narrowly passed the Lower House and then was defeated in the Upper House on August 8, 2005. It was the negative votes or abstentions by LDP members, breaking with the party's normally tight discipline, that created the problem. Determined to punish those party members who had impeded the progress of his pet legislative project, Koizumi treated the defeat as a de facto no confidence vote, dissolved the Lower House and called for elections.

Koizumi proved a tactical master in orchestrating the run-up to the election. He began by denying the party's official endorsement to those party members who had impeded his postal reform proposal in the Lower House (even though it had passed narrowly in that body). Even more dramatically, in most cases he ran fresh new LDP candidates, known as assassins, against these opponents, thereby forcing them to run as independents or as members of some new party. This strategy managed to obliterate, or at least to weaken, the party's bloc of internal dissidents, replacing them where possible by pro-reformers loyal to him and his policy agenda.

The strategy was hardly without risks. At least two were obvious. First, the election created vitriolic competition between the incumbent dissidents and new official LDP challengers in 33 of Japan's single member districts (two additional dissidents chose not to run). Such head-to-head competition enhanced the possibility that the potential LDP vote would be split two ways, leaving the door open for candidates from the opposition Democratic Party of Japan (DPJ) to capture many of these multiply contested seats. There was a genuine prospect that the DPJ could win enough seats to gain a parliamentary majority, thereby shutting the now fragmented LDP out of power. A second risk was that many of the dissidents could rely on long-standing electoral strength within their districts, win election as independents, rejoin the LDP, and carry out a purge of a thus weakened Koizumi and his "pro-reform" followers. Under either scenario the LDP could have splintered in several ways, leading to a much deeper party reorganization that would effectively diminish or even eliminate the LDP.

As it turned out, Koizumi's strategy proved to be tactically brilliant (although he was no doubt helped by parallel ineptitude of the DPJ). He transformed the election into a battle, not between the LDP and the DPJ, but into one between "reform" and "resistance." This turned most voter attention to the intra-LDP battles and away from a choice between the LDP and the opposition parties. Essentially he managed to equate "reform" with "pro-Koizumi" and the results were astonishing. Going into the election, the LDP held 212 seats in the Lower House; in the election the party won 296 seats (61.7 percent), a level never before enjoyed by any single political party in Japan. The opposition DPJ meanwhile was devastated, falling from 177 to 117 seats. Moreover, the Koizumi reform forces also won spectacularly: there were 33 dissidents who were denied party endorsement and against whom Koizumi dispatched his generally young, personable and media savvy assassins (a tactic made possible by Japan's relatively new single member district system). A substantial number were women (popularly dubbed "lipstick ninja"). Only 15 of the 33 dissidents survived and successfully defended their seats (two others were defeated in their single seat constituencies but were returned through proportional representation). Meanwhile, 14 of the assassins won (and another 12 gained seats through PR) (*Asahi Shimbun*, September 12, 2005). And with 296 LDP members in parliament after the election, Koizumi had a two-thirds majority never before achieved by the LDP and giving him no incentive whatsoever to allow those dissidents who had won seats to rejoin the party after the election. The anti-reformers were frozen out of political power, leaving Koizumi and the LDP with a more powerful LDP, a powerful executive, and a more explicitly pro-productivity base. Clearly, Koizumi and the productivity wing of the LDP had carried out a successful purge of their major opponents and after the election the party was transformed into one that was hard pressed not to support reform- and productivity-oriented proposals.

Koizumi's victory in the September 2005 election seemed to resolve the intra-party debate in favor of "reform" and economic productivity. "Pork" had been defeated; "productivity" was ascendant. In practice this also meant an expanded and somewhat new constituency for the LDP along with economic policies designed to focus official attention on reinvigorating productivity and downplaying pork. Following the September 2006 Lower House elections, it was quite conceivable to envision a return to, albeit with different structural components, a new regime that would be capable of retaining the LDP's political control while generating positive economic performances that might allow Japan to return to the ranks of the world's industrial leaders. Bolstering this view was a growing awareness that many of Japan's private companies had gone through, and were beginning to reap the benefits of, significant corporate reforms involving streamlined workforces, greater openness to non-bank sources of capital including foreign capital, efficiency-inducing mergers and acquisitions, new boards of directors, enhanced stockholder rights, and greater focus on creativity and efficiency among other things (Vogel 2006).

Any such optimism was pulverized in the early months of the Abe Shinzo administration. With a political tone deafness that contrasted dramatically with Koizumi's astuteness, Abe readmitted most of the so-called "postal rebels" back into the LDP, reinstating a politics predicated on factional accommodation and a priority to pork. He also brought in a cabinet of cronies, avoided most discussions of economics in favor of grandiose right-wing foreign policy posturing, and presided over a series of crony-driven financial scandals and policy gaffs that drove his and party's popularity to lows unseen for years. Electoral vengeance was soon delivered in the Upper House election of July 29, 2007. In contrast to the LDP's stunning Lower House win only a year earlier, the 2007 election saw the LDP lose its controlling majority in the Upper House for the first time since its formation in 1955. Only half of the 242 seats (121) were up for contestation but the DPJ gained 11 seats and won a total of 60 seats to the LDP's 37, jettisoning the previously limp opposition party upward with a total of 109 and transforming it into the largest single party in the Upper House and taking that role from the LDP for the first time it its history. Despite his stunning defeat, Abe originally refused to resign, clinging to office until finally capitulating in September 2007.

With a majority in the Upper House the DPJ enjoyed a position where it could effectively block government-induced legislation as well as hold potentially embarrassing hearings on any number of government and administration activities (the Lower House can constitutionally overrule the Upper House opposition by a two-thirds majority, however, which the LDP and its coalition partners still enjoyed). Such powers for the opposition made it exceptionally difficult for the LDP to govern without continual compromise with an opposition salivating at the prospect of another rapidly-called election.

The LDP did not have to call a Lower House election until September 2009, and with its huge majority it obviously sought to delay the election as long as possible. Yet, policy stalemates throughout the Fukuda administration led to his early resignation, and the selection of Aso Taro as the LDP's head, and the next prime minister with his long roots in the pork segment of the LDP gave few signs that he would attempt to recreate the LDP as a reform-minded party focused on returning the country to high levels of productivity. Instead, his initial policies, formulated in the turmoil of a rapidly expanding global recession, concentrated on a return to Keynesian stimulus monies aimed at Japan's most pork-dependent regions and sectors. As of early 2012 the political situation has the DPJ in control of the Lower House and the LDP controlling the Upper Chamber. While both politics and economics can often turn very quickly, at this point it is exceptionally difficult to visualize conditions under which political majorities and economic productivity would emerge as the probable combination for Japan in the near future. Vastly more likely is some combination of vacillating political leadership and economic sluggishness, except for those Japanese companies that do not depend heavily on political actions for their bottom line success.

Conclusion

At least as of this writing, power within Japan has shifted is several important ways:

- Within the LDP parliamentarians favoring productivity over pork held preponderant power briefly but surrendered that agenda shortly after Koizumi left office.
- Within policy-making circles, power has shifted from numerous vertically insulated "iron triangles" toward the Prime Minister's Office and the Cabinet, but it is not at all clear that such power will be used to recatalyze the country's most productive industries.
- Among political parties, the once limping LDP enjoyed a Lower House majority never seen before but the party under Abe squandered its advantages and now finds the opposition DPJ controlling the Lower House, the LDP ironically in charge of the Upper House, and the entire political leadership fragmented.

There was some return in the national political bias toward industries and investments most likely to generate higher levels of economic productivity but it is no longer clear that this bias is sufficiently institutionalized as to prevent a reinvigoration of pork barrel politics and protection. A host of reforms at both the governmental and corporate levels, while not yet returning Japan to anything like the productivity the country enjoyed in the 1970s or 1980s, suggest that the country's most global companies have turned a difficult corner and may be poised to lead the country to moderate levels of productivity in the near future. But the recent political situation – with the LDP being forced to share power with the opposition DPJ – makes it increasingly unlikely that any single and sustained economic direction will be pursued. Combined with the global recession, the prospects for an economic resurgence in Japan look dismal.

It appeared that the election of September 11, 2005 had "resolved" the tension between pork and productivity in favor of productivity; power and productivity were reforged as the driving logic in Japan's production regime. Anti-reformists had hardly been eliminated from the party's ranks, even if they have been hobbled, by Koizumi's actions. But quickly the party's pro-productivity bias was eradicated as Abe with his roots in the pork segment of the party squandered his economic and political opportunities. In particular, Abe's reversal of the Koizumi purge undercut any serious moves toward a return to productivity. It is hard to imagine the anti-reform groups in the LDP holding quite the stranglehold over productivity enhancing policies as they did for much of the period 1994–2005. However, unless the LDP can regain its mantle as the party of economic productivity and structural reform, and bring forth a leader able to epitomize that orientation, it is unlikely that it can again return to power. For a brief period, power and productivity appeared to have been reconnected under the LDP and Koizumi. But as of this writing, the links appear to have been shattered and show little promise of being reintegrated.

140   *T. J. Pempel*

References

Albert, Michel (1993) *Capitalism vs. Capitalism*. New York: Four Walls Eight Windows.

Amyx, Jennifer (2004) *Japan's Financial Crisis: Institutional Rigidity and Reluctant Change*. Princeton: Princeton University Press.

Berger, Suzanne and Ronald Dore (eds.) (1996) *National Diversity and Global Capitalism*. Ithaca: Cornell University Press.

Dore, Ronald (2000) *Stock Market Capitalism: Welfare Capitalism—Japan and Germany Versus the Anglo-Saxons*. Oxford: Oxford University Press.

Economist, The (1998) "Public Prudence," April 23: 107.

Esping-Andersen, Gosta (1990) *The Three Worlds of Welfare Capitalism*. Princeton: Princeton University Press.

Esping-Andersen, Gosta (1999) *Social Foundations of Postindustrial Economies*. Princeton: Princeton University Press.

Estevez-Abe, Margarita (2008) *Welfare and Capitalism in Postwar Japan*. Cambridge: Cambridge University Press.

Gourevitch, Peter J. (1986) *Politics in Hard Time: Comparative Responses to International Economic Crises*. Ithaca: Cornell University Press.

Hall, Peter A. and David Soskice (eds.) (2001) *Varieties of Capitalism: The Institutional Foundations of Comparative Advantage*. Oxford: Oxford University Press.

Krauss Ellis, S. (2007) "The Prime Minister, Cabinet, and Policymaking: The Changing 'Core Executive' and 'Presidentialization' in Japan," paper presented at the conference on Changes in Japanese Policymaking, Vancouver, Canada, August 27–29.

Maclachlan, Patricia L. (2004) "Post Office Politics in Modern Japan: The Postmasters, Iron Triangles, and the Limits of Reform," *Journal of Japanese Studies* 30(2): 281–314.

Mulgan, Aurelia George (2002) *Japan's Failed Revolution: Koizumi and the Politics of Economic Reform*. Canberra: Asia Pacific Press at The Australian National University.

Muramatsu, Michio and Noriyuki Yanagizawa (2002) "Sengo nihon ni okeru seisaku jissetsu: seitô to kanryô" [The True Story of Policy in Postwar Japan: Parties and Bureaucracy], in Michio Muramatsu and Masahiro Okuno (eds.), *Heisei baburu no kenkyu* [Research on the Heisei Bubble], vol. 2. Tokyo: Tôyô Keizai Shimpôsha, 87–126.

Noguchi, Yukio (1995) "The Role of the Fiscal Investment and Loan Program in Postwar Japanese Economic Growth," in Hyung-ki Kim, Michio Muramatsu, T. J. Pempel and Kozo Yamamura (eds.), *The Japanese Civil Service and Economic Development: Catalysts of Change*. Oxford: Oxford University Press, 261–287.

Nonaka, Naoto (2007) "Koizumi's Postal Service Privatization and the Core Executive in Japan," paper presented at the conference on Japanese Policymaking Network in Transition, Vancouver, August.

Ôtake, Hideo (1996) *Sengo Nihon no ideorogii tairitsu* [Ideological Conflict in Postwar Japan]. Tokyo: San'ichi Shobo.

Park, Gene (2011) *Spending Without Taxation: FILP and the Politics of Public Finance in Japan*. Palo Alto: Stanford University Press.

Pempel, T. J. (ed.) (1990) *Uncommon Democracies: The One-Party Dominant Regimes*. Ithaca: Cornell University Press.

Pempel, T. J. (1998) *Regime Shift: Comparative Dynamics of the Japanese Political Economy*. Ithaca: Cornell University Press.

Pempel, T. J. (1999) "Structural Gaiatsu: International Finance and Political Change in Japan," *Comparative Political Studies* 32(8): 907–932.

Pempel, T. J. (2006) "A Decade of Political Torpor: When Political Logic Trumps Economic Rationality," in Peter J. Katzenstein and Takashi Shiraishi (eds.), *Beyond Japan: The Dynamics of East Asian Regionalism*. Ithaca: Cornell University Press, 37–62.

Pempel, T. J. and Keiichi Tsunekawa (1979) "Corporatism without Labor? The Japanese Anomaly", in Philippe Schmitter and Gerhard Lehmbruch (eds.), *Trends Towards Corporatist Intermediation*. Beverly Hills: Sage, 231–270.

Reed, Steven R. (2002) "Evaluating Political Reform in Japan: A Midterm Report," *Japanese Journal of Political Science* 3(2): 243–263.

Rogowski, Ronald (1989) *Commerce and Coalitions: How Trade Affects Domestic Political Alignments*. Princeton: Princeton University Press.

Samuels, Richard J. (2003) *Machiavelli's Children: Leaders and Their Legacies in Italy and Japan*. Ithaca: Cornell University Press.

Scheiner, Ethan (2002) "Democracy Without Competition: Opposition Failure in One-Party Dominant Japan," unpublished Ph.D. dissertation, Duke University.

Scheiner, Ethan (2006) *Democracy Without Competition in Japan: Opposition Failure in a One-Party Dominant State*. Cambridge: Cambridge University Press

Schlesinger, Jacob (1997) *Shadow Shoguns: The Rise and Fall of Japan's Postwar Political Machine*. Palo Alto: Stanford University Press.

Streeck, Wolfgang and Kozo Yamamura (eds.) (2001) *The Origins of Nonliberal Capitalism: Germany and Japan in Comparison*. Ithaca: Cornell University Press.

Vogel, Steven (2006) *Japan Re-Modeled: How Government and Industry are Reforming Japanese Capitalism*. Ithaca: Cornell University Press.

Weiner, Robert James (2002) "Opposition Disappearance in Japan: Post-Realignment Evidence Supports Theoretical Pessimism," paper delivered at the annual convention of the American Political Science Association, August 31.

Yamamoto, Masao (ed.) (1972) *Keizai kanryô no jittai: Seisaku ketteir no mekanizum* [The Realities of the Economic Bureaucracy: The Mechanics of Policy Formation]. Tokyo: Mainichi Shimbun.

Yamamura, Kozo and Wolfgang Streeck (eds.) (2002) *Embedded Capitalism: Japan and Germany in the Postwar Period*. Ithaca: Cornell University Press.

7 Divergent fate of left parties in political economic regime transitions

Italy and Japan in the 1990s

Hideko Magara

Introduction

Similar backgrounds, contrasting outcomes

The political earthquakes of Italy and Japan in the 1990s provide political scientists with a set of important puzzles: why did large-scale political changes take place almost at the same time in Italy and Japan? Why did some large postwar parties disappear (Democrazia Cristiana: DC; Japan Socialist Party: JSP) while other dominant parties either successfully transformed themselves into new parties (Partito Comunista Italiano/Partito Democratico della Sinistra/Democratici della Sinistra: PCI/PDS/DS) or found a way to survive (Liberal Democratic Party: LDP)?

Italy and Japan have several similar backgrounds specific to them: defeat in World War II and a rapid economic growth led by the state in the 1950s and 1960s; long uninterrupted conservative rule reinforced by informal institutions, namely clientelism and consociativism;[1] the exclusion of the leading leftist parties – the PCI in Italy and the JSP in Japan – from office for almost 50 years although they were the second largest parties in each country's party system. After the 1970s Italy and Japan faced new issues commonly shared by other advanced capitalist countries: post-industrialization; changes in world politics (democratization, the removal of Berlin Wall) and in the world economy (globalization). Then in the early 1990s both Italy and Japan experienced the massive exposure of political scandals almost simultaneously.

Political parties in both countries reacted to these scandals by changing electoral laws, from the pure PR (proportional representation) system in Italy and the semi-PR system in Japan,[2] to very similar systems based mainly on majoritarianism (yet mixed with PR to some extent – 25 percent in Italy, 40 percent in Japan).[3] The Italian and Japanese outcomes were quite different. In Italy, after its historic victory in the 1996 elections, the ex-communist party (PDS) took office for the first time in Italian electoral history by successfully building a center-left coalition. On the other hand, the DC, once a powerful conservative party which had dominated Italian politics since the postwar era, disappeared after its devastating defeat in the 1994 elections. Instead, the center-right space was filled with a newly born party (Forza Italia) and an ex-neofascist nationalist party (Alleanza Nazionale). In Japan, it was the JSP, the second largest postwar party, that disappeared after participating in several ephemeral coalition governments. Instead, the Democratic Party, a new centrist party created under the initiative of several liberal-conservative politicians who had left the LDP, absorbed some liberal groups of ex-socialist politicians and came to confront the LDP. The LDP, which had continuously ruled Japanese politics on its own from 1955 to 1993, returned to office in 1994 after playing an oppositional role for a short period. Due to electoral reforms, Japanese politics moved further to the right; now the large conservative LDP competes with the centrist Democratic Party. There have been rhythmical government alternations in Italy since the second half of the 1990s, while in Japan such events were absent until 2009.

Why do parties initiate important reforms? When threatened by new challenges in the polity, particularly in the electoral arena, parties initiate reform in order to survive. Large-scale reform is often preceded by party leaders' perception of serious organizational crisis. In many cases, governing parties decide to change the rules of the game in order to maximize their representation, if no old party enjoys a dominant position (Boix 1999). Similarly, when office alternation is distributed evenly among the largest parties, reform are more likely, because politicians think supporting reform would generate support from a small number of middle-class voters. When office alternation is distributed unevenly among the largest parties, reforms are not likely, because the majority party does not have any incentives for reforms (Geddes 1991, 1994).

Yet, there are possibilities, in which either the dominant ruling party or the opposition does initiate reform. In Italy, the largest opposition party (PCI/PDS) held the initiative of electoral reform in the early 1990s, while in Japan the strongest faction within the governing LDP promoted reform. It should be noted that, unlike the cases treated by Boix in which electoral systems shifted from plurality/majority to PR, in the Italian and Japanese cases, the electoral systems shifted from PR/semi-PR to mixed systems based mainly on majoritarianism in the 1990s. Large parties, either in office or out, certainly have strong incentives in modifying electoral systems from PR to majority. This does not explain, however, why in Italy the DC failed to achieve reform, and why in Japan the JSP could not play an important role. These parties were on the verge of collapse. What prevented these parties from promoting reform? What made their rational responses difficult?

Focusing on the left

In order to understand fully the nature of Italian and Japanese electoral reforms and political realignments which peaked in 1993–1994, it is necessary to examine not only their party systems from the inside, but also the impact of social economic changes on political transformation. This does not necessarily mean, however, that political realignments and shifts in party systems can be explained only by economic and policy-related motives. Some stress economic factors in explaining the recent political restructuring in Japan. One argument is that weakened political mobilization and policy convergence between the governing parties and the opposition parties made the cross-cutting realignment of Japan's party system possible. According to this perspective, the neoconservative reforms during the 1980s rendered viable the restructuring of the party system (Hiwatari 1995). Another economic argument underlines the international pressures for change. The export sector, which feels increasingly vulnerable to the global competition with the existing domestic institutions, urged the conservative government to reduce protection of the least efficient sectors of the economy. The conservative party in office thus needed to change the electoral rules under which it had secured the support of the protected sector (Rosenbluth 1996). A similar explanation is that the new logic of the conservative governing party in the 1990s forces the "regime" – the composite of socioeconomic coalitions, political institutions, and public policy profiles – to deviate drastically from the earlier forms that were appropriate during the rapid economic growth of the 1960s (Pempel 1998).

Japanese politics specialists often attempt to account for political changes in the 1990s by analyzing the LDP's reactions to the new economic circumstances. These analyses of the strategic choices of the LDP, which heavily emphasize economic factors, however, fail to solve more general puzzles for comparative political scientists: why did Japan and Italy, exceptional among affluent societies, undergo such drastic changes in the 1990s? Why did the LDP return to power and why did the JSP disappear in Japan, while in Italy the conservative DC vanished and the leftist PDS at last took office? Why did Italy and Japan end up with completely different results despite many historical, political, and economic similarities? The above arguments do not offer any persuasive answers to these puzzles, probably because they underestimate the crucial roles played by another important actor, the leftist parties.

These arguments also fail to recognize the uncertainty particular to the significant system changes, in Bull and Rhodes' words, "completely unpredictable nature of crisis" (Bull and Rhodes 1997) which could produce an unexpected and ephemeral outcome and could multiply the dimensions of the crisis. In the 1980s, almost every advanced country not only implemented neo-liberal policies but also attempted to respond to contextual changes in the global market. Yet such drastic political changes as Japan and Italy experienced during the first half of the 1990s were rather exceptional. During the system changes, the factors that are different from those functioning under normal and stable conditions play an important role. When analyzing these changing situations, it is necessary to use more appropriate tools which are distinguished from those used to analyze static situations. Actually the traditional main actors such as the DC and the JSP suddenly disappeared and completely new actors emerged to take office.

The Italian and Japanese political scandals in the early 1990s hit the DC and LDP similarly. The demise of the former and the survival of the latter can be better explained by both extra- and intra-parliamentary dimensions: (1) varieties of capitalism, i.e., how markets are structured, whether or not managers are rigidly organized, where unions' coordination take place; and (2) the success and failure of parties in strategically responding to opportunities for change. Their success and failure not only reflect the type of capitalism but also derive from their preceding efforts to reform themselves both organizationally and ideologically. Party leaders' cost-benefit calculations and opportunity structures may well vary according to differences in the structure of capitalism, and their relations with supporting groups.

In the absence of social democracy

At the root of the political changes in the 1990s, there was an explosion of chronic and wide-ranging dissatisfaction among citizens owing to the dissolution of the factors which had restricted their ability to speak out after the drastic shift in the world political economy in the 1990s (Morlino and Tarchi 1996). From a long-term perspective, however, this dissatisfaction came not only from moral disapproval but also from the erosion of the material base which had been supporting the postwar political-economic regime. The loss of the system's legitimacy was caused by the dysfunction of interest representation in each society.[4]

One of the most important attributes of democracy is that it causes governments to be responsive to the interests of voters (Przeworski *et al.* 1999). Yet in Italy and Japan democratic performance is poorer than in other affluent countries. For the Italian and Japanese left, postwar politics characterized by the predominance of informal (undemocratic) institutions, such as consociativism and clientelism, were contingent outcomes. The Italian and Japanese voters were long unable to switch their governments in the absence of feasible alternatives. Looking at postwar politics in Italy and Japan, the lack of government alternation and limited legitimacy can be understood as unintended consequences brought about by the large left parties: they neither anticipated nor desired these outcomes when they made choices at the beginning of the democratization process. Yet being highly constrained by miscalculation at the critical juncture (Collier and Collier 1991) in which new institutions were founded, they after all chose (JSP) or were forced (PCI) to be isolated when a drastic change in international politics occurred – the initiation of the Cold War. Since then, both countries lacked any relevant government alternation and social democratic practices (Magara 1999). Italy and Japan were anomalies among affluent democracies in that social democracy was long absent.

A typical pattern of social democracy can be observed in actualizing and maintaining the welfare state through political exchange (Pizzorno 1977) between the social democratic governments and supporting trade unions. The social democratic government was able to develop the welfare state by universalizing their policies and thus by getting support of non-workers. Comprehensive unions' self-restraint contributed considerably to this process (Shalev 1983; Esping-Andersen 1985). The unions, however, pursued their own exclusive interests when post-Fordist transformation and the recession and intensification of international competition triggered the crisis of the welfare state.[5] In this situation, social democratic parties try to redefine themselves in response to social and economic changes, but such renewal contradicts the interests of unions that have been their financial, organizational, and electoral base. At the same time, social democratic parties, which have too strong a tie with the unions, are unpopular in elections. In many cases, the toughest barrier that the parties face in redefining their basic principles derives from the corporatist unions in cooperation with the social democrats.[6]

Italy and Japan have followed a different path. Strictly speaking, neither Italy nor Japan has neo-corporatist unions. In Italy and Japan, neither a social democracy nor a so-called social democratic welfare state was realized. It was the conservative parties that invented the "Italian style" and "Japanese style" welfare states. Although leftist parties count unions as their key allies in both countries, they never took office as the primary party until the 1990s, and did not provide unions with benefits that social democratic governments usually produced.

It is important to distinguish the circumstances surrounding these leftist parties from those surrounding social democratic parties in analyzing transformations of the former. For the PCI and the JSP, reaching decisions to change their ideologies and reorganize themselves was difficult. Parties are institutions. They have durability (Aldrich 1995). In many cases, only exogenous shocks can trigger their reforms. Reformers easily encounter intensified reactions from the most conservative factions within them. Moreover, they will face different situations from those social democratic parties face, when reorganizing themselves. The fact that they did not take office for a long time – except a very short period after World War II – makes their conditions more severe than those of social democratic parties in terms of human and financial resources and access to information, which are asymmetrically distributed (Manin *et al.* 1999). Parties without any record in office encounter much stronger resistance to win a measure of power, because the exclusion of outsiders by the incumbent leaders is much more determined. Compared to social democratic parties, they have fewer possible allies inside the regime. Since they confront much more powerful conservative regimes in the sense that incumbent parties have been able to routinize and structurize their dominance thanks to the lack of government alternations, outsiders may well need to seek stronger and more broadly based support if they want to force their way into the political system (Shefter 1994). Unlike the United States, another affluent society without social democracy, Italy and Japan had no significant government alternations. Both Italy and Japan were long ruled by conservative governments, which created and maintained limited consensus among vested interests by demobilizing potential voters for the left. The incumbent parties continuously provided their supporters with selective incentives. This limited, partial consensus, however, turned out to be too costly to maintain, not only because it never develops into any explicit, fully national consensus but also because it is simply inefficient in the phase of economic downturn in which voters become more cost-conscious.

The PCI and the JSP considered the citizens' hatred of the "party government" and the political corruption caused by a quasi-permanent conservative rule as the impetus to change the entire party system. The Italian left launched a political realignment, calculating that the risk of maintaining the status quo would be greater than a risk of reform, even though the latter was considerably high. This calculation was partly owed to the failure of the DC and PSI, their major electoral rivals and the leading actors in a series of *Tangentopoli* scandals. The left reasoned that their big chance had come to redraw the political map of Italy, recognizing the voters' resentment toward conservative politics. Although similar scandals happened in Japan, the JSP never took the initiative of political reform. They could not react quickly to a drastic change in the political world after 1989. In regard to the political realignment, they could not obtain even intra-party consensus, and merely reluctantly followed the scenario for change advocated by conservative forces. This variance rendered a drastic difference in both countries' political outcomes.

These two similarly situated countries produced two contrasting outcomes. While the so-called left lost legitimacy in Japan, the Italian left, which initiated political reform to dismantle the conservative dominance, discovered a way to survive. The Italian left tried to respond to post-industrial social economic changes and made an effort to promote reforms based on new ideas, and was successful in remaining in the electoral arena. In contrast, the Japanese conservative realignment stemmed from the failure of the left to respond appropriately to post-industrial social economic changes. Although the JSP recognized the breakdown of the Fordist base, it was involved in political realignment without preparing any alternative ideas.

The next section develops a stylized model to characterize leftist parties under highly fluid, uncertain circumstances in which most parties have lost their legitimacy but have not yet established alternative norms. It explains why it is crucial for parties to present new ideas in such unstable situations in order to survive at all. It also shows that new ideas advocated by party leaders are not easily politicized and actualized without effective organizational backing, no matter how attractive they are to voters. Party structures matter. Supporting groups' preferences heavily constrain leaders' choices. The importance of varieties of capitalism lies here. Voters' preference may well reflect how and under what circumstances the economy is managed in each country.

Uncertainty under political economic regime transition

The Italian and the Japanese parties were on the verge of breakdown in the early 1990s. In both countries, the right completely lost its legitimacy after the revelations of disgraceful scandals. Also the left was seriously injured by the breakdown of East European economies. Without reforming themselves, it seemed very likely that all of them would collapse. At a glance the political earthquakes of Italy and Japan in the 1990s may appear to be limited to the electoral arena. Yet in this chapter I view these upheavals as transitions of the political economic regime under democracies with limited legitimacy. In depth, the electoral reforms in both countries involved significant interactions between political parties and civil society.

The political economic regime here consists of two interdependent and inter-locking "partial regimes," the varieties of capitalism and party politics regime – the most fundamental dimensions of capitalist democracies.[7] Political economic regime transition is a process in which political actors attempt to change political and economic institutions by massively politicizing their new ideas in order to mobilize voters for their broad support. It may involve significant institutional changes that are determined by interplay among actors. The outcomes can be highly contingent, and heavily dependent on the ability and choices of actors.[8]

In analyzing the Italian and Japanese political economic regime transitions, in which the democratic games are characterized by strong uncertainty, it would be necessary to emphasize the following three points. First, institutional impacts certainly are crucial, but more important is the dynamics demonstrated by the strategic actors in breaking and reforming the excessive institutional constraints and in building new institutions (Piven 1991: 12). Actually, the Italian and Japanese cases indicate that institutions cannot alone explain political transformation, since they ended up with totally opposite outcomes despite their similarities in electoral reforms and long-standing conservative political control strengthened by informal institutions since the postwar era to the beginning of the 1990s.

Second, the limits of actors' ability to pursue rationality should be underlined. The short-term rationality for individual politicians (in many cases, short-term re-election) and the organizational, long-term rationality of their parties do not necessarily coincide (Tsebelis 1990; Koelble 1991). Each politician often calcu-lates that it is more rational to secure voting blocs by protecting particular inter-ests of certain groups and regions. Such a calculation, however, may well gradually endanger the parties' organizational credibility (Panebianco 1988). It is also clear that the actors' pursuit of rationality becomes more difficult in such dynamic phases as political economic regime transition than under normal con-ditions. In the process of regime shift in which situations rapidly change and uncertainty grows to the maximum, actors' miscalculation and less reliable information make rational choices more difficult. Political transformations in Italy and Japan fit this case exactly. Under greater uncertainty dependence on norms becomes essential (Offe 1996: 682). It is very possible that unexpected factors bring uncertainty to the party system and indispose the conventional way of recognition and decision-making process. When uncertainty increases, polit-ical leaders can no longer resort to their traditional actions. They are compelled to redefine the very structure of competition. In such a phase, a party's own iden-tity becomes the object of the game (Vassallo 1995: 52–53).

The third point, which is closely related to the second, concerns the role of party leaders in establishing norms, a necessary premise for political actors to pursue long-term rationality. Establishing norms does not mean that parties adapt themselves to both the internal and external conditions of party systems. Rather it requires (1) the creation of new environment by proposing new ideas on their initiative, and (2) the politicization of their ideas though effective interaction with society in order to obtain a broad consensus of the citizens. Party leaders' creation of new ideas and interaction with civil society – these factors become significant in political economic regime transitions. Electoral strategies thus can be perceived as attempts to mold the preferences of voters in order to establish coalitions broad enough to secure parliamentary majorities (Boix 1998: 42).

Ideas, structures, and parties' choice

Political parties are composed of ambitious office-seekers who abuse, reform, or abandon parties when doing so furthers their goals and ambitions (Aldrich 1995). Extra-party actors who hold, or have access to, critical resources that office-seekers need to realize their ambitions are also important. The changed incentives of these groups have played a significant role in the fundamentally altered nature of the contemporary party. Parties are highly constrained by these actors. When analyzing transitions of political economic regimes, impacts of these extra-parliamentary actors, such as trade unions and business associations, on choices taken by parties need to be fully examined.

My hypothesis is that the success and failure of party transformations in fluid, uncertain situations are determined by leadership – the competence of party leaders to create new ideas and to politicize them effectively. Yet leaders' choices are constrained by the party structure – the intra-party balance of power, and the relationship between the party and supporting interest groups.

Parties want to maximize their votes to win elections (Downs 1957). Not all possibilities, however, are open to parties. Parties often fail to adopt attractive policy packages despite their leaders' serious advocacy (Koelble 1991: 26). Party leaders and activists work under various constraints coming from exogenous as well as endogenous variables when fixing their policy ideas. While political parties are able to develop new ideas and electoral strategies adaptive to new situations, they also face the difficulty in following such new political lines because of intense conflicts within parties concerning their new ideas. In-party opposition to the new ideas, which would become popular among the electorate, is in many cases obdurate and parties often fail to follow public opinion (Koelble 1991: 25–28). The intra-party structure heavily constrains party leaders' choices.

Creating new ideas certainly involves inter-sectoral alliance strategies. Parties' choices can often be full of tensions: their coalition strategies occasionally contradict interests of core voters who they have materially relied on. Certain material bases, such as unions' backing, are so rigidly institutionalized that they compose an integral part of party organizations. Even organizational resources can be objects for party leaders to change. Party leaders, however, can hardly stop relying on the existing resources and find new resources. They try to maintain existing resources, while seeking new ones; but they may lose the old resources they still need without finding new ones.

Similarly important is to recognize the role played by business leaders. In retrospect, leftist parties and unions in advanced countries make use of institutionalized power. The left has maintained its power by forming an implicit alliance with the dominant groups among capitalists (Swenson 1991: 515). In Italy, where capitalists historically failed to establish a monolithic, powerful capitalist

Table 7.1 Varieties of capitalism: Japan and Italy

	Japan	*Italy*
Market structure	hierarchical	pluralist
Managers' organization	rigid	loose
Unions	decentralized corporatism (Ido)	national coordination

organization (Hellman 1993; Lanzalaco 1998), the *Confindustria* recently tried to take the initiative in regime change. In Japan, capitalists had a particularly strong influence on the unions' conservative reorganization and the eventual party realignment.

Are parties able to defend the youth and women, while securing consensus of the traditional actors (e.g., the capitalists attempting maximum rationalization on the worldwide scale economic restructuring and the conservative trade unions regressing to the maintenance of their self-interests)? The degree to which party leaders can make their colleagues – particularly in-party oppositions – recognize the necessity and the viability of reducing the negative effects of post-industrial economic restructuring, and the extent to which their new ideas earn cross-sectoral support including those of capitalists and unions in spite of structural constraints, will determine their electoral fates.

Table 7.1 shows the main properties of Japanese and Italian capitalism by market structure, managers' organization, and unions. While economic coordination is deeply structured in Japan, Italian economic coordination is rather weak. It implies that even under the post-1989 situation, it is hard for the leftist parties to win elections in Japan owing to strong coordination among business and political elites. It is possible, however, for the Italian left to win elections when there are endogenous/exogenous pressures, once the Berlin Wall was already removed.

The following sections briefly review whether party leaders were successful in creating new ideas, and how internal structures of the parties and their relationships with the unions promoted/blocked leftist parties' success in Italy and Japan respectively.

The Italian case

Reforming the party, reforming Italian politics

Retrospectively, the PCI constantly sought renovation: from Berlinguer's *compromesso storico* to "democratic alternative" and Occhetto's even more radical reforms. One of the most meaningful contributions of Berlinguer was that he urged the PCI to reform itself by showing the possibility to take office through an alliance with other parties (Hellman 1986; Sassoon 1981). Changes of the PCI encouraged by Berlinguer consolidated its image as a political force that played a game based on democratic rule and created a space in which other parties seriously considered the PCI as a potential member of government. Berlinguer's claim – commitment of the PCI to political pluralism and to democratic institutions, approval of NATO, criticism of the Soviet political system – fully renovated the PCI. It grew to become a significant political force. However, it was impossible that the PCI represented the Italian left as a whole. The *compromesso storico* which excluded the PSI broke down. And a shift to the "democratic alternative" alone could not cancel out a confrontation with the PSI. The possibility to overcome internal conflicts within the Italian left came about only after the complete party reform by Occhetto was realized.

The renovation of the PCI/PDS was a process in which the party integrated the two affluents, its own in-party renewal on the one hand and an overall party realignment with external political forces on the other, into one mainstream of Italian political reform. Upon being elected Secretary of the PCI in June 1988, Occhetto immediately proclaimed a "discontinuity." He was extremely active in promoting reforms, and appointed young and talented people with middle-class intellectual backgrounds including Walter Veltroni and Massimo D'Alema as his advisors. He advocated "strong reformism" and argued that the party should not ignore but transcend the traditional class cleavages. Following the British case, he constructed a "shadow cabinet" by which he criticized the existing government and proposed a realistic alternative to the conservatives. He tried to redefine his party as a "liberal" party (Weiberg 1995).

Such a scenario led by the middle-class intellectuals incurred a strong reaction from the in-party laborists. There were four major factions within the party at that time. Napolitano's faction on the right asserted an alliance with the PSI. At the center, Occhetto was seeking further support for the party renewal. On the left, the Ingrao-Natta faction insisted on limited reform only within the PCI framework. Also on the left, Cossutta's faction still believed in Marxism-Leninism and was strongly opposed to any scenario of reforms.

Occhetto and his young advisors actively responded to this opposition by campaigning enthusiastically and persuasively around the party's local branches all over Italy. The CGIL, the union closest to the PCI, initially was skeptical of Occhetto's reform scenario, and four-sevenths of its sub-federations were opposed to it. However, Luciano Lama and Bruno Trentin, leaders of the CGIL, recognized the significance of Occhetto's efforts and strongly supported them. Backing by the foremost leaders in the labor sector like Lama and Trentin was definitely important for the self-renewal of the PCI/PDS. In addition to the active support by eminent thinkers and unionists, opinion among the leftist youth which was initially divided showed increasing sympathy for Occhetto, particularly for his assertions on ecology, global interdependence, peace, and disarmament (Weiberg 1995).

Occhetto placed electoral reforms high on his objectives when he promoted the transformation of the PCI into the PDS. He embraced a scenario that a leftist government would become a reality by way of electoral reforms, a shift from PR to majoritarianism. His party's renovation was inseparably related to the reforms of Italian politics. For him, therefore, the success of electoral reforms was a necessary precondition for the success of his own party's renewal and survival.

The stream of radical change in Italian politics up to the March 1994 elections can be divided into three phases. The first is the period between 1990 and 1992 in which traditional parties tried to renovate their own identity (e.g., PCI/PDS), and at the same time, relatively new forces (la Lega, i Verdi, la Rete) expanded their power. The second phase, 1992–1993, saw the extinction of the traditional parties which had already been involved in a blizzard of confusion and had lost their *raison d'être*. In the third phase, 1993–1994, more radical and definitive transformation of the parties and the party system became a reality. Adoption of the new electoral laws, no doubt, heavily influenced such an overall collapse of the old party institutions (Di Virgilio 1994: 497).

The dramatic shift of Italian politics up to the 1994 elections can be grasped as a process of identity-redefinition and pact-building among various political parties. In this process, the Italian elites' pursuit of new ideas was significant. After the breakdown of Berlin Wall, leftist leaders seriously attempted to create new ideas that would attract broader voters beyond the old class lines.[9] Particularly important is the fact that they strategically aimed to gain support of capitalists and unorganized post-industrial voters. The Italian left argues that it is necessary to make new pacts among Italians which would change the very social hierarchy, breakdown a suffocative network of vested interests and powers, and transfer resources from the protected sectors to the productive sectors. These were the new pacts between the state and markets, between the public and private.

Just like the PDS that emphasizes its ties to new social movements, Bruno Trentin, then Secretary General of the biggest Italian union CGIL, pointed out the significance of solidarity with voluntary groups. He insisted that unions must change themselves in establishing networks among separate new actors (Trentin 1994). Under his leadership, the CGIL tried to become a legitimate interlocutor for all kinds of voluntary, political, social, and cultural groups. The Italian unions in the early 1990s recognized themselves as a political actor (*un soggetto politico*) beyond mere interests groups.[10]

In March 1994, however, the *progressisti* lost and the rightist alliance that included the National Alliance (Alleanza Nazionale, AN) stemming from a neo-fascist trend, won an overwhelming victory. The 1994 elections showed a stereotype of "dualism of democracy" in Bobbio's term (Bobbio 1994: 47). The votes for the left were, in total, no more than 34 percent: a very discouraging result. While the PDS did not have the capacity to engage the hopes of the youth and the unemployed, it simultaneously lost trust among people who had voted for the PCI.[11] Such a devastating defeat was mainly due to the PDS's inability to develop effective electoral campaigns that would attract voters (Biasco 1994: 15–17). Although their electoral programs contained many meaningful ideas with regards to the reforms of the state, finance, and labor markets (PDS 1994), the PDS was unable to promote itself effectively at the polls.

The PDS does not lack policy advisors, most of whom are scholars and journalists specialized in the fields of economics and social policies and political institutions. However, the PDS was unable to fully utilize their advice. There

was a strong group within the PDS who were still inclined to traditional ideological and cultural values instead of substantive policies. This group tended to
hinder the development of many practical ideas in the actual electoral campaigns. Yet, the outcome of the 1994 elections was still transitional. Just after
the elections, Massimo D'Alema, the would-be successor of Occhetto, keenly
recognized the sheer necessity to form a broad center-left coalition in order to
govern Italy from the left.

New strategies to survive

What actually mattered under the new electoral systems concerns how the left
shows its self-identity as an alternative to the right. The PDS in particular needed
to show what kind of relationship it would build with the old guards (PPI and
PSI), on the one hand, and with the new forces (i Verdi) on the other, especially
how it would strategically place the centrists in its future scenario.

Massimo D'Alema, leader of the PDS, recognized that the Italian right was
formidable (D'Alema 1996: 12). As a matter of fact, the right represented by
Silvio Berlusconi of Forza Italia, Gianfranco Fini of the Alleanza Nazionale
(AN), and Rocco Buttiglione of the Cristiano Democratici Uniti (CDU) continued to offer a populist anchor. The center-left itself was divided. Lamberto Dini,
former prime minister, was close to the center-right. Dini showed a political
position different from a moderately left-leaning centrist stance. The fact that
two confrontational forces coexisted in the center-left (D'Arcais 1996: 16–17)
constantly contained the possibility of further centrists' turn to the right and,
thus, a further conservatization of Italian politics as a whole. This difficult situation for the center-left could become even more severe due to the existence of
the hard-liner Partito Rifondazione Comunista (PRC). The moderate left was
faced with Przeworski's dilemma (Przeworski 1985) here again.

It was not impossible to overcome such a structural vulnerability on the part
of the moderate left by advocating new ideas and by practicing them through
actual policies. Radical liberalism, which is based on the concept of free markets
and self-reliance, was the very opposite of the Italian public sector excessively
protected by the state and the type of Italian capitalism that has evolved in the
form of local family enterprises. Advocates of liberalism were found most in the
area of the center-left. The ex-republicans, socialists, and ex-Christian democratic liberals shared this value. Even the PDS, which had not been liberal, now
recognized the principle of liberalism (Salvati 1995: 91–93). The problem for
the center-left to solve, therefore, was how to attract moderate voters with the
still influential PRC existing to its left and how to build radical liberalism in both
ideological and practical terms.

The PDS's new leader, Massimo D'Alema, who concentrated his energies on
forming an anti-Berlusconi alliance, chose economist Romano Prodi, a catholic
leftist and ex-president of the IRI, as leader of the new center-left alliance. Professor Prodi, who kept relations with various political forces miraculously well,
seemed capable of uniting centrist and leftist forces. The PDS decided not to

make electoral programs on its own but to leave them subject to the discretion of Prodi's staff and then follow his programs. In so doing, the PDS aimed at absorbing moderate votes.

Reorganizing the welfare state also was one of the most important themes of the regime transition for the PDS. Before the April 1996 elections, Massimo D'Alema presented an image of new post-industrial welfare state:

> In Italy, the crisis of the welfare state created deep cleavages. On the one hand there existed people who were protected by the welfare state – a strange combination among a certain part of the labor movement, the traditional or matured industrial sector, the wide-ranging strata of bureaucrats and professionals, managers of social policy organization, and big enterprises which enjoyed great merits by the social buffer policies. The other block composed of more dynamic sectors of capitalism (small enterprises, new professions) includes the young and women, who have never been protected by the traditional formula of welfare redistribution and have formed an anti-welfare social block. If this cleavage deepens further and if we side with the old block, the left will lose, because the old block is practically and culturally based on a civic category we can no longer accept, i.e., , a category of male, adult, employed union members. Such a formula excludes not only the young and women but also the weak and newcomers. We want a welfare state which invests more in the future and for new generations, turns resources for innovation, provides more opportunities of life and chances, and eliminates the vacuum of security and guarantee. We need to get rid of the old social democratic compromise – in Italy a distorted form of social security provided by the DC – to create a new welfare state against excessively competitive individualism and cruel ultra-liberal culture.
>
> (D'Alema 1996: 33–35)

In the April 1996 elections, the Italian center-left achieved a better outcome than expected. The elections resulted in a narrow victory margin for the center-left. The victory, as a matter of fact, was an "historical success"[12] for the Italian left. The March 1994 elections, the first elections under the new electoral law, were won by the rightist alliance, il Polo della Libertà'. In the April 1996 elections, the second elections after the electoral law amendment, the center-left alliance, l'Ulivo, rose to power. The Italian transition to a new regime, thus, cleared one crucial hurdle for a more advanced democracy in that it realized a government alternation.

The elections provided the PDS with the status of a primary party. D'Alema immediately expressed his intention to remove the sickle and hammer from the party symbol, which showed that the PDS had become a "normal" party. The leftist goal to directly take part in the government was finally realized for the first time since *Risorgimento*. This is an historical shift that required a long and difficult transformation including radical changes in identity and the establishment of a broad system of social and political coalition building.[13]

During the transition from the First Republic to the Second Republic, not merely the issues of electoral reform and political realignment, but also a more essential issue concerning the management of Italian capitalism hereafter was discussed by various social actors such as politicians, managers and capitalists, labor unionists and intellectuals. The Italian transition questioned the very nature of the political economic regime of Italy, and it was in the field of economic reform that the capitalists took the initiative. The capitalists' reform project was firmly grounded with the focus on the constitutional reform issue.

They occasionally organized managers' conferences and strongly appealed for constitutional reform which would secure the deregulation of the markets, insisting that Italy needed to liberate itself from the unsustainable burdens of the state and to build a new model of capitalism, a new model of world economy. Ineffective state finance, European integration, a distorted welfare state, excessive statism, inefficiency – all of these things that characterized Italian capitalism under *partitocrazia* were now targeted for reforms. They stressed that Italy needed a new constitution that would reduce state intervention, cut public expenditure, and secure the autonomy of the central bank. The entire Italian economy had now become a target for an "emergent" argument. The Italian capitalists hoped not for gradual but bold and immediate economic reforms. Their reform proposal was clearly one which emphasized the liberalism of the market maximizers.

On the other hand, another difficulty for leftist parties is that unions tend to be more conservative under economic restructuring. Actually, after taking office, the Italian center-left government faced difficulties in protecting the interests of unrepresented, unorganized post-industrial groups while maintaining cooperative relationships with traditional actors, i.e., unions and business associations. Unions' veto power remains a big threat for the government, especially when the left, backed by labor, takes office. Italian unions supported the leftist parties' reorganization and subsequent political realignment. Were they able to continue such support even after the realization of the center-left government?

The Japanese case

Unsuccessful party reform

The JSP has traveled a difficult course in terms of ideology, organization, and policies. Since the early 1950s the party had been dominated by an aggressive group of Left Socialists, whose dogmatic program bound the party for quite a long period after the 1960s. Another problem was that a strong tie to the biggest trade union, the Sohyo (the General Council of Trade Unions of Japan), was reinforced in the era of Left Socialist expansion. The Sohyo positively supported the Left Socialists, a hard left faction, and began to provide financial and human resources. From the very beginning, the Sohyo strongly committed itself to party politics. Heavy dependence of the JSP on the allied unions continued until its demise. Despite several realistic leaders' attempts for social democratization of the JSP, objections from the in-party left were strong enough to block any efforts for party renewal.

In such a context, the emergence of Doi Takako as the new party leader in the mid-1980s was significant. She declared that she would commit herself to post-industrial policies: (1) to turn the JSP into a party open to every citizen's participation; (2) to make policies of the JSP with the citizen's cooperation; (3) to promote women's political commitment. She wanted to show new ideas different from old laborist ideas.

The rise of Doi, who had never belonged to the in-party factions, created a wave of popularity beyond the JSP's expectations. She earned citizens' support by showing a straightforward political stance against the LDP in regard to the problems of corruption and consumer taxes. In the July 1989 Upper House election, the JSP gained many ex-LDP votes thanks to the Doi boom. The JSP's proportional share of the vote was 35.05 percent, much higher than that of the LDP at 27.32 percent. Doi's JSP, however, was faced with limits to its promotion of the government alternation project by the opposition parties just after its epoch-making electoral victory. Although the JSP's leader, Doi, did want to establish new, post-industrial ideas, she was unable to get the internal backing of her party owing to most politicians' excessive dependence on unions.

Owing to the rival LDP's notorious scandals, the possibility for opposition parties to take office increased overnight. The JSP executives' enthusiasm seemed boundless. Nevertheless, Japanese politics took a conservative turn which was contrary to the initial aim of the JSP, i.e., a social democratic convergence despite the fact that the LDP government collapsed in 1993 and that the JSP participated in the anti-LDP coalition government as the primary party. Although Doi's emergence was epoch-making and held great potential, she had certain limitations because according to the conventional logic of the JSP she was an "amateur leader" without the experience of Diet administration and policy activities and had nothing to do with the party's leadership (Shiihashi 1989: 60–64).

Retrospectively, the movement of the JSP and Sohyo bloc did not expand beyond the framework of labor unions. The JSP, which ended up representing only the interests of limited categories of workers, therefore became the permanent opposition. However, the 1989 election indicated a possibility that the increase in non-union support could bring a great victory to the JSP. Doi Takako, who was particularly interested in developing new political supporters, tried to approach various groups including women's groups, citizens' groups, consumers' groups, and cooperatives (Takabatake 1989).

By clearly showing the primary opposition party's political direction as different from that of the LDP, Doi responded to citizens' expectations. Activists in citizens' and social movements who had been estranged from the JSP gradually became attracted to her. The JSP was remaking its image and expanding its support. It was truly a perfect occasion to form new social bases in fields outside the labor movement (Igarashi 1994: 51). Nonetheless, Doi's in-party base was vulnerable, partly because she had never belonged to factions. On the other hand,

Doi adopted many activists of the citizens' movements, university professors, and intellectuals as an external think tank, which provoked a reaction from the traditional party executives, most of whom came from unions. It was not known how they would react if Doi made a mistake (Shiihashi 1989: 63; Igarashi 1994: 51).

The JSP failed to catch the radical-liberal trend beyond social democracy and came along a non-European way in which it continued to be dependent on labor unions led by conservative leaders who sided with the conservative post-industrial economic restructuring advocated by capitalists. In the July 1995 Upper House election, the JSP visibly relied on unions: 43.8 percent of the successful JSP candidates, and almost 80 percent of all the new successful candidates, came from unions.[14]

In retrospect, the presence of Doi Takako, who aimed at strengthening the JSP's ties with the citizens, was thought possibly to assist the JSP to a radical-liberal post-industrial transformation by breaking the socialists' stalemate with the labor unions, who became more conservative during the 1980s, and so deprived the JSP from advocating social democracy. Doi's citizen-oriented project, however, collapsed because of its inability to secure cooperation from within a party that was excessively dependent on unions.

Conservative political restructuring

In Japan, unions and business associations were influential in the conservative political restructuring. A series of political reforms may have resulted from the Japanese establishment's recognition of the limit of the LDP's politics and attempt to break such politics from within the regime. The conservative scenario of Ozawa Ichiro, head of the strongest faction of the LDP and protagonist of Japan's political realignment, reflected a big contribution on the part of business leaders, as well as his own ambitions. The leaders of the big enterprises, who were frustrated from the late 1980s with the dullness of LDP's one-party control of the government, thought that a conservative two-party system would be more acceptable. What they hoped for was not the European type confrontation between two forces, i.e., the conservatives versus the social democrats, but the American type of confrontation between two conservative parties. They said, "A two party system with the radicals on one pole is not acceptable," and "The American type two conservative party system is ideal. With the West European Social Democratic type, economic policies would be crushed." More concretely, they hoped for a two-party system with the liberal democratic mainstream on one pole and some part of the LDP, the Komeito (the Clean Government Party), the DSP (the Democratic Socialist Party) plus rightist socialists on the other. They also agreed to the electoral reform on the basis of a majoritarian system. At the same time, business leaders strongly requested administrative reform and thorough deregulation. Recognizing the inappropriateness of Japan's traditional institutions in the international political economic context of the post-Cold War era, they fully realized the sheer necessity of reorganizing Japan's political and economic order on a global but conservative basis. Thus, political reform was indispensable in order to realize a politics strong enough to cope with such a crisis (Watanabe 1994: 405–418).

Unlike the Italian case, Japan's political reform resulted in a fatal fiasco for the left. One reason can be found in a strategic failure of the JSP and the Rengo (Japanese Trade Union Confederation). The JSP and Yamagishi Akira, president of the Rengo, tried to break the LDP's one-party control of the government and create a government alternation with a slogan called "political reform." The biggest problem with the JSP was that it never tried to hold the initiative for change throughout the process of political reform. Rengo's president Yamagishi barely held such an initiative at the very beginning of the reform. Nonetheless, he could not obtain consensus for his project not only from the JSP but also from his conservative colleagues within the Rengo. His project, thus, went in a different direction from his own original social democratic ideas. In fact, unions themselves had internal conflicts. Social democracy-oriented leaders were defeated by realistic centrist union leaders, who were simultaneously seeking alliances with capitalists and conservative parties with regard to the prospects for the forthcoming political economic regime. The Japanese game was literally multilayered in nature.

What characterized Japanese regime transition was the absence of new ideas and of a center-left leadership capable of restricting each candidate's pursuit of short-term rationality by directing them toward the long-term rationality of party organization. The gradually growing rate of abstention and the increasing number of voters who did not have any party identification indirectly supported this fact.

The course of Japanese politics since 1992 was turbulent. In May 1992, the Nihon Shinto (Japan New Party) was created. With the Lower House election of 1993, the 38-year history of the LDP's one-party control of government came to an end, and the LDP split. The Shinseito (Japan Renewal Party) and the Shinto Sakigake (New Party Harbinger) were formed and created the Hosokawa anti-LDP coalition government. In June 1994, however, the situation was reversed and the Murayama government was established by the JSP (Japan Socialist Party), the LDP, and the Sakigake. In January 1996, the three-party coalition government was transferred to the hands of the liberal democratic Prime Minister Hashimoto Ryutaro. Meanwhile, the Shinseito, the Komeito (Clean Government Party), the DSP (Democratic Socialist Party), and the Nihon Shinto merged to create the Shinshinto (New Frontier Party) in 1994. Throughout this series of events, the JSP was self-destructing. It devolved from the primary party in the Hosokawa anti-LDP government to merely a minor party supplementing conservative forces under the Hashimoto LDP-led coalition government. Owing to the breakdown of the Cold War structure, the relationship between the economic growth-oriented LDP and the egalitarian JSP turned into a symbolic one (Hayano 1996: 14).

The strategic failure of the conservative "reformists" coming from the very core of the old regime to nullify the socialists within the anti-LDP government helped the status quo seekers of the old regime recover hegemony in the party system. Meanwhile the center-left forces devoted themselves to satisfying their short-term interests without seeking long-term rationality based on new ideas. The status quo seekers' success in recapturing the legitimacy of the conservative ideology was brought about by the lack of ideological redefinition, or long-term rationality, on the part of center-left forces.

The JSP's devastating electoral retreat and subsequent demise due to the process of Japan's political restructuring and realignment can be explained by several factors. Among them, the lack of leadership and the lack of an in-party system to support the leaders were particularly significant. In order to hold the initiative in a process of drastic political changes, the JSP needed to have promoted its own reorganization along with the macro reform of Japanese politics. The generational renovation within the party, the development of young new leaders, the presentation of new ideas reflecting the socioeconomic changes in the post-industrial transformation – the JSP was not able to satisfy these preconditions to survive. Moreover, the conservatization of the labor unions during the political reshuffling in response to the economic restructuring championed by the business leaders was a decisive factor in the decline of the JSP.

In fact, the former socialist unions' pattern of support drastically changed from those in the previous election. The LDP's officially approved candidates who were supported by the Jichiro, the Zendentsu, the Denkirengo and the Zentei reached no less than 60 candidates in the 1996 election. The unions' electoral policies became extremely fluid. For the LDP, unions' backing could increase their votes in majoritarian districts. Moreover, the LDP expected the unions, which had ties to both the SDP and the LDP, to function as a bonding agent in the government consultation after the election. The LDP calculated that the unions "at least were able to prevent the Democratic Party from allying with the *Shinshinto* for office," and the LDP also aimed at becoming an "urban party which spoke to salaried men directly, not through their managers."[15]

The managers' attitudes to the election also contained something particular. The Keidanren (Federation of Economic Organizations) on October 16 sent to its 1,200 member corporations and organizations letters from the chair, Toyota Shoichiro, seeking their votes. According to Mr. Toyota, the coming election was extremely important for determining the policies of business in the twenty-first century, including the reforms of administrative structures, public finance, and tax reform. He claimed that each individual manager and executive must actively participate in order to avoid a low turnout that could weaken the meaning of each party's official electoral promises.[16] The appeal of the Keidanren for its members' votes was very exceptional, but the Keizai Doyu Kai (Japan Committee for Economic Development) also made the same kind of appeal. Such behavior by Japanese managers clearly showed their strong concern and misgivings over how the politico-economic regime would evolve after the election.

The October 20 election, which was conducted in 300 majoritarian districts and 11 PR blocks, recorded the worst voter turnout in history: 59.6 percent. This turnout, which was 8 percent worse than the record of 67.2 percent of the 1993 election carried out under the old electoral system, provoked many political commentators to warn of a crisis in parliamentary democracy. The numbers of seats obtained by each party were the LDP's 239, the Shinshinto's 156, the Democratic Party's 52, the JCP's 26, the SDP's 15, the Sakigake's 2, others and the independents 10, totaling 500 seats. The LDP gained more seats than it had before the election, although the number of seats did not reach the majority of 251. The Shinshinto finished far behind the LDP. The SDP, which had been an important actor in the 1955 regime, ended its historical role and was demoted to a minor party.[17]

It was ironic enough that, just as the Italian founding elections of 1994 indicated, in Japan too, forces which had been promoting electoral reforms retreated and those who had opposed such reforms like the LDP won the election. This was the election which extinguished the Socialist Party. The Socialist Party, once the protagonist of postwar Japanese politics, changed its party name and finally slid down the rankings to even below the JCP.

Since the SDP split on the eve of the election, the former socialist candidates were divided into three parties, the SDP, the Democratic Party, and the New Socialist Party. Although the ex-Sohyo member unions such as the Jichiro worked out an electoral policy to back the Democratic Party, the local unions' reactions were inconsistent. The Socialist Party–Sohyo bloc, which had countered the LDP under the 1955 regime, completely broke down. Although the former socialist unions felt relieved to hear that the Democratic Party retained its original seats, most candidates who directly represented the unions lost the election.[18]

Conclusion

The nature of unions and political parties' relationships with them strongly influenced political changes. In Japan, where social democratic union leaders were defeated by centrist union leaders, unions abandoned the JSP and switched their support from the JSP to a new centrist party called the Democratic Party. Being heavily dependent on unions, and without any powerful party machine, the JSP disappeared. Consequently, Japanese politics turned toward the American brand of electoral politics, in which conservatives and centrists confront each other. In the Italian case, the PCI/PDS was not so dependent on allied unions as the JSP was. Unions provided significant support to the transformation of the PCI/PDS. Parties and unions maintained interdependent relationships throughout the process of political change.

In the 1996 elections the PDS successfully established a center-left coalition and took office as the primary party for the first time in Italian history. To the contrary, the JSP broke down after participating in the LDP-led coalition government. These contrasting results were brought about by the difference between the Italian and Japanese capitalisms, and leftist leaders' ability to politicize new ideas and by the strength of constraints coming from unions' vetoes.

The Italian center-left leaders were relatively successful in creating new ideas, and on this basis they could develop coalition strategies rationally. (Yet it is obvious that the grand project of European economic and monetary unification favored the Italian left in presenting new social visions compared to those of the right.) In Japan, political restructuring and electoral reform started before the leftist leaders attempted to create new ideas. It was all individual politicians could do to seek their own short-term rationality and self-interests, e.g., continuously depending on particular interest groups such as unions and industries, and thus these parties' organizational long-term rationality was lost.

In the countries where social democracy has produced good economic performances, there is a great deal of uncertainty concerning how to establish post-social democratic values. In Italy and Japan, however, where there was little social democratic practice, two contrasting political forms emerged. In Italy, the PCI successfully transformed itself into a governing party by presenting new ideas which can be shared cross-sectorally and by building broadly based center-left coalitions. In Japan, the JSP was not able to survive despite a devastating loss of credibility on the part of the LDP after the scandals. It disappeared from political scene without playing an important role of a reformer. The success of the Italian left and the failure of the Japanese left – these contrasting results of two countries whose environments and institutional backgrounds have many similarities indicate that external factors alone are not able to predict political outcomes. Varieties of capitalism, i.e., whether market structures are hierarchical or pluralist, whether managers are organized rigidly or loosely, whether the role of the bureaucracy is directive or moderate, produced divergent results in Italy and Japan. At the same time, political leaders' ability to develop strong strategies in order to survive the internal and inter-party competitions becomes significant under rapidly changing conditions. Their competence in presenting new political agendas and in politicizing them despite structural constraints coming from both allied unions' and business elite's vetoes is imperative in order to secure the broad-based support of voters (Therborn 1991: 118).

Parties on the verge of collapse take part in a very uncertain game, because the game's results are unknown. Yet some actors positively participate in this game while others do so reluctantly (or are forced to participate). The former joins this game, calculating that the entry into this democratic game can increase its own interests. The Japanese political economic transition in the 1990s demonstrates one typical pattern of the strong hegemony of the capitalists. The unions, in a defensive posture, sided with the capitalists and became conservative. This, in turn, caused the JSP – the largest leftist party in Japan – to vanish from the political scene. The Italian case provides another pattern of the class compromise between the traditional unions and the post-industrial capitalists. Beside this compromise, the leftist parties are trying to establish a new social alliance between traditional actors and new actors.

Notes

1 The Italian word consociativismo is different from the English word consociationalism.
2 In this chapter I use Sartori's categorization of Japan's old electoral system, i.e., semi-PR, which places Japan in a comparative, general framework (Sartori 1994). Many political scientists call Japan's old electoral system (1947–1993) the SNTV (single non-transferable vote). Although the SNTV explains why one party can maintain office for a considerably long period (Cox 1997), it does not explain why that was the LDP. Some Japanese politics specialists attribute the success of the LDP and/or the long decline of the JSP to a single factor, namely the SNTV, without fully examining ideological dimensions of party politics. They fail to account for the conditions under which such an electoral system was created and maintained, often without recognizing that the SNTV itself was a product of earlier actions taken by parties and party leaders that again reflected the balance of power among them.
3 The Italian electoral system changed again to be a more proportional one in 2006.
4 For the argument stressing that the legitimacy of a regime is based on the interests, see Przeworski (1986).
5 Pontusson (1992). Yet some argue that the Scandinavian unions have maintained universalistic stances even in the phases of economic downturn. See Pierson (2000).
6 For a different view, see Pierson (1996). Yet Pierson's argument is only based on the American and British cases in which unions are not so influential compared with Scandinavian and Continental European countries.
7 For the notion of partial regime, see Schmitter (1992 and 1995).
8 For an argument focusing on actors' interplay and contingent outcomes, see Przeworski (1991).
9 See, for instance, Adornato (1993); Bobbio (1994); Bosetti (1993); D'Arcais (1994); Martinelli and Salvati (1993); Paci (1993); Salvati (1992).
10 Author's interview with Mr. Bruno Trentin, at the CGIL, Rome, June 21, 1994.
11 *L'Espresso*, April 15, 1994, 54.
12 Author's personal interview with Prof. Roberto D'Alimonte at his office of the University of Florence, April 22, 1996.
13 Ibid.
14 *Nihon keizai shinbun*, July 24, 1995, evening.
15 *Asahi shinbun*, October 17, 1996, "Shiji ryudo-ka o shimesu."
16 *Asahi shinbun*, October 17, 1996, "Keidanren kaicho mo tohyo yobikake."
17 *Asahi shinbun*, October 21, 1996, "Jimin fukucho, shusho keito e."
18 *Asahi shinbun*, October 21, 1996, "Kyu-Shato kei no roso wa ando."

References

Adornato, F. (1993). *Oltre la sinistra*, Milano: Rizzoli.
Aldrich, J. H. (1995). *Why Parties? The Origin and Transformation of Political Parties in America*, Chicago: University of Chicago Press.
Bobbio, N. (1994). *Destra e sinistra: ragioni e significanti di una distinzione politica*, Rome: Donzelli.
Boix, C. (1998). *Political Parties, Growth and Equality: Conservative and Social Democratic Economic Strategies in the World Economy*, New York: Cambridge University Press.
Boix, C. (1999). "Setting the Rules of the Game: The Choice of Electoral Systems in Advanced Democracies," *American Political Science Review*, 93(3): 609–624.
Bosetti, G. (1993). "Introduzione: La crisi e significati di una distruzione politica," in Giancarlo Bosetti (ed.), *Sinistra punto zero*, Rome: Donzelli editore.

Bull, M. and M. Rhodes (1997). "Between Crisis and Transition: Italian Politics in the 1990s," in M. Bull and M. Rhodes (eds.), *Crisis and Transition in Italian Politics*, London: Frank Cass, 1–13.

Collier, R. B. and D. Collier (1991). *Shaping the Political Arena: Critical Junctures, the Labor Movement, and Regime Dynamics in Latin America*, Princeton: Princeton University Press.

Cox, G. (1997). *Making Votes Count: Strategic Coordination in the World's Electoral Systems*, Cambridge: Cambridge University Press.

D'Alema, M. (1996). *Progettare il futuro*, edited by G. Cuperlo and C. Velardi, Milan: Bompiani.

D'Arcais, P. F. (1994). *Il disincanto tradito*, Torino: Bollati Boringhieri editore.

D'Arcais, P. F. (1996). *Il populismo italiano: da Craxi a Berlusconi*, Rome: Donzelli editore.

Di Virgilio, A. (1994). "Dai partiti ai poli. La politica delle alleanze," *Rivista italiana di scienza politica*, 3: 493–547.

Downs, A. (1957). *An Economic Theory of Democracy*, New York: Harper & Row.

Esping-Andersen, G. (1985). *Politics against Markets: The Social Democratic Road to Power*, Princeton: Princeton University Press.

Geddes, B. (1991). "A Game Theoretic Model of Reform in Latin America," *American Political Science Review*, 85(2): 371–392.

Geddes, B. (1994). *Politician's Dilemma: Building State Capacity in Latin America*, Berkeley: University of California Press.

Hayano, T. (1996). "Fukai yami o saku no wa dare ka: Eden no sono o deta Nihon seiji," *Ronza*, March.

Hellman, S. (1986). "The Italian Communist Party between Berlinguer and the Seventeenth Congress," in *Italian Politics: A Review*, vol. 1, London: Frances Pinter, 47–68.

Hellman, S. (1993). "Italy," in M. Kesselman and J. Krieger (eds.), *European Politics in Transition*, Washington, DC: Heath.

Hiwatari, N. (1995). "55nen seito sei henyo no sei-kan kankei," in Japanese Political Science Association (ed.), *Nenpo Seijigaku: Gendai nihon sei-kan kankei no keisei katei*, Tokyo: Iwanami Shoten, 77–105.

Igarashi, J. (1994). "Hosokawa renritsu seiken to Shakaito," *Ohara shakai mondai kenkyujo zasshi*, 428: 46–62.

Koelble, T. A. (1991). *The Left Unraveled: Social Democracy and the New Left Challenge*, Durham, NC: Duke University Press.

Lanzalaco, L. (1998). "Le associazioni imprenditoriali," in G. P. Cella and T. Treu (eds.), *Le nuove relazioni industriali*, Bologna: Il Mulino.

Magara, H. (1999). "Anti-System Parties and Decay of the State: Protracted Democratic Consolidation in Italy and Japan," paper presented at the annual meeting of the American Political Science Association, September 2–5, Atlanta, USA.

Manin, B., A. Przeworski, and S. Stokes (1999). "Introduction," in A. Przeworski, S. Stokes, and B. Manin (eds.), *Democracy, Accountability, and Representation*, New York: Cambridge University Press, 1–26.

Martinelli, A. and M. Salvati (1993). "What is Left: La sinistra disincantata," *Il Mulino*, 346: 227–235.

Offe, C. (1996). "Political Economy: Sociological Perspective," in R. E. Goodin and Hans-Dieter Klingemann (eds.), *A New Handbook of Political Science*, Oxford: Oxford University Press, 675–690.

Paci, M. (ed.) (1993). *Le dimensioni della disuguaglianza: Rapporto della Fondazione Cespe sulla disuguaglianza sociale in Italia*, Bologna: Il Mulino.

Panebianco, A. (1988). *Political Parties: Organization and Power*, Cambridge: Cambridge University Press.

Partito Democratico della Sinistra (1994). *Programma di Governo del PDS: Per ricostruire un'Italia più giusta, più unita, più moderna*, Rome: L'Unità.

Pempel, T. J. (1998). *Regime Shift: Comparative Dynamics of the Japanese Political Economy*, Ithaca: Cornell University Press.

Pierson, P. (1996). "The New Politics of Welfare State," *World Politics*, 48: 143–179.

Pierson, P. (2000). "Coping with Permanent Austerity: Welfare State Restructuring in Affluent Democracies," in P. Pierson (ed.), *The New Politics of the Welfare State*, Oxford: Oxford University Press, 369–406.

Piven, F. F. (1991). "The Decline of Labor Parties: An Overview," in F. F. Piven (ed.), *Labor Parties in Postindustrial Societies*, Cambridge: Polity, 1–19.

Pizzorno, A. (1977). "Scambio politico e identità collettiva nel conflitto di classe," in C. Crouch and A. Pizzorno (eds.), *Conflitto in Europa: Lotta di classe, sindacati e stato dopo il '68*, Milan: Etas Libri, 407–433.

Pontusson, J. (1992). *The Limits of Social Democracy: Investment Politics in Sweden*, Ithaca: Cornell University Press.

Przeworski, A. (1985). *Capitalism and Social Democracy*, Cambridge: Cambridge University Press.

Przeworski, A. (1986). "Some Problems in the Study of the Transition to Democracy," in G. O'Donnell, P. Schmitter, and L. Whitehead (eds.), *Transitions from Authoritarian Rule: Comparative Perspectives*, Baltimore: Johns Hopkins University Press, 47–63.

Przeworski, A. (1991). *Democracy and the Market: Political and Economic Reforms in Eastern Europe and Latin America*, Cambridge: Cambridge University Press.

Przeworski, A., S. Stokes, and B. Manin (eds.) (1999). *Democracy, Accountability, and Representation*, New York: Cambridge University Press.

Rosenbluth, F. M. (1996). "Internationalization and Electoral Politics in Japan," in R. O. Keohane and H. V. Milner (eds.), *Internationalization and Domenstic Politics*, New York: Cambridge University Press, 138–155.

Salvati, M. (1992). "Eguaglianza ed efficienza," in AA.VV. *Le idee della sinistra*, Rome: Editori Riuniti.

Salvati, M. (1995). "The Crisis of Government in Italy," *New Left Review*, 213: 76–95.

Sartori, G. (1994). *Comparative Constitutional Engineering: An Inquiry into Structures, Incentives and Outcomes*, London: Macmillan.

Sassoon, D. (1981). *The Strategy of the Italian Communist Party*, New York: St. Martin's Press.

Schmitter, P. C. (1992). "The Consolidation of Democracy and Representation of Social Groups," *American Behavioral Scientist*, 35(4/5): 422–449.

Schmitter, P. C. (1995). "The Consolidation of Political Democracies," in G. Pridham (ed.), *Transitions to Democracy*, London: Routledge, 535–570.

Shalev, M. (1983). "The Social Democratic Model and Beyond: Two 'Generations' of Comparative Research on the Welfare State," *Comparative Social Research*, 6: 315–351.

Shefter, M. (1994). *Political Parties and the State: The American Historical Experience*, Princeton: Princeton University Press.

Shiihashi, K. (1989). "Kore ga Shakaito da," in M. Takabatake (ed.), *Shakaito: Mannen yato kara nukedaseru ka*, Tokyo: Iwanami Shoten, 43–103.

Swenson, P. (1991). "Bringing Capital Back In, or Social Democracy Reconsidered: Employer Power, Cross-Class Alliances, and Centralization of Industrial Relations in Denmark and Sweden," *World Politics*, 43(4): 513–544.

Takabatake, M. (1989). "Shakaito wa ima nani o nasu bekika," in M. Takabatake (ed.), *Shakaito: Mannen yato kara nukedaseru ka*, Tokyo: Iwanami Shoten, 107–152.

Therborn, G. (1991). "Swedish Social Democracy and the Transition from Industrial to Postindustrial Politics," in F. F. Piven (ed.), *Labor Parties in Postindustrial Societies*, Cambridge: Polity Press.

Trentin, B. (1994). *Lavoro e libertà*, Rome: Donzelli.

Tsebelis, G. (1990). *Nested Games: Rational Choice in Comparative Politics*, Berkeley: University of California Press.

Vassallo, S. (1995). "La politica della coalizioni. Da un sistema partitico all'altro," in G. Pasquino (ed.), *L'Alternanza inattesa. Le elezioni del 27 marzo 1994 e le loro conseguenze*, Messina: Rubbettino editore, 49–97.

Watanabe, O. (1994). *Seiji kaikaku to kenpo kaisei: Nakasone Yasuhiro kara Ozawa Ichiro e*, Tokyo: Aoki Shoten.

Weiberg, L. (1995). *The Transformation of Italian Communism*, New Brunswick: Transaction Publishers.

Part III

Emergence of new VoC in new and non-democracies

8 A macro-historical analysis

Globalization, party-state, and capital in China's emergent capitalism

Christopher A. McNally

The case of China: theoretical pointers

The development of a capitalist political economy has in most cases preceded a democratic transition. This implies that capitalism is historically prior to the development of a democratic polity. There are some exceptions to this rule, such as Switzerland and Israel, but in most cases this temporal relationship holds true. In keeping with the insights of Philippe Schmitter and Arpad Todor in Chapter 2 of this volume, we can therefore infer that the form capitalist development takes influences the structure of social interest alignments, and, in turn, the shape that democratic governance takes. Put differently, Varieties of Capitalism (VoC) could be causally related to certain types of party systems and organizations, at least in the initial phases of a democratic transition. After all, capitalist development generates social interest alignments that shape the timing, nature, and dynamics of future political evolution.

Theoretical inquiries along these lines have generated two important strands of literature in comparative politics. The first ties certain initial conditions of industrialization, such as an economy's degree of backwardness, social structure, or global environment, to the institutional configurations and social interest alignments that shape a VoC. This literature encompasses pioneers such as Gerschenkron (1962) and Shonfield (1965), as well as the contemporary literature on VoC (cf. Hall and Soskice 2001). The concern here is how historical conditions facing capitalist developers can generate alternate institutional arrangements over time and space.

The second literature emphasizes how institutional configurations and social interest alignments can influence trajectories of democratization. These often structural analyses agree that capitalist development gives rise to new social classes that struggle for political change to serve their chiefly material interests. Alliances driving capital accumulation therefore can influence the type of democracy that emerges. Classic works include Schumpeter (1950) and Moore (1966). More current efforts in comparative politics follow in the footsteps of these scholars to probe the relationship between capitalist development, social interest alignments, and democracy (cf. Cusack *et al.* 2007).

This volume seeks to link these two strands of literature. Its focus rests on exploring the interrelationships between changes in VoC and party systems as globalization impinges on both. Evidently, the manner in which a country sets up institutions to effectively compete in the global capitalist system is likely to influence the nature of its political regime.

In this regard, Gerschenkron's (1962) classic investigation is pertinent. His central insight rests on how the timing of a political economy's entry into the global capitalist system directly influences the institutional arrangements shaping its capitalism. "Late developers," such as Germany, Japan, Italy, and Russia in the late nineteenth century, faced fierce market competition from established enterprise institutions in more advanced economies. They had to catch up and undergo a rapid process of industrialization. As a result, their institutional arrangements supporting capital accumulation were quite different from earlier developers. The role of the state was magnified and state coordination much more closely linked to finance and industry. These institutional arrangements, in turn, shaped different social interest alignments; in particular, as Barrington Moore Jr. (1966) noted, a close alliance between state and capital laid the foundation for the fascist regimes that emerged in Italy, Germany, and Japan.

The causality linking institutional arrangements supporting capital accumulation to subsequent political developments, however, is not straightforward. As Wolfgang Streeck argues regarding Japan and Germany, there is a certain autonomy of political events:

> Total mobilization before and in war, and the need to rebuild the nation after total defeat, offered states and politics opportunities to reassert their primacy over economy and society and make decisions that were determinative of future events for a long time to come.
>
> (Streeck 2001: 35)

As a result, the "gradual formation in the 1950s and 1960s of the German and Japanese 'models' can be best conceived as a process of successful institutional hybridization" (Streeck 2001: 33).

Undoubtedly, there is a degree of path dependency in how institutional arrangements in the economy influence political interest alignments; yet, there is no definitive link between the institutional legacy of capitalist development and the type of democracy that emerges. "Critical junctures," crises, wars, foreign occupation or influence, and unintended consequences arising from earlier institutional choices can all shape the form party organizations and systems take.

Consequently, this chapter does not attempt to use the People's Republic of China's (PRC) incipient capitalist institutions to predict that country's political future. Leadership choices and more generally the degree of autonomy that the politics of China's one-party system still possess could influence future political trends. Despite these caveats, contemporary China can be used as a rare opportunity to, in a quasi-experimental fashion, trace the evolution of a form of capitalism under conditions of intense globalization.

I argue here that China may be best viewed as a late developer with a "competitive state coordinated economy."[1] Mirroring Eva Bellin's (2000) arguments on how late development under a state-guided economy may undermine public pressures for democracy, I argue that in China both the capitalist class and labor are relatively weak. Capitalists, the budding bourgeoisie, depend on the state for finance, protection, and favorable regulation. They also are becoming politically embedded in the Chinese party-state. And as in other late developers, organized labor tends to be a small percentage of the labor force in China and dependent on the state for its privileged status relative to unorganized workers. Finally, large wealth gaps commonly found in late developers under globalized conditions prod bourgeois and small middle classes to fear giving the poor majority (farmers and unorganized workers) voting rights in a democratic regime.

It thus seems that the relationship between economic development and democracy is stronger in earlier developers than in later developers.[2] China is experiencing the rapid growth of a capitalist class, but these entrepreneurs depend in part on their close connections with the ruling regime for their prosperity and security. As a result of this situation, capitalists exhibit little enthusiasm for democracy, while organized labor is weak and materially dependent on the authoritarian state.

Following these insights, this chapter uses the case of China to explore how globalization affects the process of capitalist development and, with this, the reorganization of a political party's structure and policies vis-à-vis new and emerging social interests. For example, what are the possible translation mechanisms by which globalization influences capitalist institutions, social interest alignments, and the Chinese Communist Party's (CCP) policies and structure? Indeed, how is the CCP adjusting and adapting to socioeconomic change and class formation? How are the party and its political mechanisms of control changing?

While this chapter cannot conclusively answer these questions, I proceed by first examining the institutional arrangements characterizing China's emergent capitalism.[3] This leads to an analysis of the social interest alignments that China's capitalism is engendering. I then highlight the continued role that China's party-state performs in managing globalization, guiding capitalist development, and, ultimately, influencing China's political evolution. In the concluding remarks I elaborate on some of the implications of the Chinese case for the study of late capitalist development under globalization.

Institutional arrangements

Capitalism as a socioeconomic system is not cast in stone. In part, differences in institutional arrangements between advanced and developing economies can be traced back to at which point in world historical time an economy enters the global capitalist system. This is the central thesis of Alexander Gerschenkron's *Economic Backwardness in Historical Perspective*. He argues that "significant interspatial variations in the process of industrialization are functionally related to the degree of economic backwardness that prevailed in the countries concerned on the eve of their 'great spurts' of industrial growth" (Gerschenkron

1962: 1). Late developers invariably used already developed economies as their models, often copying a variety of institutional arrangements and technologies. Nonetheless, late developers, "by the very virtue of their backwardness, tend to differ fundamentally from that of an advanced country" (Gerschenkron 1962: 7).

First-comers such as Great Britain and the United States faced no established competitors and could therefore industrialize gradually with relatively slow technological advances and institutional change. Late developers that began industrialization in the late nineteenth century did not have this luxury. Firms in countries such as Germany, Japan, Italy, and Russia faced fierce market competition from established firms in more advanced economies. The result of this pressure was that they undertook a much more rapid process of industrialization. It also influenced the institutional solutions pursued to enable industrialization, "for which there was little or no counterpart in an established industrial country" (Gerschenkron 1962: 7).

Germany, for instance, built large-scale integrated firms within the span of only one decade that adopted technologies from earlier developers in cutting-edge industries like chemicals, steel, and electronics. To undertake such a growth spurt in capital-intensive branches of industry new institutional solutions were created, such as the universal bank and cartelization. These institutional solutions hinged on the greater role of the state in coordinating finance and industry. Moreover, state-led transformations in the late nineteenth century were not only limited to purely economic activities, but also included top-down reforms of educational institutions, bodies of law, and bureaucratic structures to support capitalist development. In other words, the role of the state was magnified considerably in late developers when compared to earlier instances of industrialization.

In some cases, the state even became the primary force driving industrialization. The Japanese state in the late 1870s invested directly to establish many large-scale enterprises in shipbuilding, steel, and mining. As the historian Peter Duus put it, at the outset of industrialization it was clear to Japanese leaders "that the government would have to play a major role in building a modern commercial and industrial economy." The result: "the government embarked on a policy of state capitalism" (Duus 1976: 84). However, as the economic crisis of the early 1880s hit, many of these state-sponsored firms were privatized. During the late 1920s and 1930s, the Soviet Union followed in the steps of its Tsarist predecessors and implemented a highly state-centric model of late development. However, an overemphasis on planning and state investment occurred at the expense of competition and dynamic capital accumulation. Despite considerable successes in establishing integrated industrial complexes, Soviet central planning ended as a failure (Kornai 1992).

Do these patterns of late development hold true for China? The perhaps most obvious manifestation of China as a late developer concerns the speed of China's capitalist development. Chinese economic growth, industrialization, and infrastructure development are outpacing that of earlier capitalist developers, even those in East Asia just a generation earlier. The speed of China's industrialization and continental infrastructure development thus follow closely the general patterns of late development. Gerschenkron's insights hold true in this respect. China's breathtaking process of industrialization is also occurring on a scale seldom witnessed before (McNally 2008b). As a continental-sized country, China is so far the only major civilization outside Europe and North America that has shown signs of a massive and potentially successful transformation into an advanced capitalist political economy.

China's size complicates somewhat direct comparisons to earlier capitalist developers. While most of the world's earlier developers were relatively homogenous economically, China encompasses considerable divergences in regional endowments, including disparities in access to global markets and capital. China's unique historical-geographical heritage also introduces a further layer of variation. Regional merchant cultures, for example, continue to influence contemporary economic arrangements on the local level. Nonetheless, patterns of late capitalist development hold true throughout the Chinese political economy.

Globalization

China's entry into the global capitalist system occurred during an era of intense globalization. This stands in contrast to the situations faced by the economies of Japan, South Korea, Taiwan, Hong Kong, and Singapore during the immediate postwar period. These late developers faced a fairly tightly managed system of economic exchanges and benefited as front line states in the Cold War from privileged access to US markets and technology. China, on the other hand, belongs to a more contemporary wave of industrialization in East Asia, a wave that roughly began in the 1980s during an intensified period of globalization.

Strengthening forces of globalization offered both opportunities and challenges for China and directly shaped policy. Compared to earlier developers in East Asia, China adopted more free-market principles (Ten Brink 2010; Lee *et al.* 2002). These principles include substantial access by foreign capital to China's manufacturing and retail sectors; the relatively rapid development of stock markets and intensive use of Hong Kong's internationalized capital markets to take large state firms public; and the fact that Chinese banks are not allowed to own shares in industrial firms. Finally, despite China's socialist legacy, concerted efforts have been made to increase labor market flexibility, especially the hiring and dismissal of employees.

China's opening to foreign direct investment is especially noteworthy. At the beginning, overseas Chinese capital played a crucial role, with more than 70 percent of all foreign investment in China coming from overseas Chinese sources between 1982 and 1994 (Hsing 1998: 147). Later, more globalized players used China's coastal areas as manufacturing platforms, servicing customers in advanced industrial societies – the "Wal-Mart Economy." China therefore has emerged as one of the world's leading traders with a highly internationalized export sector. Indeed, China's GDP to trade ratio at 72 percent is very high for a continental sized economy, and Chinese efforts at trade liberalization have been larger and proceeded quicker than those undertaken by earlier capitalist developers in Asia (Edmonds *et al.* 2008).

Put differently, the Chinese government has deliberately stirred China toward developing one of the highest "absorption capacities" for the forces of globalization among developing economies. Some of China's developmental policies, especially in terms of openness to foreign investment and trade, stand in marked contrast to East Asia's earlier developers. However, in other respects, Chinese policy has followed East Asia's earlier developers, especially Japan, Taiwan, and South Korea. Like these economies, China has used exchange rate controls to maintain an undervalued currency to foster export performance (Edmonds *et al.* 2008). More broadly, China's development policies, despite some liberal impulses, feature a substantial role for the state in directing development.

All in all, China would have faced enormous costs in seeking to insulate itself from globalization. As a result, Chinese policies have openly endorsed certain aspects of globalization, especially providing cheap labor and land with few regulatory strings attached to multinational manufacturing concerns. To some extent, China has been able to select those aspects of globalization beneficial to its development while excluding those aspects seen as dangerous to economic and political stability. China's size probably played a crucial role in allowing China to pick and choose. Globalization might have opened China to the world, but on Chinese terms.

China's size and increasing economic weight are also making the country a rapidly rising global player. This, in turn, gives China a substantial measure of international economic influence. Historically, late developers have had very little influence over how the global capitalist system functioned and thus had to adjust to its rules, institutions, and power relations. China's aggregate economic heft means that the country's political economy will have an impact on the global competitive landscape at an early developmental stage. In fact, the global system will be faced with an economy that contains considerable capacities, yet remains a developing state coordinated transition economy.

The state

The most pertinent insight of Gerschenkron's analysis is how the role of the state was magnified in late developers. The adaptation of new institutional solutions hinged on the capacity of states to coordinate or even directly manage "great spurts" of industrialization. In this respect, China has been no exception. It was undoubtedly the Chinese Communist Party (CCP) under Deng Xiaoping which ushered in capitalist development and mustered the political will to sustain disruptive developmental dynamics. The Chinese state also has played an enormously important role in guiding and directly managing economic development during the reform period. However, the magnified role of the Chinese state is not only due to the fact that China is a late developer – the Gerschenkronian thesis. China's state-coordinated economy must be traced back to China's historical heritage, especially the socialist period that immediately preceded China's capitalist development.

Since its founding in 1949, the PRC attempted to establish a command economic system modeled after the Soviet Union. This system never functioned as well as in the Soviet and Eastern European instances. China's command economy operated with a considerably lower degree of centralization and was permeated by a jumble of authority relations. As Barry Naughton (1995: 51) remarks, "Planners gave commands to the system, but what actually emerged bore little resemblance to those commands."

This weakness in the planning apparatus facilitated moves toward a market-based system of resource allocation. Equally important, authority over a majority of state firms had devolved to provincial and sub-provincial governments, which allowed various local experiments to take off once the party leadership gave the green light. This occurred when Deng Xiaoping in 1978 de-emphasized ideological correctness and political education to focus on economic growth as the principal means to ensure the CCP's legitimacy.

Deng's reforms strengthened and legitimized already existing autonomies on the local level, giving local cadres political space for economic experimentation. Reforms also created incentives for cadres to improve local economic performance. This occurred via the CCP's *nomenklatura* system – the system that is responsible for party personnel appointments. Rather than emphasizing ideological correctness ("being red"), the maintenance of social stability and local economic performance emerged as the principal yardsticks by which the performance of local cadres was evaluated (Huang 1996; Edin 2003). Finally, local governments received decreasing amounts of financial support from higher levels, forcing them to look for new sources of revenue.

The combination of these measures, especially the Leninist incentives focused on improving economic performance, incentivized local governments to compete vigorously for investment capital. Intense inter-jurisdictional competition emerged as local cadres circumvented central rules restricting market transactions, foreign investment, and local capital accumulation. With this inter-jurisdictional competition cycles of induced reforms unfolded, since each small step at liberalization created pressures for further liberalization (Naughton 1992, 1995; Solinger 1989).

However, despite the gradual liberalization of China's economy and increased private capital accumulation, the Chinese party-state continues to retain control over the commanding heights of the economy via large state firms. State firms and state research institutes dominate the state's direct developmental interventions, undertaking projects fraught with risks or long repayment horizons (Nolan 2001). In addition, an ambitious effort at state enterprise reform starting in the mid-1990s under the policy of *zhuada fangxiao* ("To grasp the big and let go of the small") created a much more profitable state sector. Under this policy most small- and medium-sized state firms have been privatized. Large state enterprises, on the other hand, have undergone corporate restructuring and state ownership diversification under continued state control. As a result, the Chinese state sector is populated by very large enterprises that in 2007 produced profits of about 6.2 percent of GDP, an astounding number (Naughton 2008: 19)!

Evidently, the state sector continues to loom large over the Chinese political economy. While state firms retreated from the most competitive and least profitable sectors, they have kept a tight grip on a wide range of critical industries. These include upstream extraction of natural resources (e.g., oil, gas, and mining), production of basic materials (e.g., non-ferrous metals, steel, and petrochemicals), and essential network industries in telecommunications, transportation, and utilities. In 2006, state-controlled firms made up only 8 percent of all industrial firms, but produced 36 percent of industrial value added and 44 percent of industrial profits (Wildau 2008: 27). The state also controls all major banking and financial institutions in China and, after several waves of bureaucratic reforms, possesses an administrative structure much more amenable to regulating a developing and globalizing market economy (Zheng 2004; Yang 2004).

By and large, Gerschenkron's insights on the magnified role of the state in late developers holds quite true for China. Nonetheless, China's state can hardly be conceived of as following in the footsteps of the "developmental states" present during Japan's, South Korea's, and Taiwan's high growth phases (Johnson 1982; Amsden 1989; Evans 1992). These developmental states are conceived to have perfected market-conforming methods of state intervention in the economy. This image hardly holds up in the face of Chinese reality. Intense rivalries among the Chinese state's agencies and jurisdictional levels put considerable implementation constraints on indicative planning and market-conforming state interventions. In fact, overlapping and incongruous features have created a complex "polymorphous" state apparatus in China (Howell 2006). This is expressed by the manifold local government interventions that run counter to central policies and general market norms.

To sum up, top-down Leninist incentives conveyed via the party-state, the control of the commanding heights via state firms, and the substantial regulatory purview of local and central state formations have all played crucial roles in guiding China's capitalist transformation. Combined with private capital accumulation and the development of a relatively internationalized economy, China's VoC thus seems to fit the image of a state coordinated economy. Yet, any conceptualization of China's emergent capitalism must draw attention to the very unique duality of its institutional arrangements.

The unique duality of China's emergent capitalism

Although China resembles a state coordinated economy, there are certain twists. While state intervention has played a key role in China's capitalist transition, industrial policy implementation has been frustrated by the complex and polymorphous nature of China's state apparatus. China thus might best be conceived of as a competitive state coordinated economy, where multiple agencies and levels compete to create a relatively competitive market economy with diffuse state guidance. Indeed, the Chinese political economy contains a distinct duality: the state controls finance and the commanding heights of industry while most competitive sectors in retail and manufacturing are populated by private (both foreign and domestic) or hybrid ownership firms. The Chinese state's continued dominance over crucial aspects of the economy is therefore tempered by the dynamism of China's entrepreneurial producers. Successful institutional hybridization has allowed these two dissimilar types of capital accumulation to coexist and feed on each other.

Put differently, top-down China's capitalist development is, indeed, driven by state guidance and state firms. But bottom-up it is powered by a myriad of often small- and medium-scale capitalist ventures. This entrepreneurial sector benefited from a particular set of social institutions that happened to exist in China and which were employed in the process of capitalist accumulation. Specifically, *guanxi* practices – the establishment of long-term informal reciprocal personal relationships that create enduring trust – have allowed budding entrepreneurs to link up with state officials, creating personal ties that are both instrumental and affective (McNally 2011). In addition to *guanxi* practices, private entrepreneurs also used family connections and hybrid forms of ownership to access finance, overcome government indifference, and compensate for institutional uncertainty (International Financial Corporation 2000: 20–34; Wank 1999).

There are deep historical reasons for why China's emergent capitalism is developing this way. The combination of vibrant entrepreneurship and a dominant state bears a certain resemblance to the political economies of the Song to late Qing dynasties. In this imperial era, government had stifled high finance and reinforced a reliance on personalized ties to undertake business dealings (Faure 2006; Gates 1996). Rather than the sanctity of contracts and the rule of law, "ritual and patronage had a strong place in Chinese business institutions" (Faure 2006: 5). State officials viewed impersonal business dealings that could lead to the amassing of large fortunes as a potential threat to state dominance. A preference for interpersonal accommodation undermined China's attempts to develop well-functioning bureaucracies with formalized and universally applicable rules (Mann 1987; Boisot and Child 1996).

As a result, the late imperial era was characterized by the dominance of a state-managed tributary system overseeing a system of commodity production by kin corporations (Gates 1996: 7). Although these two modes of production displayed a tendency to grow more sophisticated and complex over the course of history, the duality of a state dominant mode juxtaposed with small-scale family-based production units remained intact. The scholar officialdom that ruled the imperial state harnessed both capital and markets for its own purposes – the maintenance of ritual order.

While China's political economy differs in many respects from the late imperial period, the PRC might be slipping back into this pre-communist history of capitalist accumulation harnessed for state purposes. As then, the state-dominant and private entrepreneurial modes of capital accumulation are quite unlike. One relies on oligopolistic competition with enormous support from state agencies, especially in terms of financing; the other depends on the savvy of individual entrepreneurs exposed to market pressures with little state aid. Nevertheless, these two modes meet at the lower levels of the state-administrative apparatus, where local cadres have played a crucial role in accommodating entrepreneurial capitalist practices. Many of China's private entrepreneurs, especially those in charge of bigger private firms, also are becoming embedded in the local party-state (McNally and Wright 2010; Dickson 2008).

Put together, the use of informal *guanxi* practices has allowed China's private sector to move from an object of state discrimination to forging a symbiosis with various individuals and agencies situated within the party-state. This has changed the relative powers of state and capital over time: the power of the private sector has continuously improved and put it in a stronger position to negotiate with local governments. Nonetheless, continued CCP rule and the existence of the state dominant mode of economic governance encourage a degree of ambiguity and decentralization in business dealings (McNally 2011). Market, legal, and regulatory rules are only partially institutionalized, while state officials wield considerable leeway to intervene in private firms and markets. China's party-state is therefore not a "constitutional state." High degrees of institutional predictability and certainty for large-scale business dealings among private parties remain a work in progress.

All told, China resembles a competitive state coordinated economy with various levels, agencies, and interests competing. China's historical legacy, size, and exposure to the forces of globalization, however, have given rise to unique institutional arrangements. As elaborated, China's emergent political economy is characterized by a distinct duality: state-led capitalism in which the state owns and guides the commanding heights of the economy stands in contrast to vibrant networks of entrepreneurial capitalist producers.

This duality is further reflected in how China has harnessed globalization. Strong incentives for local governments to attract international capital have created industrial parks that are tailored to the needs of multinational corporations. These parks are segregated from the domestic economy at large and provide excellent hard and soft infrastructures. In the process, economic spaces that are divorced from China's domestic economy but highly integrated into global production networks have been created.

Interest alignments

Causality in the social sciences is inherently spurious. Using a political economy argument to highlight the congruencies between China's distinct form of capitalism and emerging social interest alignments is thus open to interpretation. Nonetheless, I argue that institutional arrangements – the duality of a state dominant mode juxtaposed with vibrant capitalist producers and globalization pressures – are echoed in the shape that China's class structure is taking. In fact, as China has become more affluent it also has become a more deeply divided society.

This is expressed by statistical indicators for inequality. Official data from 2007 by the United Nations indicate that China's Gini coefficient is 0.469, placing China among countries with the widest wealth gap in the world. No advanced industrial economy has a bigger rich–poor gap than China. The United States, well known for having considerable inequality, has a coefficient of 0.408. Several Latin American countries are more unequal than China, with Brazil at 0.570 and Chile at 0.549. Besides Latin America, countries with a rich–poor gap that is worse than China's are among the poorest in the world, mainly in Africa (UNDP 2008).

China's Gini coefficient indicates a highly stratified class structure. This is even more significant in view of the fact that China was considered at the outset of reforms in 1978 to have one of the most even distributions of wealth in the world (albeit at very low levels of wealth). Although space considerations do not allow for a full analysis of the shape of China's stratified class structure, I briefly lay out its main contours.[4] In terms of wealth, a narrow upper and middle class includes owners of medium and large private enterprises, managers in both foreign and private domestic enterprises, family members of the state elite, and various types of professionals, such as lawyers, accountants, and engineers.

These upper strata generally have strong incentives to perpetuate the political status quo. Due to China's polarized social structure, the wealthy minority tends to fear the political empowerment of the poor, which could threaten their economic privileges. Bruce Dickson's (2003, 2008) work further highlights how private entrepreneurs and college-educated urban residents do not seek to distance themselves from the party-state. Rather, they view the regime as a flexible and relatively open collection of organizations and institutions wherein individuals and social groups can expect to find some genuine representation of their interests. This implies that so far the CCP has successfully incorporated individuals and groups that are primarily concerned with economic matters.

In addition, many in China's upper strata have garnered their wealth via their embeddedness and *guanxi* with the ruling party-state. First of all, many private entrepreneurs in charge of large firms are party members. Official surveys indicate that roughly one third of all private business people are party members, with the percentage among the bosses of large private firms even higher (*Xinhua* 2005). Another segment of entrepreneurs are directly related to top party members via family ties, especially the growing group of "princelings" in Chinese finance and industry. Therefore, most private entrepreneurs in charge of large firms are somehow affiliated with the CCP, giving them direct access to political power brokers.

Similar to entrepreneurs, many urban professionals also have sought to embed themselves in the party-state. This is even the case for professionals, such as lawyers, who would be expected to have pro-liberal and anti-CCP tendencies. However, in a legal system that continues to be dominated by the party-state, Chinese lawyers must build *guanxi* with the political establishment to give them access to information and relative immunity from harassment. Only in this manner can they successfully represent their clients. As Ethan Michelson notes, those who succeed are "precisely the lawyers most folded into the state and the party" (Michelson 2007: 401).

The embeddedness of the wealthy in the party-state might suggest that the bottom strata of Chinese society are less inclined to support the CCP. However, this is generally not the case. The bottom of China's class structure is composed of rank and file state and private sector workers, self-employed small-scale entrepreneurs, migrant workers, and farmers. These groups tend to have many grievances, but they still support "socialist" economic ideals, something the CCP has nimbly exploited by retaining some commitment to socialist economic values.

Moreover, there are really no viable alternative political options for these groups, since many would expect a more liberal order to also be more pro-capitalist. As a result, when relatively poor citizens engage in protest, rather than calling for an end to CCP rule, they urge the party to live up to its socialist rhetoric. This is especially the case for rank and file state sector workers, many of whom experienced harsh economic conditions beginning in the mid-1990s. Privatization and retrenchments in the state sector triggered a loss of secure employment and privileged pay and social status for these workers. Nonetheless, even if laid off, state enterprise workers tend to remain dependent on the state for part of their livelihood. And those that still have jobs tend to be better off than the vast majority of migrant workers.

At the low end of China's class structure sit rural migrants and the bulk of Chinese farmers. Rural migrants have migrated to the cities in search of employment, often finding work in private firms and small-scale operations such as street-side stalls. While they endure exacting working conditions and receive minimal income, they have moved up a step from their rural lot, and thus perceive themselves as improving their and their children's life chances. In fact, the discrimination of rural migrants by urban governments is diminishing, giving them continued reason not to upset the status quo.

Farmers, as in ancient China, are at the very bottom of the class structure. Despite several good years in the 1980s, the incomes of most farmers have improved little starting in the 1990s. As a result, they show only tenuous support for the existing political system. Their relative autonomy and grievances have created pressures for policy actions on the part of the central government. Rural land taxes have been abolished, school fees drastically cut, and a new rural medical insurance system initiated. Even so, as of the late 2000s, farmers continue to be China's most volatile and politically dissatisfied group.

The overall image of China's class structure is that of a truncated bell with a big bottom. At the very top sits a small minority, most of which are closely affiliated or deeply embedded in the party-state. They are followed by a small middle class, a larger formal urban working class, and then in the expanding bottom part rural migrants and the biggest group of all, Chinese farmers. Roughly 15 percent of the population occupies the narrow upper level, while the remaining 85 percent form the wide base. Evidently, the most important feature of China's interest alignments at present is the development of a highly polarized class structure. In fact, China's wealth gap has emerged under the same political system that until recently castigated the evils of economic polarization.

How has this stratification occurred? Put in general terms, late capitalist development under globalization has transformed one of the most egalitarian societies in the world to one of the most unequal in the short time span of 30 years. First of all, China has since the early 1990s embraced certain forces of globalization such as attracting multinational capital with weak regulations, cheap land, and a quiescent, yet disciplined, labor force. This has given unskilled Chinese laborers new chances for economic advancement, but exposed them to the vicissitudes of the global market. Globalization also provided Chinese entrepreneurs and skilled professionals with new economic opportunities. As in the large majority of capitalist political economies, globalization has increased returns on skills and economic connections (*guanxi*), leading to a widening wealth gap in China.

Capitalist development under globalization also influenced China's regional income gaps. Due to China's large size, different regions possess different endowments, especially in terms of access to foreign markets and capital. The more globalized a region economically, the wealthier it tends to be.

Finally, China's status as a transition economy influenced growing wealth differentials. State sector reforms have focused on closing down or selling off loss-making enterprises. Rank and file state workers suffered considerably as a result, while skilled professionals and managers gained. Another socialist legacy, tough restrictions on the migration of farmers to cities based on residency permits, also contributes to income gaps, since those with urban residency enjoy social welfare benefits that migrant laborers cannot access.

China's highly stratified social structure mirrors to some extent the institutional arrangements of China's capitalism. As in China's institutional arrangements, the dominant state sits above the class structure. This state is ruled by a technocratic class, which are the leading cadres of party and government bodies (Zheng 2006). In essence, this elite sits atop both society and economy. It manages the large state sector – the commanding heights of the economy. It also has co-opted private entrepreneurs and emerging professional classes. Since both private entrepreneurs and professionals lack political autonomy and constitutional guarantees, they face strong incentives to embed themselves in the party-state to create a modicum of institutional certainty and predictability. Nonetheless, they straddle two worlds: a state-dominated world ruled by command; and a much more competitive landscape infused by global professional and entrepreneurial interests.

Consequently, China's societal structure contains a degree of congruence with the institutional arrangements defining China's emergent capitalism. As China's political economy is marked by a distinct duality in which a state-led mode of production contrasts with vibrant networks of capitalist producers, so is China's society characterized by a technocratic state elite that co-opts and is influenced by new professional and entrepreneurial elites.

The vast majority of Chinese citizens, though, remain far beyond these elites in a polarized social structure. But even here, some lower class cleavages parallel the duality of China's capitalist institutions. A narrow formal urban employment sector made up primarily of employees in state and large private firms (both foreign and domestic) contrasts with a large army of wage laborers working in services and small-scale private firms. The bulk of this second group tends to consist of rural migrants, which face much worse working conditions, pay, and social welfare benefits than the prior group.

Overall, China's capitalist development has set in motion a process whereby the social power of capital is gradually strengthening. This is expressed by concerted efforts on the part of the CCP to co-opt business interests. A state-led logic harnessing capital accumulation for the purposes of CCP legitimacy has evolved in which the party continues to remain at the political center. An analysis of the institutional arrangements and social interest alignments underlying China's emergent capitalism must thus come back to the party, especially the policies and structural changes it has adopted.

Back to the party

The CCP is a gigantic political party. With about 70 million members it is now the largest ruling party in the world. As such, the CCP stands at China's power center and has been central to the changes experienced by China's political economy. Its structure, policies, and reactions to the combined forces of globalization and private capital accumulation cannot be ignored.

CCP leaders are keenly aware that the fate of the CCP is of crucial importance to the success of China's modernization drive. Indeed, since 1989 the CCP has been able to manage capitalist development without engendering increased public pressure for liberal political reforms. The CCP has adapted its policies and structure so as to attract popular support, at least among critical social interests. As a result, most social interests in China either accept or want to perpetuate CCP rule. How has the CCP-led political system accomplished this?

Several analyses have noted that the CCP has been able to introduce various reforms at the grassroots level while strengthening the capacity of central party and state institutions. The result has been a form of "authoritarian resilience" (Nathan 2003), "illiberal adaptation" (Pei 2007), "nimble authoritarianism" (Kroeber 2007), or "dynamic stability" (Shambaugh 2008). Although the CCP remains fundamentally "authoritarian," it has changed dramatically in the reform era.

First, the CCP has abandoned its utopian socialist ideology in favor of a highly pragmatic modernization vision. It also has eschewed charismatic leadership and focused on a more meritocratic and rule-bound selection process for political leaders. One key aspect of this is the ability of the CCP to institutionalize a peaceful, orderly transition of power from Jiang Zemin to Hu Jintao, a rather unusual situation in the history of authoritarianism (Nathan 2003).

Second, in order to promote economic growth and manage globalization, the CCP has empowered a technocratic class. Technocrats are now the "ruling elites or power holders in China" (Zheng 2006: 233). Starting with Deng Xiaoping, the CCP has made efforts to recruit younger and better educated cadres into leadership positions. The average age has dropped, and educational levels and backgrounds of leading cadres improved. This was accomplished by conscious policies adopted by the CCP's *nomenklatura* system.

Third, administrative reforms spearheaded by the CCP have created much greater institutional certainty and predictability compared to the Maoist period. Party and state institutions have become functionally specialized and differentiated, and the party-state as a whole is becoming more organizationally coherent. Administrative reforms have allowed the party-state to address a host of challenges starting in the 1990s. For example, comprehensive tax and fiscal reforms strengthened the central government's control over revenue, thus enabling "major increases in social spending" (Yang 2003: 44). In waves of bureaucratic reforms, various administrative and state institutions also were substantially streamlined and downsized, resulting in a more efficient and effective regulatory state. Overall, these administrative reforms display a successful adaptive response to the challenges created by capitalist development and globalization. They have also increased the party-state's capacity to respond to public sentiments and grievances (Yang 2004).

Fourth, despite a heavy reliance on coercion to repress any form of organized political dissent, the CCP has opened some aspects of the political arena. As Andrew Nathan argues, the CCP

> has developed a series of input institutions (that is, institutions that people can use to apprise the state of their concerns) that allow Chinese to believe that they have some influence on policy decisions and personnel choices at the local level.
>
> (Nathan 2003: 14)

This includes village elections (when competitive and free of corruption), citizens' right to sue the state, and an increased willingness by government institutions to accept and address public complaints. It also includes feedback provided by a more independent and market-driven media as well as by China's burgeoning Internet culture.

Finally, and perhaps most importantly, the CCP has been able to restructure its social support base. With the start of the reform era, the party devoted itself to fostering rapid economic development and integration with the global capitalist system. This meant that the CCP moved away from its traditional social support bases – peasants and workers – to incorporate new social strata that had benefited from capitalist development. This process culminated in 2001 when Jiang Zemin implemented his theory of the "Three Represents." According to this concept, the CCP represents the most advanced forces of production, the most advanced cultural elements, and the interests of the majority of the people. As a result, the CCP opened its door to admitting new social strata as party members, especially private entrepreneurs and skilled professionals.

With greater political recognition, private entrepreneurs have become an important force in the party-state's political advisory and legislative bodies. They also have participated in local elections on the village level (Dickson

2003). Overall, private entrepreneurs have become more politically embedded in the polity as the reform era has progressed (McNally and Wright 2010). A process of "informal institutional adaptation" unfolded that enmeshed capitalists in the party-state's process of decision-making and policy implementation, especially on the local level (Tsai 2007). Similarly, many skilled professionals have benefited economically from reform policies via the privatization of professional units and the introduction of greater market competition. Many professionals advanced politically as well, especially if their technical expertise is in demand by state and economy.

Rising social strata such as professionals and private entrepreneurs thus are quite supportive of the present regime. On the one hand, the CCP's economic policies have facilitated their upward socioeconomic mobility. On the other hand, the state-led nature of China's capitalism and continued CCP economic and political controls give these groups incentives to maintain ties with the party-state.

This cannot be said for China's lower classes, but even here the party has deftly used rhetoric and policy to address grievances. The most recent effort in this regard has been the enunciation of the concept of a "Socialist Harmonious Society" under the leadership of Hu Jintao and Wen Jiabao. This concept reflects an awareness of the massive stresses generated by China's capitalist development, especially in terms of income inequalities and environmental degradation. The party leadership would like to take the lead in addressing these stresses, creating a more pro-people image. Underlying a harmonious society are serious efforts to shift the country's policy orientation, which have included strengthening workers' rights under the Labor Contract Law and giving farmers stronger claims over the disposal of their land leases (Yu 2008). Clearly, the CCP sees an urgent need to address the grievances of China's lower classes and to create a more socially encompassing policy orientation.

On the whole, the CCP has displayed a considerable degree of adaptation and resilience (Shambaugh 2008). Front and center have been efforts to continue the CCP's dominance over society, economy, and state. Reflecting on the collapse of communism in Eastern Europe, "The Decision of the Central Committee of the Chinese Communist Party on Strengthening the Party's Ability to Govern" (issued in September 2004) emphasizes the need to forestall the ossification of the CCP's governing system. Accordingly, the CCP must upgrade the quality of the party's leadership corps and become more professional, more efficient, and more adaptive to face the challenges of a globalizing world (Brodsgaard and Zheng 2006: 1–2; Shambaugh 2008). Clearly, while the CCP is continuously seeking a strong social support base, it still sees itself as the dominant and overarching force leading China. The inclusive side of the CCP must thus be seen in balance to its coercive side. China's one-party state remains an authoritarian system: any organized political opposition is resolutely crushed.

Evidently, both China's political economy and society remain subjugated to the one-party state. Despite ongoing changes, the CCP has continued to govern with an organizational capacity for imposing its will upon society. This relatively high degree of autonomy from class interests has allowed the CCP to undertake far-reaching social changes, including a restructuring of the party's social support base. The CCP thus should be perceived as constituting the backbone of the Chinese political system. It functions like mucilage, the main source of systemic coherence, binding the technocratic state elite to the various institutional tools and societal interests needed to rule China.

Concluding remarks

I have used the case of China to explore how the process of capitalist development under globalization can affect the reorganization of a political party's structure and policies vis-à-vis new and emerging social interests. In these concluding remarks I focus on elaborating the possible translation mechanisms by which globalization and late capitalist development shape institutional arrangements, social interest alignments, and political rule in China.

If one were to display a brief history of the PRC's political economy, it would start with the revolution of 1949 and the building of a socialist command economy. This initial choice of institutions created unintended consequences, especially the emergence of deep economic and political fissures by the late 1970s. As a result, Deng Xiaoping and his fellow CCP leaders reconfigured the institutions of China's political economy in a radical way, ushering in market forces, private capital accumulation, and integration with the global capitalist system.

The new configuration of institutions encompassed considerable local autonomies, giving rise to inter-jurisdictional competition for attracting private investment and access to foreign trade. Globalization arrived at China's doorstep, leading to the rapid dispersion of certain capitalist practices. Nonetheless, the state's role remained considerable. China thus emerges in the global economy as a late developer with a competitive state coordinated economy under the continued rule of an autocratic regime – the CCP.

What are the links between the institutions of China's emergent capitalism and changes in social interest alignments as well as party structure and policy? First, a caveat must be inserted. The Chinese party-state and its relations to economy and society are highly complex. There are considerable variations among Chinese regions, with differences in how the Chinese party-state's agencies and jurisdictional levels relate to economy and society. Generalizations on the institutional arrangements and interest alignments characterizing China's emergent capitalism must thus be seen against the background of a multifaceted, polymorphous state that has engendered considerable variations in state–capital and state–society relations.

Nonetheless, several general observations can be made. First, China's capitalist development has taken place under more intense conditions of globalization than faced by earlier developers in East Asia. This has influenced institutional arrangements and policies, including China's openness to international investment and trade. Institutional and policy innovations include, for instance, relatively flexible labor markets, land readily available for industrialization, and China's entry into the World Trade Organization (WTO). WTO entry in particular is binding China to international norms of commerce and investment. Institutional arrangements have also involved the proliferation of industrial parks that allow multinational corporations to access cheap Chinese labor and land, while being somewhat divorced from the direct influences of China's domestic institutions.

Both domestic and international factors have therefore interacted to accelerate China's participation in the world capitalist system. This provides a rare opportunity to trace the evolution of a form of capitalism under conditions of intense globalization. Building on Gerschenkron, I argued that China contains characteristic features of a late developer: the speed of development has been more rapid than in prior instances of industrialization; China needed to adjust to the forces of globalization as noted above; and the role of the state in China's capitalist development looms large.

In addition, China's emergent political economy is characterized by a distinct duality: a state-dominant form of capital accumulation based on China's large state sector contrasts with vibrant networks of entrepreneurial capitalist producers which form the bulk of the Chinese private sector. Globalization is partially responsible for some of the institutional arrangements of China's emergent capitalism, but not solely. China's socialist and imperial legacies also are influencing contemporary institutional arrangements.

How has globalization translated into social interest alignments? I noted that there is a degree of congruity between China's unique duality in the economic realm and relations between China's technocratic state elite and new social elites, especially private entrepreneurs. However, I would argue that this is more dependent on China's socialist and imperial legacy than the forces of global capitalism. Indeed, as in imperial times, China's political economy contains combinations of bottom-up entrepreneurial and top-down state-led dynamics. These two modes meet at the lower levels of the state-administrative apparatus, where local cadres have played a crucial role in accommodating capitalist practices. This duality also continues to be permeated by *guanxi* networks and informal norms for business dealings, an ambiguity which serves the CCP's goal of keeping absolute political power well. The CCP therefore harnesses both capital and markets for its own purposes – the maintenance of its rule.

Globalization has translated perhaps more directly into the increasing polarization of China's social order. Since integration into the global capitalist system enhances returns on skills and capital, those with skills and capital are likely to benefit. This is even more so the case in China's political economy, which has made the transition from an egalitarian socialist command economy to a capitalist system in one generation. It is therefore difficult to exactly distinguish the influence of institutions that link China's economy to the global capitalist system from the influences of late capitalist development in general, especially in the context of China's transition economy.

What is clear is that China has experienced perhaps the fastest and most extreme increase of wealth gaps in the world during the 1979–2009 period. Is this linked to globalization? Some general non-China specific studies seem to indicate this. For example, the greater openness to trade and international financial flows that globalization entails tends to prompt more conservative fiscal policies that constrain social spending (Rudra and Haggard 2005). Decreases in social welfare spending, especially in China's state sector, have been partially responsible for greater wealth gaps in China's urban areas.

Several studies also indicate that globalization has increased domestic economic inequality within less developed countries (Brune and Garrett 2005). Even so, the relationship between globalization and increasing inequality is neither fixed nor inevitable. Political leaders of developing countries sometimes increase social welfare spending to ease the "adjustment costs" of integration with the global capitalist system. In view of recent moves by the Chinese leadership to improve social welfare expenditures, such a development might be starting to unfold in the Chinese context. However, so far China indicates how late capitalist development under globalized conditions creates a polarized social structure.

Translation mechanisms of how globalization and late capitalist development affect interest alignments are clearer on how the structural power of capital has increased both vis-à-vis labor and the party-state. The CCP's promotion of economic privatization and marketization has allowed many of China's private entrepreneurs to become extremely wealthy. Since wealth is fungible and can be easily transferred to other jurisdictions, the party-state, especially on the local level, has started take the interests of capitalists into account. In fact, the requirements of a market economy have compelled the party-state to withdraw somewhat from society and to accept the increasing dominance of private ownership. The result: the CCP leadership has moved from tolerating the private sector to embracing it, even inviting private businesspeople to join the party.

Marketization, state sector retrenchment, and the influence of international competitive forces have made labor the relative loser under China's capitalist development. Nonetheless, rapid economic growth has raised "all boats." Each major socioeconomic sector has seen its economic conditions improve during the reform period. Even labor has reason to support continued CCP rule, especially given the CCP's continued adherence to socialist tenets.

Late capitalist development under globalization has therefore shifted the balance of social interests markedly in favor of capitalist interests. The party's ruling elite – the technocratic class – has benefited as well. The state sector is now much more profitable and party-state leaders better educated, more exposed to the outside world, and better remunerated. Finally, key professional groups on which the party-state relies for its modernization goals have gained in both economic and political status. Besides wealthy entrepreneurs, therefore, the party's technocratic ruling elite and, more broadly, professional groups have been major beneficiaries.

Are there parallels between China's situation and other instances of late capitalist development? In general, capitalist development gives rise to new socioeconomic interests that tend to struggle for political change. Consequently, to what extent social interests benefit from capitalist development and how they align with state power can have a bearing on the type of political regime that emerges. In early developers, capital often rose in opposition to a feudal and/or authoritarian state and possessed a degree of class autonomy. Barrington Moore Jr. (1966) thus perceived the bourgeoisie as being crucial in pressing for democratic change. However, in the late developers of Germany, Japan, and Italy a different social constellation drove capital accumulation. Development took place in a mostly top-down fashion guided by a close alliance between state and capital. This, according to Moore, laid the foundations for fascist regimes.

Pushing this structural perspective further, Rueschemeyer *et al.* (1992) argue that the working class also can champion democratic reform. Nonetheless, the authors note that the working class needs allies, especially in the context of late-developing countries with smaller and weaker urban working classes. Capitalists, professionals, and intellectuals play a crucial role, since how they align their interests can tip the balance of power in favor of or against a democratic movement.

The attitudes of labor and capital under late developmental conditions are therefore contingent and variable, a point emphasized by Eva Bellin (2000). In her view, both the capitalist class and labor tend to be weak in late developers. Capitalists, faced with enormous international competitive pressures, often depend on the state for finance, market protection, and favorable regulation. Similarly, organized labor tends to be a small percentage of the labor force in late developers and dependent on the state for its privileged status relative to unorganized workers.

In view of their weak status and the generally large wealth gaps found in late developers under globalized conditions, capitalists and small middle classes may fear giving the poor majority voting rights in a democratic regime. Even organized labor often perceives itself as a relatively advantaged group. The inclusion of a poor majority could, therefore, hurt the interests of capitalists, small middle classes, and organized labor, driving them into the arms of authoritarian stability. Bellin, in keeping with Moore's insights, holds that the relationship between economic development and democracy appears stronger in earlier developers than in later developers

China's experience mirrors Bellin's argument on how late development under a state coordinated economy may undermine public pressures for democracy. When the state controls key economic resources, individuals and groups that are dependent on the state for their material livelihood have an interest in perpetuating the political status quo, even when the political regime is harshly authoritarian. As Bellin notes, this has been the case in other state-led late developers with authoritarian political regimes such as Brazil (mid-1960s through the mid-1980s), Singapore (1960s through the present), and South Korea (1960s through the 1980s). In these political economies, capitalists prospered as a result of their close connections with the ruling regime and exhibited little enthusiasm for democracy. In several instances, organized labor also was materially dependent on and supportive of the authoritarian state.

Similarly in China, large wealth gaps and dependence by capitalists, professionals, and part of the labor force on the state indicate a small chance for a democratic breakthrough in the near future. China's emergent capitalism has resulted in a state–capital symbiosis, especially at the lower levels of the party-state. Although the state-dominant mode of capital accumulation and the highly networked entrepreneurial mode of capital accumulation differ, the two mesh socially and depend on each other economically.

China's competitive state-coordinated economy thus creates a degree of path dependency concerning how the structure of social interest alignments might evolve. A dominant state paired with dependent but rising capitalist and professional classes will see little interest in changing the political status quo. This is even more so the case in view of the resilience and adaptability of the CCP, which has been crucial in guiding capital accumulation and in shaping social interest alignments. Although not embedded in a competitive electoral process, the CCP is partially accountable to the populace, since the party is resolutely focused on remaining a leading element in society.

It is here that globalization re-enters the picture. Enormous competitive pressures emanate from the global capitalist system. The CCP has therefore worked hard to establish a competition-enhancing environment for Chinese businesses, something that aids China's private sector. Rapid capital accumulation within China's borders also serves the party-state to establish internal legitimacy and enhance China's standing in the world. As a consequence, CCP hegemony does not stand above the perceived need for economic expansion. There is a direct link between capital accumulation, social stability, and the CCP's political legitimacy.

This could provide an opening for social interests to assert themselves politically vis-à-vis the CCP. As China's political economy increases in complexity and sophistication, the top-down Leninist mode of governance could run into trouble. It is no wonder that the CCP has focused on the ossification of the Leninist systems in the former Eastern Bloc countries as its major challenge to overcome. Indeed, the CCP will have to be very nimble in dealing with the escalating challenges in China's governance system, such as mounting instances of corruption, environmental degradation, and the country's increasing social polarization.

Changing its mode of governance might necessitate the CCP to include social interests on a more equitable basis in its decision-making. It might also necessitate concerted efforts to narrow the wealth gap, giving the upper social strata incentives to contemplate a more open political system. Jianjun Zhang (2008), for example, argues that in the highly capitalist city of Wenzhou private entrepreneurs are largely independent of the state and wealth is distributed in a relatively equitable fashion. This has increased public pressures for local democratization. However, he also notes that the bulk of China is characterized by a polarized class structure and elite collusion.

One possibility is therefore that differing developments in China's regional political economies could create alternative political futures, pushing the national system in one direction or another. Ultimately, political events possess a high degree of autonomy, putting gradual democratization, the persistence of a resilient authoritarian system, and even a more nationalistic and xenophobic political regime all within the realm of the possible.

Notes

1 I am indebted to Philippe Schmitter for coining and conceptualizing the term "competitive state coordinated economy."
2 This point was first put forward by Moore (1966) and refined by Bellin (2000).
3 In the following I treat China as undertaking a form of capitalist development. I therefore conceive of China's political economy as based on capital accumulation, market competitive forces, and the gradual institutionalization of rules and norms governing a capitalist market economy. For more on the nature and logic of China's capitalist transition see McNally (2008a).
4 The following builds on Zheng (2006), Chen (2008), McNally and Wright (2010), and Wright (2010).

References

Amsden, Alice H. (1989). *Asia's Next Giant: South Korea and Late Industrialization*, Oxford: Oxford University Press.

Bellin, Eva (2000). "Contingent Democrats: Industrialists, Labor, and Democratization in Late-Developing Countries," *World Politics*, 52(2), 175–205.

Boisot, Max, and John Child (1996). "From Fiefs to Clans and Network Capitalism: Explaining China's Emerging Economic Order," *Administrative Science Quarterly*, 41, 600–628.

Brodsgaard, Kjeld Erik, and Yongnian Zheng (2006). "Introduction: Whither the Chinese Communist Party," in Kjeld Erik Brodsgaard and Yongnian Zheng (eds.), *The Chinese Communist Party in Reform*, New York and London: Routledge, 1–14.

Brune, Nancy, and Geoffrey Garrett (2005). "The Globalization Rorschach Test: International Economic Integration, Inequality, and the Role of Government," *Annual Review of Political Science*, 8(June), 399–423.

Chen, An (2008). "Why Does Capitalism Fail to Push China Towards Democracy," in Christopher A. McNally (ed.), *China's Emergent Political Economy – Capitalism in the Dragon's Lair*, New York and London: Routledge, 146–165.

Cusack, Thomas R., Torben Iversen, and David Soskice (2007). "Economic Interests and the Origins of Electoral Systems," *American Political Science Review*, 101(3), 373–391.

Dickson, Bruce J. (2003). *Red Capitalists in China*, Cambridge: Cambridge University Press.

Dickson, Bruce J. (2008). *Wealth into Power: The Communist Party's Embrace of China's Private Sector*, Cambridge: Cambridge University Press.

Duus, Peter (1976). *The Rise of Modern Japan*, Boston: Houghton Mifflin Company.

Edin, Maria (2003). "State Capacity and Local Agent Control in China: CCP Cadre Management from a Township Perspective," *The China Quarterly*, 173, 35–52.

Edmonds, Christopher, Sumner J. La Croix, and Yao Li (2008). "China's Rise as a Trading Power," in Christopher A. McNally (ed.), *China's Emergent Political Economy – Capitalism in the Dragon's Lair*, New York and London: Routledge, 169–189.

Evans, Peter (1992). "The State as Problem and Solution: Predation, Embedded Autonomy and Structural Change," in Stephen Haggard and Robert R. Kaufman (eds.), *The Politics of Economic Adjustment*, Princeton: Princeton University Press, 139–181.

Faure, David (2006). *China and Capitalism: A History of Business Enterprise in Modern China*, Hong Kong: Hong Kong University Press.

Gates, Hill (1996). *China's Motor: A Thousand Years of Petty Capitalism*, Ithaca: Cornell University Press.

Gerschenkron, Alexander (1962). *Economic Backwardness in Historical Perspective: A Book of Essays*, Cambridge, MA: Harvard University Press.

Hall, Peter A., and David W. Soskice (2001). *Varieties of Capitalism: The Institutional Foundations of Comparative Advantage*, Oxford: Oxford University Press.

Howell, Jude (2006). "Reflections on the Chinese State," *Development and Change*, 37(2), 273–297.

Hsing, You-tien (1998). *Making Capitalism in China*, New York: Oxford.

Huang, Yasheng (1996). *Inflation and Investment Controls in China: The Political Economy of Central-Local Relations During the Reform Era*, Cambridge: Cambridge University Press.

International Financial Corporation (2000). *China's Emerging Private Enterprises: Prospects for the New Century*, Washington, DC: International Financial Corporation.

Johnson, Chalmers (1982). *MITI and the Japanese Miracle*, Palo Alto: Stanford University Press.

Kornai, Janos (1992). *The Socialist System: The Political Economy of Communism*, Princeton: Princeton University Press.

Kroeber, Arthur (2007). "The Durable Communist Party," *China Economic Quarterly*, 11(1), 14–18.

Lee, Keun, Donghoon Hahn, and Justin Lin (2002). "Is China Following the East Asian Model? A 'Comparative Institutional Analysis' Perspective," *The China Review*, 2(1), 85–120.

McNally, Christopher A. (2008a). "Reflections on Capitalism and China's Emergent Political Economy," in Christopher A. McNally (ed.), *China's Emergent Political Economy – Capitalism in the Dragon's Lair*, New York and London: Routledge, 17–35.

McNally, Christopher A. (2008b). "Conclusion: Capitalism in the Dragon's Lair," in Christopher A. McNally (ed.), *China's Emergent Political Economy – Capitalism in the Dragon's Lair*, New York and London: Routledge, 228–244.

McNally, Christopher A. (2011), "China's Changing *Guanxi* Capitalism – Private Entrepreneurs between Leninist Control and Relentless Accumulation," *Business and Politics*, 13(3).

McNally, Christopher A., and Teresa Wright (2010). "Sources of Social Support for China's Current Political Order: The 'Thick Embeddedness' of Private Capital Holders," *Communist and Post-Communist Studies*, 43(2), 189–198.

Mann, Susan (1987). *Local Merchants and the Chinese Bureaucracy, 1750–1950*, Palo Alto: Stanford University Press.

Michelson, Ethan (2007). "Lawyers, Political Embeddedness, and Institutional Continuity in China's Transition from Socialism," *American Journal of Sociology*, 113(2), 352–414.

Moore, Barrington Jr. (1966). *Social Origins of Dictatorship and Democracy*, Boston: Beacon Press.

Nathan, Andrew (2003). "Authoritarian Resilience," *Journal of Democracy*, 14(1), 6–17.

Naughton, Barry (1992). "Implications of the State Monopoly Over Industry and Its Relaxations," *Modern China*, 18(1), 14–41.

Naughton, Barry (1995). *Growing Out of the Plan: Chinese Economic Reform, 1978–1990*, Cambridge: Cambridge University Press.

Naughton, Barry (2008). "SOE Policy – Profiting the SASAC Way," *China Economic Quarterly*, 12(2), 19–32.

Nolan, Peter (2001). *China and the Global Economy: National Champions, Industrial Policy and the Big Business Revolution*, Basingstoke: Palgrave.

Pei, Minxin (2007). "How Will China Democratize?" *Journal of Democracy*, 18(3), 53–57.

Rudra, Nita, and Stephan Haggard (2005). "Globalization, Democracy, and Effective Welfare Spending in the Developing World," *Comparative Political Studies*, 38(9), 1015–1049.

Rueschemeyer, Dietrich, Evelyne Huber Stephens, and John D. Stephens (1992). *Capitalist Development and Democracy*, Chicago: University of Chicago Press.

Schumpeter, Joseph A. (1950). *Capitalism, Socialism and Democracy*, New York: Harper & Row.

Shambaugh, David (2008). *China's Communist Party: Atrophy and Adaptation*, Berkeley and Los Angeles: University of California Press.

Shonfield, Andrew (1965). *Modern Capitalism – The Changing Balance of Public and Private Power*, New York: Oxford University Press.

Solinger, Dorothy J. (1989). "Capitalist Measures With Chinese Characteristics," *Problems of Communism*, 38(1), 19–33.

Streeck, Wolfgang (2001). "Introduction: Explorations into the Origins of Nonliberal Capitalism in Germany and Japan," in Wolfgang Streeck and Kozo Yamamura (eds.), *The Origins of Nonliberal Capitalism – Germany and Japan in Comparison*, Ithaca: Cornell University Press, 1–38.

ten Brink, Tobias (2010). "Structural Characteristics of Chinese Capitalism," mimeo, Max Planck Institute for the Study of Societies, Cologne, Germany, May.

Tsai, Kellee S. (2007). *Capitalism without Democracy: The Private Sector in Contemporary China*, Ithaca: Cornell University Press.

UNDP (2008). "World Development Report," available at: http://hdrstats.undp.org/indicators/147.html (accessed February 3, 2008).

Wank, David L. (1999). *Commodifying Communism: Business, Trust and Politics in a Chinese City*, Cambridge: Cambridge University Press.

Wildau, Gabriel (2008). "Enterprise Reform – Albatross Turns Phoenix," *China Economic Quarterly*, 12(2), 27–33.

Wright, Teresa (2010). *Accepting Authoritarianism: State-Society Relations in China's Reform Era*, Palo Alto: Stanford University Press.

Xinhua (2005). "One Third of China's Private Businessmen are CPC Members," *Xinhua News Agency*, February 10, available at: news.xinhuanet.com/english/2005–02/10/content_2569317.htm (accessed February 3, 2008).

Yang, Dali (2003). "State Capacity on the Rebound," *Journal of Democracy*, 14(1), 43–50.

Yang, Dali (2004). *Remaking the Chinese Leviathan*. Palo Alto: Stanford University Press.

Yu, Verna (2008). "China's Farmers Can Bank On Land," *Asia Times Online*, October 10, available at: www.atimes.com/atimes/China/JJ10Ad01.html (accessed October 15, 2008).

Zhang, Jianjun (2008). *Marketization and Democracy in China*, New York and London: Routledge.

Zheng, Yongnian (2004). *Globalization and State Transformation in China*, Cambridge: Cambridge University Press.

Zheng, Yongnian (2006). "The Party, Class, and Democracy in China," in Kjeld Erik Brodsgaard and Yongnian Zheng (eds.), *The Chinese Communist Party in Reform*, New York and London: Routledge, 231–260.

9 Political regime types and varieties of post-socialist capitalism in the era of globalization

Laszlo Bruszt

For the former state socialist countries 1989 was the year of the starting of the simultaneous transformation of their political regimes and economic systems. This entailed attempts at remaking simultaneously the political and economic institutions of these countries under the conditions of opening up their economies and entering the "era of globalization." These countries have ended a developmental model that was built upon the combination of authoritarian political regime, state control of the economy combined with limited links to the global markets. In 1989 they started their pathways toward some uncertain other, away from autocracy, command economy and autarchy.

The goal of this chapter is to provide a description of and an explanation for the diverging pathways of the post-socialist countries that have combined different political regime types with specific varieties of capitalism and have ended up with dramatically different patterns of insertion into the global markets.

The questions discussed in the introduction to this volume about the various causal links between VoC, ToD and globalization were raised in the post-socialist countries in the very basic form as questions about the relationship between political regime type, type of capitalism and pattern of insertion in the global economy. The first question in this setting was whether a democratic or a non-democratic political regime was more conducive to successful economic transformation? The answer to this question primarily depended on the way one answered the second question of how one could conceptualize variation in post-socialist capitalism. The central question about the right policies during economic transformations was about the role of the state, whether the key task was to liberate the economy from the state, or to transform its role in the economy. While some in that debate expected the coming variety of capitalism to be based primarily on the level of freedoms from the state, others have expected variation based on the differences in the outcomes of efforts to create the capacity of post-socialist states to set and enforce public rules for the private economy. Finally, the third question was how would the interplay between economic and political change affect the insertion of these evolving market economies into the global markets?

The first question was about the relationship between the simultaneous extension of property rights and political rights: is the building of "any kind of democracy" (AKD) compatible with, or is it inimical to, building a functioning capitalism in these countries? Which of the former communist countries will have a functioning market economy? Those that will have governments constrained by democratic politics or those countries where governments will not be bothered by democratic rights and procedures?

From the start, the question about the link between political regime type and economic system was answered based on differences in the understanding of what a "functioning market economy" was, how one could meaningfully conceptualize variation among differently functioning capitalist economies in evolving market economies. Depending on the answer to this question, researchers of post-socialism arrived at diametrically opposing results on the link between AKD and variation in the outcomes of capitalist transformation. According to the dominating neo-liberal view in the 1990s, the levels of freedom from the state defined functioning market economies. Variation in capitalism from this perspective meant variation in the level of liberalization of prices, trade and privatization. For the neo-liberals AKD, at least in the short term, was a liability from the perspective of the necessary reforms that were supposed to lead to a functioning market economy. The right sequencing of reforms for them was the following: market reforms should come first; democracy and state building should come later.

Market reform → democracy → state building

Institutionalist approaches to post-socialist transformation called attention to variation in the extent and mode of social regulation of evolving markets. According to this approach differences in the regulative capacities of post-socialist states were expected to be the basis for capitalist variety. Representatives of this approach could not make much use of the refined institutionalist perspective of the VoC literature. In the VoC literature the two basic types of capitalism, LMEs and CMEs, differ in the ways firms acquire their finances and labor, or in the way they organize skill formation. Variation on these dimensions is the function of how these countries regulate their financial markets and labor markets, or how they set the rules framing skill promotion. LMEs and CMEs differ in the specific rules of the market. On the other hand, they have in common the existence of robust state capacities to make, uphold and change the public rules of the private economy. This is to say that they have one generic thing in common: they are both regulated capitalist economies (RCE).

For the study of post-socialist transformations, the existence of such robust regulative states could not be taken as granted. In the post-communist countries capitalism was built from scratch in the presence of weak states, fledgling civil societies and, at least in the initial stage, no capitalist class. For the institutionalist students of post-socialism, the question was not whether the outcome of the economic transformation would be something resembling an LME or a CME. Rather, the question was whether the outcome of economic change would be an RCE of any kind, or some kind of crony capitalism in which the state cannot control the setting of the rules of the economy and the strongest economic or political players can set arbitrarily the rules of the game in the private economy. Whereas neo-liberals expected capitalist diversity based on the degree of liberalization from the state, institutional approaches expected variation based on state capacity to set public rules for the private economy.

For the institutional approach then the question was whether AKD helps or hinders the building of RCEs? Can RCEs be built without AKDs, leading also to the question of whether there are non-democratic ways of arriving at RCE? This later question needs some explanation in the light of the success of the Chinese experience of building a robust form of capitalism in the framework of a non-democratic regime. In most of the post-communist countries, unlike in China, one could not take as granted the presence of a stable and robust state with the capacity to control economic change. The demise of the old regime in most of these countries meant that economic transformation and political change had to go hand in hand with the rebuilding of states. Therefore the question for the institutionalist approach was whether these countries could rebuild their states and remake their economies successfully without AKD. The answer of the institutionalist approach was that the remaking of states and endowing them with the capacity to regulate the private economy presupposed pluralist political framework. According to them, the redistribution of economic powers to private actors via privatization and liberalization, in the absence of state capacity to set the rules of the private economy, will result in the coming about of crony capitalism. Political pluralism, the extension of governmental accountability, the institutionalization of checks and balances could be the way to create political counter-balance to the increased powers of the emerging capitalists and help the coming about of state capacity to set public rules for the private economy. The suggested sequencing of transformations in this approach is the following:

Democracy → state building → market reform

Finally, the third question was how would the interplay between economic and political change affect the insertion of these evolving market economies into the global markets? The former socialist countries differed from the advanced capitalist economies not primarily at the level of their industrialization but at the level of the competitiveness of the goods they produced. Most of the former communist countries were highly industrialized but the products of their industries were not competitive in the world markets. Exposure to the markets might have been either a blessing or a curse to these economies, meaning either convergence to the core economies of the global economy or de-industrialization and convergence to the periphery. The key developmental question of the post-communist world was which of these countries will occupy better positions in the globalizing economy? Will those countries be better off that could separate the building of capitalism from creating AKD? Or, in the post-communist setting the co-evolution of democratic political institutions and economic institutions was a necessary condition for creating a competitive market economy with advantageous pattern of global insertion?

The suggested neo-liberal sequencing was the following:

Economic transformation → Global insertion → Plural Political Representation

From the perspective of the institutionalist approach this was the right sequencing:

Plural Political Representation → Economic transformation → Global insertion

This chapter will present some empirical evidence on the relationship between market reforms, state building and democracy and demonstrate that the representatives of the institutionalist approach were right in their theoretical conclusions. Moreover, early on they provided a key to a central factor of post-socialist divergence in developmental pathways.[1] Twenty years after the commencement of economic and political transformations, the former state socialist countries dramatically diverged on key dimensions of economic development. While most of them have introduced all the liberalizing reforms prescribed to them in the early 1990s, less than half have a well functioning regulatory state. One can find RCEs comparable to Western standards only in countries where in the 1990s issues of economic transformation and regulation were politicized and decided in a democratic political framework. The development of capable regulatory states in the framework of democratic institutions was the necessary condition for improving global positions in international markets while keeping social inequalities low and domestic social integration relatively high. Lack of progress in building regulatory states meant remaining in, or falling to the periphery of, the globalizing world economy, drastic increases in social inequalities and lower levels of domestic social integration (Bruszt and Greskovits 2009).

The chapter starts with an overview of the debates on what a functioning market economy is and what the politics of economic transformation in the post-socialist countries should have been.

The second part of the chapter provides some evidence on the evolution of varieties of capitalism contrasting the neo-liberal and the institutionalist perspectives. I will present evidence on the evolution of regulative state capacities and about the relationship between democracy and the evolution of state capacities. First, I will contrast the two conflicting perspectives on market making: the neo-liberal and the institutionalist. According to the latter approach, first formulated in the post-socialist setting by Linz and Stepan, the outcomes of economic reforms will differ not in degree but in kind depending on progress in state making: no state capacity, no market economy (Linz and Stepan 1996). The data to be presented below proves that Linz and Stepan were right: the development of functioning market economies in post-communist Eastern Europe presupposed state building. No market-preserving state and no regulatory state meant the absence of a normally functioning market economy.

Second, we also find that the relationship between political regime type and the construction of economic state capacities in the post-communist world worked in the way predicted by the institutionalists: no democracy, no regulatory state.

Finally, I will present evidence on the relationship between patterns of market making and patterns of insertion in the global economy. We find a strong positive relationship between the characteristics of post-socialist market making and patterns of global insertion. Countries that have remade their economies under the conditions of political pluralism and broad politicization of the questions of economic and social transformation have better quality capitalism: a stronger regulative state and a "higher" road of global insertion. At the other extreme, in a second group of post-socialist countries with autocratic political regimes we identify the "low road" of global insertion.

The debate on the politics of economic transformation

The neo-liberal discourse

At the time of the start of economic transformations in Eastern and Central Europe, in the early 1990s, most policy-makers and advisors agreed that priority should be given to economic change, understood as neo-liberal reforms. Political reform and especially state reconstruction, in that view, should wait until the consolidation of liberalizing reforms.

There were several interlinked arguments used by international developmental agencies and domestic neo-liberal reformers for sequencing reforms that way, starting with liberalizing the economy. The economic part of the argument was based on the then dominant assumption that markets were realms of protected freedoms from the state, and creating markets was about liberating economic action from the state. The key political argument of the proponents of neo-liberal reforms was that only the rapidly executed economic reforms could create the foundations for progress in political reforms. The essence of that view was that people cannot make inter-temporal trade-offs, and that if economic reforms imposed social hardships on voters, they would use the political opportunities offered by democracy to halt reforms.[2] The suggested solution to this dilemma was to use shock therapy and/or insulate the making of economic reforms from democratic political interventions.

The political dominance of the neo-liberal ideas throughout the first half of the 1990s was strongly linked to the perceived failure of any kind of developmental model that was based on the idea of politicizing economic issues and involving states in the running of the economy. During the 1980s, partly as a result of the failure of the state-based developmental models in several Latin American countries and the collapse of the state socialist model in Eastern and Central Europe, states began to be perceived more as part of the problem itself than as part of the solution. While there remained some scholarly interest in the sources and ways of changing and upgrading developmental state capacities, the mainstream turned toward such questions as the sources of the state capacity for "de-statization," meaning the introduction of neo-liberal reforms.[3] For some time the capacity to "introduce and sustain the right policies" of liberalization, privatization, and stabilization – the mantra of the international financial institutions (IFI) – was the sole cited challenge on the pathway of economic transformation and development. The yearly progress reports of the IFIs ranked transforming countries according to the capacity of their states to make progress in the introduction of the policies of "de-statization." In that context, state capacity to further market reforms was pictured as being the function of success in de-politicizing economic reform (Haggard and Kaufman 1995).

At the beginning of economic transformation in Eastern and Central Europe, these were the dominant views both in scholarly and in policy circles. The idea that making a functioning market economy has something to do with social regulation was rarely, if at all, mentioned. Building RCE was clearly not on the agenda of most of the first reformist governments and this idea was absent from the policy suggestions of the IFIs until the second half of the 1990s. The policy suggestions of IFIs were shaped by an amalgam of the "capture theory of regulation" and by libertarian pre-New Deal ideas of constitutionalism stressing the importance of preserving the pre-political status of "private ordering."

According to the capture theory of regulation, first proposed by George Stigler and later to become the basis for broader public choice models of the state, markets have to be saved from regulations. Regulations are closer to conspiracies by rent-seeking groups than to expressions of something that could be called public good. In the popularized version of this thesis, interest groups and other political participants will use the regulatory and coercive powers of government to shape laws and regulations in a way that is beneficial to them. Attempts at politicizing economic issues and giving the state regulatory powers are the surest way to the corruption of states and markets. Liberating the markets from social and political regulations was in this framework pictured as liberating the state from the hold of rent-seeking groups.[4]

Behind the policy advice given by IFIs in the initial period of economic transformation one can also detect the revival of the laissez-faire ideas from pre-New Deal era constitutionalism.[5] Until the mid-1930s, US Supreme Court decisions tried to restrain the legislature and the executive from politicizing market ordering and rejected a large part of regulatory interventions with arguments referring to the superiority of private ordering (Sunstein 1987). For the Spencerian proponents of laissez-faire, market order was the outcome of millions of private contracts. The most important goal of the state was to uphold the maximum freedom of contracting and maintain the "pre-political" status of economic transactions. Public interventions in free contracting were pictured as unjust redistributions of wealth and opportunities, as arbitrary "taking" (Sunstein 1987). State neutrality meant staying away from private ordering, leaving it to courts and the judiciary branch to deal with conflict. It also meant minimizing the possibility of politicizing economic transactions by way of interventions of the executive or the legislature (Sunstein 1987). In this perspective, the key task of states was to preserve markets by upholding the key economic freedoms: the freedom of property and freedom of contracting.[6]

At around the mid-1990s reports on the progress in market making prepared by the IFIs started to rank countries based on elementary state capacities to uphold market freedoms. Typical was the study commissioned by the World Bank that made the first inter-regional comparative study on the capacity of states to uphold property rights, enforce contracts, maintain a stable and predictable policy environment for businesses, and to combat corruption (Brunetti *et al.* 1998). While these reports were still silent about regulations, they were the first to depart from the public choice assumption of a uniform state and thus were the first to represent post-communist states as variable and changeable entities.

Bringing the regulatory state back in

The idea of the regulatory state, and with that the building of a RCE as the final goal of economic transformation, had been brought back in by the second half of the 1990s, and the list of (missing or weak) state capacities grew in the meantime. Until the second half of the 1990s the talk about state capacity to regulate the economy was not politically correct in serious economic developmental circles. However, the European Bank for Reconstruction and Development (EBRD) in 1997 had already introduced measures in its progress report showing the highly uneven capacity of the transition countries to introduce extensive and effective regulation of their financial and capital markets.

While the World Bank and the EBRD were very active in the second half of the 1990s in propagating the necessity of building regulatory capacities, theoretical reflections on regulations and the need for regulatory state were in short supply throughout the decade. Until the collapse of the Russian financial markets in 1998 and the publication of the first studies on the uneven development of capital markets in the leading post-communist reform countries, there were very few theoretically oriented reflections on the role of regulatory institutions in post-communist market building (Stiglitz 1999; Coffee 1999). That markets are neither self-constituting nor self-regulating was perhaps not news to many economists. Still, arguments for developing regulatory institutions as the precondition for making functioning markets were largely invisible until the late 1990s in the discussions among economists dealing with economic transformations.

Students of comparative capitalism, on the other hand, took the existence of robust regulatory states as granted as they were concerned primarily with understanding persistent divergences among well functioning regulatory regimes that have differed only in the content of regulations (Hall and Soskice 2001). The issue of the politics of making regulatory institutions and developing regulatory states in formerly communist countries was thus mainly absent in the theoretical literature on economic transformation. In a footnote, Linz and Stepan approvingly cite a leading North American economist to claim that "neglect of the role of the state in the transformation by economists borders on the criminal" (Linz and Stepan 1996: 253, fn 42).

The political arguments for building regulatory states in Central and Eastern Europe represented first in Linz and Stepan's *Problems of Democratic Transition and Consolidation* could only be weakly linked to ongoing debates among economists or students of political economy. When making their theoretical arguments, Linz and Stepan cited only one economist participating in the debate on the goals and means of economic transformation. On the issues of regulations and the regulatory state, they cite classics from political economy and political science, such as Adam Smith and Robert Dahl (Linz and Stepan 1996: 12–13). Linz and Stepan's argument for the political crafting of socially acceptable public rules for the private economy, what they called economic society, was linked to their claims about the economic conditions of a consolidated democracy. The crux of this argument was that there cannot be a consolidated democracy in a command economy, and that a completely free market economy cannot coexist with consolidated democracy. The second part of the argument is of relevance here. Linz and Stepan gave three reasons why a completely free market economy cannot coexist with consolidated democracy. "No regulatory state – no free market" was their first argument. Market economies "could neither come into being nor be maintained without a degree of state regulation" (Linz and Stepan 1996: 12). Their second argument extended the previous one: public rules are necessary for the creation of the market, and they are also necessary for the correction of eventual market failures. The third argument, finally, was linked to the key aspect of a well functioning democracy, namely that public rules are contestable and they are contested. The very working of a modern democracy leads to the development and changing of norms, regulations, policies and institutions that constitute economic society.

Note that in this framework the creation of public rules for the private economy was both a precondition of democratic consolidation and a sine qua non of successful economic transformation. The latter part of the argument concerns us more here. As we saw above, at the time of the writing of *Problems of Democratic Transition and Consolidation*, the mainstream literature linked the success of economic transformation exactly to the diametrically opposed condition, namely to the depoliticizing of economic reforms. Picturing functioning markets as a contestable structure of norms, policies and regulations, and defining market-making as the institutionalizing of public rules for private economic action was clearly deviating from the conventional definitions of the goals and expected outcomes of mainstream market reforms.

This is where Linz and Stepan bring in the state. Without an effective state that has the capacity to uphold rights, enforce norms and rules, and implement policies, neither economic society nor a functioning economy can come about. To summarize the argument thus far: no effective state → no regulated economy → no sustainable democracy and no functioning market.

The position of Linz and Stepan on the link between democracy and the construction of such a capable state follows from the definition of the goals and expected outcomes of market reforms discussed above. If the creation of economic society is the issue for modern democracies, and a coherent regulatory environment combined with rule of law is required to transform command economies into economic societies, "then a major priority must be to create democratic regulatory state power" (Linz and Stepan 1996: 435).

Linz and Stepan were, of course, not the first to stress building RCE as the major goal of market reforms. Their concept of economic society and their arguments in favor of regulations can be traced back to the political program of the post-New Deal constitutional political economy and to the ordoliberal views of the founders of the German social market economy. The effects of the later ideas can also be detected in the framing of the EU conditionality and assistance programs during the extension of transnational market-building within the European Union to the CEE countries.[7] Common among these thinkers was the rejection of the libertarian ideas that (1) social and economic order could be the outcome of free private contracts and (2) that freedom of contracting and property are natural rights that have to be protected from political interference. Both of these approaches saw markets as based on politically constructed and socially accepted norms that can be politicized and contested. While post-New Deal constitutionalism was primarily about extending regulatory state interventions after a period of laissez-faire, the "soziale Marktwirtschaft" of the post-Second World War ordoliberals was based on the idea that democracy cannot coexist with a command economy or with laissez-faire capitalism.

Both of these approaches saw freedom of contracting and property as politically crafted and socially legitimated rights that were created and upheld with reference to a public good that therefore did not enjoy a pre-political status. Both approaches saw public interventions in the free contracting as necessary measures to constitute the market order, correct market failures, and maintain competition. They have rejected the views of the libertarians who saw public regulations as unjust redistribution of wealth and opportunities. For the representatives of post-New Deal constitutionalism and ordoliberalism, non-intervention would have meant toleration of the misuse of asymmetries in economic power, which would have resulted in the public sanctioning of unfair redistributions. State neutrality for both of these approaches meant not staying away from unjust or unfair private ordering. According to both of them, political society cannot be prevented from politicizing and contesting the public rules of the private economy.

During the first period of economic transformation in the post-communist countries the above ideas seemed to have been forgotten, at least in the world of IFIs advising these countries how to go about creating markets. The originality of Linz and Stepan was to bring these ideas back based on democratic theory and linked to the idea of democratic consolidation. In the debate on post-communist transformation, Linz and Stepan were the first to make the theoretically based claim that if the ultimate goal of reforms was to have both functioning markets and sustainable democracies, then building a regulatory state under democratic conditions was the way to start. To make democracy and market reforms compatible, the reforms should create the conditions for the orderly politicizing and regulating of economic action.

While among the Washington-based IFIs each and every little step of moving away from neo-liberal orthodoxy was celebrated as a paradigmatic change, the EU, the other key external player in the Eastern European transformations, did not make a big fuss about regulation and regulatory state capacities. Brussels and the Eurocrats never participated in the ongoing global debates about the relationship between success in market reforms and building state capacities. Without much ado in the mid-1990s, the Commission posted tens of thousands pages of regulations to the aspiring applicant countries. These regulations were supposed to be introduced in the national legal systems and implemented as a condition for being considered a functioning market economy ready for EU membership. The EU demanded not the mere transposition of thousands of pages of EU laws to the domestic law books. It also insisted on building state capacities to implement and adjust these norms on the ground.

Just a year after the publication of *Problems of Democratic Transition and Consolidation* in 1996, the Commission issued its Agenda 2000. Agenda 2000 insisted on the necessity for the candidate countries to build regulatory state capacities, including the judicial and administrative capacities to enforce and monitor the European public rules of the regional market economy. The way the EU translated the dominant neo-liberal paradigm to non-negotiable conditionality is unique and still unmatched by other transnational integration regimes, such as NAFTA or Mercosur. Agenda 2000 implied the need to combine the building up of the institutional conditions for meeting EU demands with the adoption of 80,000 pages of EU institutional standards and regulations detailed in 31 chapters or policy domains ranging from consumer protection to corporate governance, from banking regulation to state aid policies, and from environmental protection to public procurement. EU conditionality documents made it clear that market building, besides liberalization, means building up institutional capacity – remaking administrative and regulatory state capacities and creating developmental state capacities (Bruszt 2002).

At least as important, and similar to the ideas advanced in *Problems of Democratic Transition and Consolidation*, the EU also used extensive assistance programs to build what Stepan and Linz called economic society. Various assistance programs throughout the 1990s and early 2000s empowered diverse public and private actors, not simply via resources but particularly by enhancing their political and functional participation in institution building efforts. By the late 1990s, the EU had built up a diversified and complex assistance program (Bruszt and McDermott 2009). With an overall budget of around €28 billion, these programs targeted building capacity both within and outside of the state and involved the direct participation of thousands of experts and policy-makers from the EU member states.

Finally, one can detect a third similarity between the ideas in *Problems of Democratic Transition and Consolidation* and the developmental interventions of the EU in the CEE countries. By connecting political with economic conditionality and closely monitoring the upholding of political rights and the rules of fair political competition, the EU helped to keep constant domestic democratic rights to contest policies and rules while at the same time giving a clear and unambiguous directionality to domestic bottom-up pressure in the form of accession conditionality. The embedding of CEE domestic markets in a broad transnationally monitored regulatory frame has strengthened the bargaining position of domestic states vis-à-vis rent-seeking domestic firms and TNCs. It has also improved the political opportunities of diverse weaker economic actors and has contributed both directly, through assistance programs, and indirectly, through increased political opportunities, to the building of economic societies in these countries.

Post-socialist varieties of capitalism

In the VoC literature, variation in the rules of doing business, organizing finances, labor relations or skill formation are used as the key dimensions to conceptualize different types of capitalism. This framework perfectly fits the advanced market economies with their robust regulative states but it is of little use to understanding variation in the outcomes of post-socialist economic transformations. As in these countries it was exactly the variation in the capacity of states to make, impose and change the public rules in the private economy, this should also be the key dimension for conceptualizing variation in the emerging types of capitalism. Figure 9.1 represents a first attempt to do so. I have included

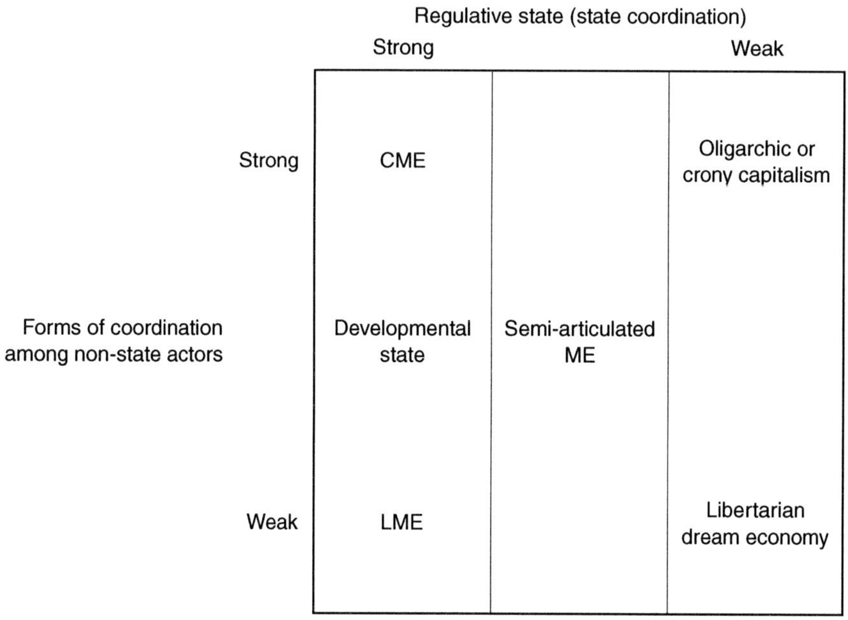

Figure 9.1 State capacity, forms of non-state coordination and varieties of capitalism.

the capacity of economic actors to coordinate as a second dimension since this is the key dimension to account for studying variation in the VoC literature.

In this analytical space we can differentiate among five types of capitalist economies. In the upper left and the lower left parts of the grid we can find the LMEs and CMEs, the two basic types of capitalism prevalent within the OECD economies. These economies differ in the forms of coordination among non-state actors but they have in common the existence of robust regulative states. The lower right corner of the grid, "Libertarian Dream Economy" is a non-existent type of capitalism that has no regulative state and has atomized private actors. The upper right corner is the location of one of the typical versions of post-socialist capitalism. In the Oligarchic or Crony Capitalist Economies a small group of well-coordinated economic actors dominates the setting of the rules of the game in the economy and the distribution of wealth and opportunities through the state. If these dominating actors come primarily from the private sector then we could talk about oligarchic capitalist economy (OCE). If the dominating actors come primarily from the intertwined group of state bureaucrats and their cronies, we can talk of a crony capitalist economy (CCE).

Borrowing the expression from Ben Ross Schneider, we call Semi-Articulated Market Economies (SAME) those that start economic transformation in the middle of the grid: with states and private actors in the process of developing their capacities to coordinate their respective environment (Schneider 2004). The post-socialist transformation started in most of these cases with these conditions: with states having relatively weak administrative and regulative capacities and with private actors in the process of (re)-establishing basic forms of collaboration. This state of affairs was also the starting point for post-socialist divergence: some of the economies were moving toward the upper right corner, with their states captured by the strongest private actors, and the other economies moving toward the upper or the lower left corners, toward LMEs or CMEs with states that had the capacity to impose public rules over the private economy.

Varieties of capitalism, political regime type and developmental pathways in the post-socialist countries – some evidence

In this section I present some evidence on the relationship of market reforms, state building and democratization. I start with the link between market reforms and state building. As noted above, in the 1990s IFIs still measured progress in market reforms with various indicators of economic liberalization. In that framework the outcomes of market reform were expected to differ from each other in degree: some of the countries made more while other countries made less progress in introducing the prescribed liberalizing policies. According to the above discussed institutionalist approaches, on the other hand, creating markets had to start with state building. In their view, the outcomes of market reforms will differ not in degree, as a function of the implementation of neo-liberal reforms, but in kind depending on progress in state making: no state capacity, no RCE.

To present some evidence on this prediction we need to operationalize two concepts: progress in neo-liberal market reforms and progress in state building. To measure progress in market reforms we use the indexes constructed by Campos and Horváth (2006) that are based on the most encompassing data set put together on progress in market reforms in the 28 post-communist countries. Campos and Horváth's data set measures actual introduction of liberalizing reforms constructed from 30 variables for external liberalization and three for internal liberalization. Regarding internal liberalization, they collected data on the number of goods subject to price regulation, the share of administered prices in the consumer price index (CPI) and wage regulation. Regarding external liberalization, they used 30 measures of capital controls and trade barriers.[8] The higher the scores countries have on these measures, the fewer the number of state controls and the freer the economic transactions are from different kinds of state interventions.

We use two measures for progress in building state capacities. First we measure state capacity to maintain rule of law using data from the World Bank governance survey (Kaufmann and Mastruzzi 2005). The Rule of Law index in this survey combines several indicators to measure the subjective perceptions of the presence of an effective state: the extent to which agents have confidence in and abide by the laws of society. These include perceptions of the incidence of crime, the effectiveness and predictability of the judiciary, and the enforceability of contracts. Together, these indicators measure the success of states in developing an environment in which fair and predictable rules form the basis for economic and social interactions, and the extent to which property rights are protected. Higher scores on this index mean the presence of states with higher capacity to create stable expectations about rule of law.

Figure 9.2 presents some preliminary evidence on the relationship between progress in neo-liberal reforms and state capacity to maintain rule of law.

According to the measures of Campos and Horváth, by the early 2000s most of the post-communist countries had liberalized their economies. Twenty-one out of 28 countries were close to the extreme right on the horizontal axis, meaning that they had implemented all of the liberalizing policy measures that were prescribed by the IFIs in the 1990s. According to the measures of Campos and Horváth, Central European countries such as Slovenia and Estonia have at least as liberalized economies as post-Soviet republics such as Moldova or Georgia.

These countries differ, however, dramatically on the vertical axis, which measures rule of law using the 2004 data of the World Bank. According to these measures, post-communist countries can be clustered in three groups. In the first group are countries in which a high level of market liberalization combines with a high level of rule of law. In these countries, economic actors can have stable expectations that they can profit from rational calculative enterprise in the presence of a state that enforces their rights. The Central European countries belong

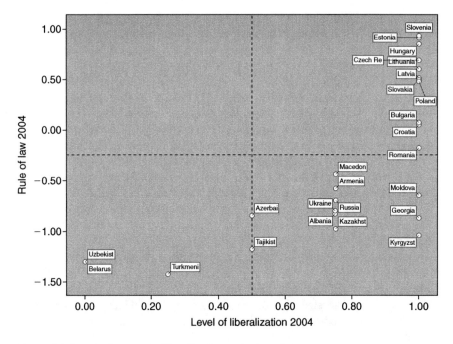

Figure 9.2 Level of economic liberalization and rule of law.

to this group. At the other extreme we find three countries, Uzbekistan, Turk-menistan and Belarus, where in the early 2000s low levels of economic liberali-zation were combined with low levels of rule of law. These countries could hardly be described as market economies.

Most of the former Soviet republics belong to the third group where a high level of economic liberalization combines with a low level of rule of law. In the early 2000s, a decade after the beginning of economic reforms, the factor that differentiated post-communist countries from each other most was not the level of freedoms from the state but the presence or absence of a state with the capac-ity to uphold these freedoms.

We find the same differentiation when we link market liberalization to the evo-lution of regulatory state capacities. To put the related argument of this chapter in a simple form: no regulatory state, no progress in market building. We measure progress in regulatory state building using the data compiled by the EBRD (2005). The EBRD data measures the capacity of a regulatory state in three dimensions: regulation of competition, the financial sector and capital markets. In each of these three dimensions, countries can get scores ranging from 1–4, with 4 equaling the presence of extensive and effective regulations. Going down from 4 to 1 means having regulatory norms on the books that are weakly enforced, not enforced at all, and finally not having regulations even on the books. For this chapter I aggre-gated the three indicators to construct an index that ranges from 1–12. The higher

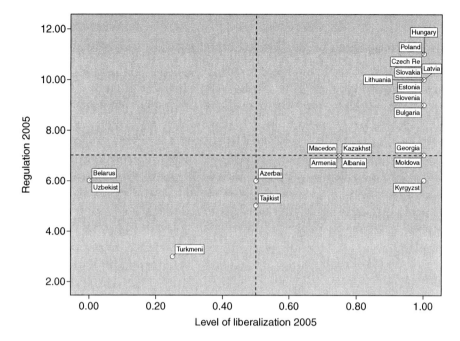

Figure 9.3 Economic freedoms and regulations.

countries score on this measure, the stronger the presence of a market regulating state. Countries with scores below 8 might have regulations on the law books but they do not have state capacities to enforce these rules.

Among the countries that we could include in this measurement we found the same differences as in the case of rule of law. The Central European countries combined high levels of economic liberalization with high levels of regulatory state capacities. In these countries, as a rule, economic actors can profit only from rational calculative enterprise and cannot use either asymmetries in economic power or information asymmetries to make rents in the markets of production or in the financial and capital markets. In the absence of such a regulatory state, the liberalized economies of the former Soviet republics had different versions of oligarchic or crony capitalism. Again, the factor that differentiated post-communist countries from each other most was not the level of freedoms from the state but the presence or absence of a state with the capacity to enforce public rules for economic transactions.

Finally, we present some evidence for the relationship between progress in regulatory state building and democratization. Linz and Stepan, in their work cited above, had two interrelated arguments on these issues. First, they argued for linking democratization with the development of regulatory states. Second, according to them, non-democratic roads to regulatory state building were not available in the post-communist countries.

We assess the level of democratization with the help of Freedom House indexes for Political Rights and Civil Liberties using the data for the initial period of economic reforms. In most of these countries this was the period of the early to mid 1990s. For the war-torn countries of the former Yugoslavia we have used the data for the postwar period starting with 1999. We count Romania as a liberal democracy at the time of reforms because after a few years of initial wavering it got the adequate Freedom House scores continuously after 1996. Also, we count Slovakia as a liberal democracy at the time of economic reforms because it was a liberal democracy in the 1990–1996 period, the key phase of economic change, and except for the short 1996–1998 period of the Meciar government, it has continued to be a liberal democracy.

We measure regulatory state capacities as above, with the aggregated EBRD indexes from the year 2005.

The findings are unambiguous: liberal democracy and regulatory state capacities go hand in hand. There is a strong association between the two variables. Countries that were liberal democracies in the period of economic transformation in the 1990s are the ones that have states that can enforce public rules in the private economy in the early 2000s. Countries that could not guarantee political rights and could not uphold civil liberties in the period of economic reforms all score below 8 in the EBRD index, i.e., below the minimum threshold of a functioning regulatory state. The aggregated low scores on this index might mean two things. First, scores below 8 might mean that while these countries have some of the rules necessary to run a functioning market economy "on the books," they do not have the needed state capacities to monitor and enforce these rules on the ground. Low scores in regulatory state capacity might also mean that some of the laws enforced in these countries reflect the interests of the strongest private actors only. Finally, even minimal regulatory state capacities are absent in the authoritarian countries. In the post-communist setting the dictum of Linz and Stepan proved to be right: no democracy, no regulatory state.

As we have elaborated in the first part of this chapter, the failed predictions about the expected negative effects of the extension of democratic rights on the success in market making were based on two interlinked assumptions. The first was that once liberated, free markets will produce strong enough economic incentives to generate the right economic institutions. The second assumption held that the politicization of economic transition might prevent both the liberation of markets and the coming about of the right institutions. Because of their flat and inarticulate social structure, runs the argument, the economic transformation would create too many losers and too rapid an increase in inequalities. The losers would not tolerate these changes and would use their newly acquired political rights to stop the process.

As it turned out, fears of the losers of market reforms proved to be exaggerated, while the dangers represented by the early winners of liberalizations, the emerging capitalist firms, were underestimated. The latter had strong incentives to set the rules of the private economy for themselves, and as a result of the fast privatization, they had concentrated economic power. In countries where states

Table 9.1 Democratization and regulatory state capacity

	1–2.5 Liberal democracies	3–5 Hybrid regimes	5.5–7 Authoritarian regimes
Political rights and civil liberties in the initial period of economic reforms. Progress in regulatory state building in 2005			
12–9 Strong to medium regulatory state capacities	Bulgaria (2) Croatia (2.5) Czech Republic (1.5); Estonia (2.5); Hungary (2); Latvia (2.5); Lithuania (2); Poland (2) Romania (2.5)* Slovakia (2.5)** Slovenia (1.5)		
5–8 Weak regulatory state		Albania (4), Armenia (4.5), Azerbaijan (6), Belarus (5), Bosnia-Herzegovina (4); Georgia (4.5); Kazakhstan (5); Kyrgyzstan (4); Macedonia (3.5); Moldova (4); Russia (3.5); Ukraine (3.5); Uzbekistan (6.5)	
Below 5 No regulatory state			Tajikistan (7); Turkmenistan (7)

Notes
In parentheses: Freedom House scores.
*From 1996 on continuously.
**Except for the 1996–1998 period.

did not have institutionalized defenses in the form of checks and balances and political pluralism was weak, early winners could capture the state and use it to redistribute wealth and opportunities amongst themselves. Political competition and the presence of mechanisms extending the accountability of incumbents, on the other hand, have helped to strengthen state capacity to introduce public rules for the private economy representing complex exchanges and accommodating diverse interests (Hellman 1998; Bruszt 2002).

This strong correlation between democracy and dimensions of development is the specific feature of the post-socialist development and it is absent in other parts of world, like Latin America where democratization started in established capitalist economies. Part of the reason for the cross-regional difference might have to do with differences in legacies of previous state-led developmental models. The state socialist regimes of Eastern Europe have left behind societies with relatively low levels of inequalities and economies with low concentration of private economic power. When market reforms in the early 1990s brought about private economies with concentrated economic power, the presence or absence of political pluralism could set these countries on divergent pathways. In Latin America, the diverse ISIs left behind extremely inegalitarian societies with highly concentrated economic power. Here, neo-liberal reforms in the 1980s and early 1990s have further decreased the chances of the weaker social groups to make effective demands on the state (Collier and Handlin 2005; Karl 2003).

Finally the last group of figures illustrates diverse patterns of insertion into global markets of the post-socialist economies. For the illustration of the specific

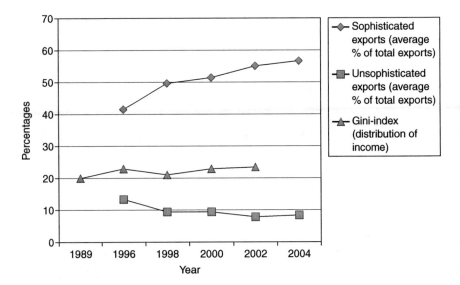

Figure 9.4 Democracies: Czech Republic. Development in "industrial upgrading," "industrial downgrading" and "inequality," Czech R, 1996–2004.

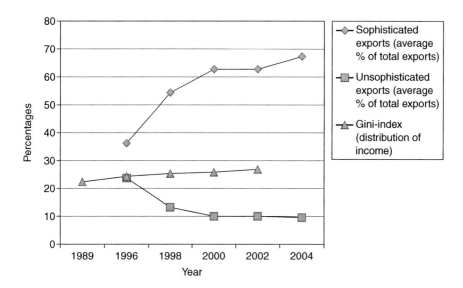

Figure 9.5 Democracies: Hungary. Development in "industrial upgrading," "industrial downgrading" and "inequality," Hungary, 1996–2004.

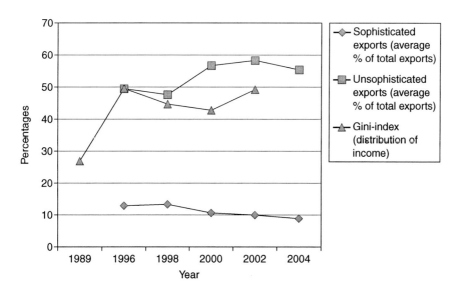

Figure 9.6 Hybrid regimes: Russia. Development in "industrial upgrading," "industrial downgrading" and "inequality," Russia, 1996–2004.

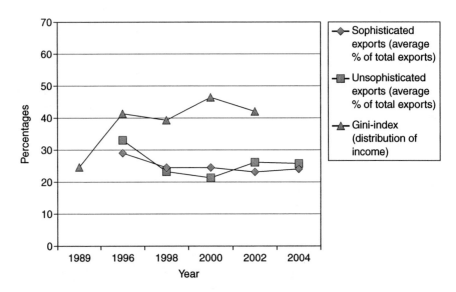

Figure 9.7 Hybrid regimes: Ukraine. Development in "industrial upgrading," "industrial downgrading" and "inequality," Ukraine, 1996–2004.

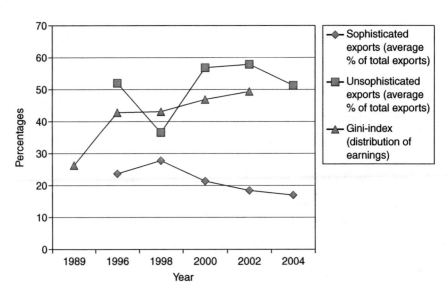

Figure 9.8 Autocracies: Kyrgyzstan. Development in "industrial upgrading," "industrial downgrading" and "inequality," Kyrgyzstan, 1996–2004.

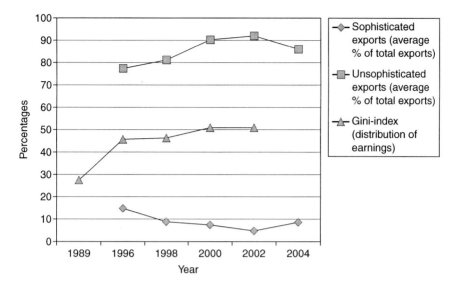

Figure 9.9 Autocracies: Azerbaijan. Development in "industrial upgrading," "industrial downgrading" and "inequality," Azerbaijan, 1996–2004.

patterns of global insertion we use indicators on the composition of the export of the country. The countries we select based on political regime type. Two countries, the Czech Republic and Hungary, represent the new democracies of Eastern and Central Europe. Azerbaijan and Kyrgyzstan represent the stable autocratic regimes. In-between we find Ukraine and Russia as hybrid regimes.

As it was mentioned in the introduction to this chapter, the major developmental question for the region was how the interplay between economic and political change will affect the insertion of these evolving market economies into the global markets? Which of these countries will occupy better positions in the globalizing economy? Will those countries be better off that could separate the building of capitalism from creating AKD? Or, in the post-communist setting the co-evolution of democratic political institutions and economic institutions was a necessary condition for creating a competitive market economy with advantageous pattern of global insertion?

The findings are unambiguous: in the post-socialist setting the construction of capable regulatory states in the framework of democratic institutions was the necessary condition for improving global positions in international markets while keeping social inequalities low. Lack of democracy went hand in hand with lack of progress in building regulatory states resulting in moving toward the periphery in the globalizing world economy, combined with drastic increases in social inequalities (Bruszt and Greskovits 2009).

Notes

1 On the diverse developmental pathways in the post-communist settings see Stark and Bruszt (1998); Bohle and Greskovits (2007); Bruszt and Greskovits (2009).
2 For a detailed presentation and critique of this approach see Hellman (1998). Some of the representatives of this approach were Fischer and Gelb (1991), Boycko *et al.* (1995) and Lipton and Sachs (1990).
3 For an excellent overview of this literature see Haggard and Kaufman (1995); see also Stark and Bruszt (1998).
4 For critical discussions of the public choice perspectives on the state see Evans (1995) and Stark and Bruszt (1998).
5 For an insightful discussion of pre-New Deal era constitutionalism see Sunstein (1987, 1990).
6 On the market preserving state see North and Weingast (1989) and Weingast (1995).
7 On post-New Deal constitutionalism see Sunstein (1987). On the ordoliberals, see Streeck and Yamamura (2001) and Borchardt (1991).
8 The indicators for capital controls include: controls on commercial credit, controls on foreign direct investment, controls on the liquidation of foreign direct investment, documentation requirements for the release of foreign exchange for imports, exchange rate taxes, interest rate liberalization, investment liberalization, multiple exchange rates, permission requirements for foreign exchange accounts held abroad by residents, permission requirements for foreign exchange accounts held domestically by residents, permission requirements for foreign exchange accounts for non-residents, repatriation requirements, repatriation requirements for invisible transactions, surrender requirements, and surrender requirements for invisible transactions. Data on trade barriers include the following: compatibility with Article VIII (current account convertibility), export duties as percentage of tax revenues, export licenses, export taxes, import duties as percentage of tax revenue, import licenses and quotas, import tariff rates, OECD and WTO membership, trade openness, share of trade with non-transition countries, tariff code lines, tariff revenues as a percentage of imports, and tax revenues on international trade (as a percentage of revenue).

References

Bohle, Dorothee and Béla Greskovits (2007). "Neoliberalism, Embedded Neoliberalism and Neocorporatism: Towards Transnational Capitalism in Central-Eastern Europe," *West European Politics*, 30: 443–466.

Borchardt, K. (1991). *Perspectives on Modern German Economic History and Policy*. Cambridge: Cambridge University Press.

Boycko, M., A. Shleifer and R. W. Vishny (1995). *Privatizing Russia*. Cambridge, MA: MIT Press.

Brunetti, A., G. Kisunko and B. Weder (1998). "Credibility of Rules and Economic Growth: Evidence from a Worldwide Survey of the Private Sector," *The World Bank Economic Review*, 12(3): 353–384.

Bruszt, L. (2002). "Making Markets and Eastern Enlargement: Diverging Convergence?" *West European Politics* 25(2): 121–140.

Bruszt, L. and B. Greskovits (2009). "Transnationalization, Social Integration and Capitalist Diversity in the East and the South," *Studies in Comparative International Development* 44(4): 411–434.

Bruszt, L. and G. McDermott (2009). "Transnational Integration Regimes as Development Programs," in L. Bruszt and R. Holzhacker (eds.), *The Transnationalization of Economies, States and Civil Societies: New Challenges for Governance in Europe*. New York: Springer Political Science Series, 35–76.

Campos, Nauro F. and Roman Horváth (2006). "Reform Redux: Measurement, Determinants and Reversals," IZA Discussion Papers 2093, Institute for the Study of Labor (IZA).

Coffee, J. C., Jr. (1999). "Privatization and Corporate Governance: The Lessons from Securities Market Failure," *Journal of Corporation Law*, 25(1): 1–39.

Collier, Ruth Berins and Samuel P. Handlin (2005). "Shifting Interest Regimes of the Working Classes in Latin America" Institute of Industrial Relations Working Paper Series. Paper iirwps-122-05, UC Berkeley.

EBRD (1998). *Transition Report 1998: Financial Sector in Transition*, available at: www.ebrd.com/pubs/econo/3542.htm.

Evans, P. (1995). *Embedded Autonomy: States and Industrial Transformation*. Princeton: Princeton University Press.

Fischer, S. and A. Gelb (1991). "The Process of Socialist Economic Transformation," *Journal of Economic Perspectives*, 5(4): 91–105.

Haggard, S. and R. R. Kaufman (1995). *The Political Economy of Democratic Transitions*. Princeton: Princeton University Press.

Hall, Peter A. and David Soskice (eds.) (2001). *Varieties of Capitalism. The Institutional Foundations of Comparative Advantage*. Oxford: Oxford University Press.

Hellman, J. (1998). "Winners Take All: The Politics of Partial Reforms in Post-communist Transitions," *World Politics*, 50(1): 203–234.

Karl T. L. (2003). "The Vicious Cycle of Inequality in Latin America," in S. E. Eckstein and T. P. Wickham-Crowley (eds.), *What Justice? Whose Justice? Fighting for Fairness in Latin America*. Berkeley: University of California at Berkeley Press, 133–157.

Kaufmann, K. and M. Mastruzzi (2005). "Governance Matters IV: Governance Indicators for 1996–2004: Worldwide Governance Research Indicators Dataset, 2004." Available at: www.worldbank.org/wbi/governance/govdata/index.html.

Linz, J. and A. Stepan (1996). *Problems of Democratic Transition and Consolidation: Southern Europe, South America, and Post Communist Europe*. Baltimore: Johns Hopkins University Press.

Lipton, D. and J. D. Sachs (1990). "Creating a Market in Eastern Europe: The Case of Poland," *Brookings Papers on Economic Activity*, 20(1): 75–147.

North, D. and B. Weingast (1989). "Constitutions and Credible Commitments: The Evolution of the Institutions of Public Choice," in L. J. Alston (ed.), *Empirical Studies in Institutional Change*. Cambridge: Cambridge University Press, 211–243.

Schneider, Ben Ross. (2004). "Varieties of Semi-Articulated Capitalism in Latin America," paper presented at the annual meeting of the American Political Science Association, Chicago.

Stark, D. and L. Bruszt (1998). *Post-Socialist Pathways: Transforming Politics and Property in Eastern Europe*. New York: Cambridge University Press.

Stiglitz, J. E. (1999). "Whither Reform?" World Bank Annual Bank Conference on Development Economics, Washington, DC.

Streeck, W. and K. Yamamura (2005). *The Origins of Nonliberal Capitalism: Germany and Japan in Comparison*. Ithaca: Cornell University Press.

Sunstein, C. (1987). "Lochners' Legacy," *Columbia Law Review*, 87(5): 873–919.

Sunstein, C. (1990). *After The Rights Revolution*. Cambridge, MA: Harvard University Press.

Weingast, B. (1995). "The Economic Role of Political Institutions: Market Preserving Federalism and Economic Development," *The Journal of Law, Economics and Organization*, 11(1): 1–31.

Index

Page numbers in *italics* denote tables, those in **bold** denote figures.